BULLETS OR BALLOTS?

The ultimate solution to crime and unemployment in South Africa

DR RUBEN RICHARDS

Mutloatse Arts Heritage Trust
101b Killarney Mall Office Towers
Riviera Road, Houghton
PO Box 2599, Houghton, 2041
Email: mutloatse@mweb.co.za
www.mutloatse.com

Trust IT5860/04

ISBN 978-0-9869833-2-0

© Ruben Richards

First published July 2010

Book design and layout: Adam Rumball
Copy editing, proofreading and indexing: Wordsmiths www.wordsmiths.co.za
Printed in South Africa by Ultra Litho
Printed on environmentally friendly paper

All rights reserved. Without limiting the rights under copyright reserved above, no part of this publication may be reproduced, stored in or introduced into a retrieval system, or transmitted, in any form or by any means (electronic, mechanical, photocopying, recording or otherwise) without the written permission of both the copyright holder and the publisher of the book.

To Joan Webber and Robert Richards, my deceased parents, who never witnessed the freedom of 1994, but practised its reality long before it arrived.

Acknowledgements

I am grateful to my wife and children who made writing this book possible. Their gift to me was time and unquestionable support. They sacrificed and adjusted their South African public school summer holiday break to accommodate my erratic writing schedule and strange levels of exhaustion. After all, I wasn't really working hard. I was just sitting in front of the computer all day long!

I owe a word of thanks to our family friends, especially those of my children, who were subjected to the central ideas of the book when they visited us. Their opinions were required as an entrance fee to our home during this period. During these occasions I received invaluable suggestions and also enjoyed the opportunity to conduct a reality check on the content of my thinking. There is nothing like the innocence and reality of youth to sober an idealistic adult.

The primary financial assistance that made this book possible came from my wife. I wish to thank her sincerely for allowing me the space and freedom to think and express myself freely through this book. Such support defies any monetary quantification and I will remain deeply grateful for such a soul mate. I received additional financial support from a trusted friend, Paul Clarence, whose financial assistance took the book to print. For this, a word of gratitude is in order.

I wish to thank my employers, colleagues and employees, especially of the past 16 years, who accommodated my sometimes off-the-wall approach to management, my obsession with "getting the job done" and my robust theorising about work completed. I know that I have managed to irritate and confuse quite a few people along the way but I hope that I have inspired and empowered even more.

A final word of thanks goes to my publisher and his technical team for giving respectable shape and order to what was originally a very wordy manuscript. With their help I am learning to be more sensitive to the reader as well as appreciate the power and economy of words.

Contents

About the author	7
Preface	8
Abbreviations	12

Part 1. Towards industrial consciousness

Chapter 1 – What unites South Africans? An exploration	16
Chapter 2 – Renewing the mind of the nation	37
Chapter 3 – The B-BBEE bombshell	57
Chapter 4 – A new fulcrum for national identity	72
Chapter 5 – A new performance standard for nationhood	84

Part 2. The emergency rescue plan

Chapter 6 – Six components of a rescue plan	100
Chapter 7 – Nine "what if" scenarios	106
Chapter 8 – Four steps to personal victory	122
Chapter 9 – How much truth can a nation tolerate?	132
Chapter 10 – Eight uncomfortable truths	144
Chapter 11 – Performance morality and the poisoned well	158
Chapter 12 – Ten do's and don'ts – the new ground rules	174

Part 3. Knife-edge transformation

Chapter 13 – Three moments of consciousness	180
Chapter 14 – Life comes full circle	192
Chapter 15 – Taming state security	218
Chapter 16 – Bringing down the elephant	234
Chapter 17 – Industrial terrorism and the Jipsa moment	252

Part 4. The way forward

Chapter 18 – Conclusion: True liberation starts in the mind	270
Postscript – For our children's sake	278
Box-thinking exercise – Determine your own list of priorities	284
Select bibliography	290

About the author

Ruben Richards is a Cape Town-born South African. Fifty years old, and married with children, Ruben began his career as a blue-collar tradesman in the marine and heavy general engineering sector. Twenty-six years after his fitter and turner apprenticeship, he returned to the same company as its CEO and a shareholder.

The intervening years were taken up by a decade of pursuing academic qualifications and experience locally and internationally. A further decade, and also the first decade of democracy in South Africa, was consumed by Ruben's full-time employment in the government sector, focusing on rebuilding a new and post-apartheid criminal justice system for South Africa. In this context he served as an executive management-leadership practitioner holding various formal employment positions including Executive Secretary (Truth and Reconciliation Commission), Executive Director – Police Practice (Technikon), and Deputy-Director General (Scorpions).

More recently, Ruben's professional activity has shifted from hard-core industrial activity as a full-time CEO to a more reflective academic arena as a Visiting Professor to Wits University's Graduate School of Public and Development Management, and an Advisor to the Manufacturing and Engineering Education and Training Authority in the areas of scarce skills and accelerated artisan training and development. He also serves as an investigative forensic specialist and mentor on anti-corruption initiatives funded by the United Nations Development Programme.

Ruben has a wide spectrum of interests and his life to date is a tapestry of seemingly incongruent career and professional activity, which spans academia, government, private industry and corporate South Africa. He brings his diverse perspectives to bear in this book, as a contribution to South Africa's quest to find lasting solutions to crime and unemployment, and ultimately the eradication of poverty in South Africa.

For more information and contact with Ruben see:
www.rubenrichards.co.za and www.strategyplusaction.co.za

Preface

There are generally two ways to solve problems in a society – either via the bullet (violently) or the ballot (non-violently). While post-colonial Africa seems to have had a preference for the former, South Africa has been an exception, leading the rest of the continent by showing that the ballot is more powerful – for now. Yet, despite the power of the ballot, we do not seem to be able to fix the crime and unemployment crisis in our country. With this book, I propose a solution for consideration by all South Africans.

Why this book?
I wrote this book in my private capacity. I live in South Africa. I am an interested, loyal, talented, male, married, black but *gatvol*[1] South African. I am not a politician. I am not pushing the agenda of a particular political party or interest group.

I am just an ordinary independent-minded South African who has had some extraordinary professional and career experiences, and I have been pondering deeply about how to fix the ongoing and deepening unemployment and crime crisis.

Why? Because South Africa is my home and it's a fantastic place to live, except for the crime and unemployment. So, instead of just mumbling abuse about easy targets such as our under-performing and sometimes corrupt politicians, and instead of walking around depressed and disillusioned with the state of affairs, I thought it wiser to channel my energies towards making a positive contribution towards solving our problems and challenges. This book is therefore a reflection of some of my thoughts and practical proposals based on my life and professional experience. In this regard I would like to think of myself as a practical person – someone with a reputation for getting the job done.

Like you, I want a safer and more prosperous South Africa where all citizens, and not just the elite few, are able to enjoy a healthier and wealthier South Africa. I want to feel proud and safe in my country. I don't want to be a complaining and criticising South African. I want to make a positive contribution to the building of a truly democratic and free South Africa where there is less crime and more jobs, and where my children and I, together with millions of other families, can live in safety and peace in our beloved country. Ordinary people like you and me have the power to change things in this country.

A new way

Our current mindset as South Africans, whether we admit to it or not, is a race-based one. On paper, South Africa is a free and equal society. However, in reality we are still deeply divided and unequal, trapped in economic bondage.

On paper, we are supposedly liberating our economy through the policy of BEE. In reality, though, we are simply creating another class of super-rich and greedy elites who are black. The poor are still getting poorer and the rich are still getting richer. Something is wrong.

To eradicate poverty we need to *change our mindset* as individuals and as a nation from a race-based consciousness and obsession, to *industrial consciousness or industriousness*.

The question is: How do we change our mindset? In this regard I propose a six-pronged emergency rescue plan. The components of the plan are (1) changing systems by considering nine "what if" scenarios and situations; (2) changing individuals by proposing a four-step change process; (3) finding and empowering our voices to speak "our" truth as we see it; (4) confronting eight hard and uncomfortable truths embedded deep in our national psyche; (5) confronting three specific moral issues which impact our performance; and (6) proposing a new set of ground rules – the 10 do's and don'ts by which we should strive to live as a rejuvenated industrially conscious South Africa.

What will it take before such a plan is activated? More often than not, we tend to respond to problems when we have absolutely no options left.

I hope that this book will inspire us to be proactive and not wait for the ultimate disaster to happen, namely the implosion of our society along traditional and racial lines.

A new fuel

The focus in this book is not on the why, but rather on the how. With this book I humbly suggest an answer to the how questions – *How do we create jobs? How do we reduce crime?* In my view, the solution is not complicated. It is a solution that says South Africa needs to actively and deliberately shift from its current race obsession towards an industrial-development obsession. I propose that South African society creates and adopts *industrial consciousness* as a basis for its national existence.

I do not share the view that some of the current South African nationally driven government-based solutions will solve our problems. The proposed and determined re-militarisation of the police coupled with granting them more fire power, a bigger social and welfare grant, and more black economic empowerment (BEE) (now known as broad-based black economic empowerment) will not solve our problems. Throwing more money at our problems is not the solution. Adopting an approach of more fire power and more money in combination with and supported by the existing race-based South African psyche will only deepen our crisis. We need a different, innovative and inspiring solution – a radical mind shift – a new way of thinking and ultimately a new way of doing.

A managerial perspective

It is important to clarify, up front, that this book is written from a managerial-leadership perspective as opposed to being an academic treatise. It derives its impetus from my own managerial-leadership perspective which I have gained while practising in various professional and career capacities directly associated with, and in some instances the primary driving force of transformation and nation building in the new South Africa. I am no different to many others who in their own way have contributed to the building of the rainbow nation. My particular contribution happens to have been located within the corridors of academia, government, as well as the manufacturing and engineering environment of the private sector. I have had a range of responsibilities and have held a range of managerial positions, including CEO of an engineering company and founding Deputy Director-General of the now disbanded Scorpions.

So the energy and spirit of this book is not that of a detached pontificating academic or intellectual, or even a party political protagonist, but rather that of an engaged (and hopefully competent) managerial leader who appreciates the nuanced debates in academia and politics. This book is a deliberate call to action. It is a call to all citizens who consider themselves patriots and loyal South Africans, to take stock of what's happening in our country and to do something about it.

What this book begins to do is identify the core requirements and elements for the emergence of a liberated economy where the majority of citizens can participate in a form of decent work and the subsequent creation of the much-needed sustainable middle class in the economy and broader South African society. Without the active creation of such a class, South Africa is likely to experience untold disharmony, given that it is currently on a development, transformation and nation-building path which is creating an ever-widening gulf between the rich and the poor. Soon, the issue won't be that of a gulf between white and black, but rather between rich black and poor black. No amount of race-based affirmative action policy will then be of any use. We are already a majority black nation. It's just a matter of time before the reality of the ballot versus the bullet will be an economic issue and no longer a race issue. What then?

Notes
1. "Gatvol" is an Afrikaans word commonly used across many language groups in South Africa to express extreme dissatisfaction and frustration.

Abbreviations

AATP	Accelerated Artisan Training Programme
AIDS	Acquired Immunodeficiency Syndrome
ANC	African National Congress
APLA	Azanian People's Liberation Army
ASGISA	Accelerated Shared Growth Initiative of South Africa
AU	African Union
AWB	Afrikaner Weerstandsbeweging (Afrikaner Resistance Movement)
B-BBEE	Broad-Based Black Economic Empowerment
BEE	Black Economic Empowerment
BLSA	Business Leadershp South Africa
BRT	Bus Rapid Transit
CEO	Chief Executive Officer
DDG	Deputy Director-General
DIY	Do It Yourself
DNA	Deoxyriboneuclic Acid
D-NDPP	Deputy National Director of Public Prosecutions
DSO	Directorate of Special Operations
DTI	Department of Trade and Industry
EMF-SA	Entrepreneurial Millionaire's Fund – South Africa
EXCO	Executive Committee
FBI	Federal Bureau of Investigation (US Government)
FET	Further Education and Training
FIFA	Fédération Internationale de Football Association
GDP	Gross Domestic Product
GEAR	Growth Employment and Redistribution Strategy
HIV	Human Immunodeficiency Virus
HRD	Human Resource Development
IDC	Industrial Development Corporation
IDOC	Investigating Directorate – Organised Crime
IDSEO	Investigating Directorate – Serious Economic Offences
IPAP	Industrial Policy Action Plan

JIPSA	Joint Initiative for Priority Skills Acquisition
MERSETA	Manufacturing, Engineering and Related Services Education and Training Authority of South Africa
MK	Umkhonto We Sizwe (military wing of the ANC)
MM	Millimetres (Unit of Measurement)
NDPP	National Director of Public Prosecutions
NEF	National Empowerment Fund
NGO	Non-Governmental Organisation
NIA	National Intelligence Agency
NICOC	National Intelligence Co-ordinating Committee
PhD	Doctor of Philosophy Degree
POCA	Prevention of Organised Crime Act
R	South African Rand (Currency)
RSA	Republic of South Africa
RDP	Reconstruction and Development Plan
SANDF	South African National Defence Force
SAPS	South African Police Service
SASOL	Suid Afrikaanse Steenkool en Olie (South African Coal and Oil)
SETA	Sectoral Education and Training Authority
SASS	South African Secret Service
SDU	Self-Defence Units
SMME's	Small, Medium & Micro Enterprises
SOE	State-Owned Enterprise
SPU	Self-Protection Units
TRC	Truth and Reconciliation Commission
TVET	Technical and Vocational Education and Training
UCT	University of Cape Town
UDF	United Democratic Front
UNIDO	United Nations Industrial Development Organisation
USA	United States of America
USD	United States Dollar

Part 1.
Towards industrial consciousness

1 | What unites South Africans? An exploration

With a magic wand in your hand, what would you change about South Africa today? How does one prioritise what is important and what needs to be changed first? Furthermore, are we a united country? On what basis do we call ourselves a nation?

We can probably list many things that divide us. But the challenge is to find those things that bind us. National unity and patriotism are key to finding a lasting solution to the frontal assault and threat of crime and unemployment to our emerging democracy. Yet, for as long as we are divided, the problem of crime and unemployment will remain South Africa's Achilles heel and may, in fact, devour us completely.

It is therefore relevant to ask, what will compel us to join hands and improve our country's appalling crime and unemployment statistics? Will we discuss issues of national unity, patriotism, sacrifice and so forth, only when there is an external threat or attack on our country, such as a war or terrorist attack? What about the internal attack from the beast of poverty through its agencies called crime and unemployment?

In this chapter I invite you to explore national unity in South Africa. I intend to show that the current basis of national unity, which is predicated on past experiences, should be replaced with a view of what the future of South Africa is envisioned to be. This chapter thus provides an overview of some of the successes of the first 16 years of democracy in South Africa. In so doing, it identifies the missing element in the democratic transformation package, namely industrial consciousness – a key element for the solution to poverty and sustained growth in the South African economy.

Nationhood and transformation score card

South Africa's 15-year nation-building performance and report card is mixed. Economics academic Polly Mashigo points out that:

> Despite progress since 1994 in socio-economic development and poverty reduction, South Africa still faces high levels of unemployment, poverty and underdevelopment, deepening inequality and rural marginalisation.[1]

It is in this context that the Jacob Zuma-led ANC adopted its 2009 Polokwane manifesto for the period 2009-2014. The five priority areas identified by the manifesto have subsequently become the five priority areas of government, namely the creation of decent work and sustainable livelihoods; education; health; the fight against crime and corruption; and rural development, food security and land reform.[2]

A worrying factor is that the economy seems unable to create decent work for its citizens. Another perspective is that there are enough decent jobs in the economy, but not enough decently qualified citizens for those jobs.

Whatever the perspective, the reality on the ground is that South Africa has incredibly high (and rising) levels of unemployment, coupled with unacceptably high levels of crime – and violent crime in particular. Furthermore, the gap between rich and poor in South Africa is the largest such gap of any country in the world.

Negative realities often overshadow and blind one to more miraculous and positive accomplishments. South Africa is a miracle nation, yet how quickly we forget the miraculous quality of the peaceful transition from apartheid to democracy. The peaceful transition may well have to do with the nature of the agreements and compromises reached behind closed doors between white-controlled business and the negotiating parties of the ostensibly black liberation movements during the last phases of negotiations at Kempton Park. I will return to this theory later.

But for now, let's remind ourselves that the incoming comrades and freedom fighters with absolutely no experience in governing a country, led by Nelson Mandela, have, under difficult circumstances, pulled off more than a small miracle for South Africa. Yes, we may be very vocal in our criticism of our leaders and representatives, but we need to acknowledge the magnitude of the challenges they faced upon taking office from the National Party led by FW de Klerk. One school of thought believes De Klerk and his cabinet bequeathed to South Africa a financially bankrupt country. The moral bankruptcy of apartheid has long since been acknowledged.[3] It is understandable then that the first phase of post-apartheid nation building needed to include changing the entire legislative framework and content in the new South Africa, guaranteeing human dignity for all, and at the same time refocusing and finding a way to rescue a bankrupt state fiscus.

In terms of the economy, a full battery of legislative measures was enacted, intended to facilitate and bring about the much-desired economic revolution. The economy needed to be stabilised and restructured.[4] New laws have subsequently restored rights to land and tenure, proscribed unfair discrimination, and introduced specific active measures to overcome the distortions in the labour market as well as provide new economic opportunities for historically disadvantaged persons. Some of the legislation introduced by the incoming Utopian-minded freedom fighters led by Mandela and later by Mbeki, Motlanthe and now Jacob Zuma, included: The Promotion of Equality and Prevention of Unfair Discrimination Act, Extension of Security of Tenure Act, Restitution of Land Rights Act, Employment Equity Act, National Empowerment Fund Act, Competition Act, Telecommunications Act, Preferential Procurement Policy Framework Act, and the Minerals and Petroleum Development Act.

In addition, government implemented various policies, strategies and programmes aimed at overcoming economic inequalities and under-development, including the Integrated Human Resources Development Strategy, Urban Renewal Programme, Integrated Sustainable Rural Development Programme, the Tourism Transformation Strategy, the Strategic Sector Plan for Agriculture and the National Small Business Development Promotion Programme.

It is worth noting that the primary driver for economic reform was that of deracialising the South African economy through the policy of BEE, a policy now widely considered to have failed (see Chapter 3). In this context there is a barrage of BEE-driven legislative and policy instruments and strategy documents.[5]

In addition to the many new laws enacted since 1994 to dismantle the apartheid machinery, we enshrined the basic human rights of all South Africans, tackled inequality in specific areas, and government enacted specific legislation to address economic inequalities throughout our society.

In 1995, a national strategy for the development and promotion of small business in South Africa was tabled in Parliament. The creation of new black-owned and -controlled enterprises was seen as a key component of the strategy. The National Small Business Act was introduced in 1996 to provide an enabling environment for SMMEs, and to establish several institutions to provide financial and other support to entrepreneurs. These institutions, Khula and Ntsika, have targeted substantial proportions of their programmes towards black entrepreneurs.

In 1997, government issued a green paper on public sector procurement reform. This policy document recognised that government, as the largest buyer of goods and services in the economy, had the responsibility to leverage this purchasing power in support of its economic policy objectives of black economic empowerment, small enterprise development and labour-intensive construction. Mechanisms were introduced to give effect to a preferential procurement policy supported by the work of the Competition Commission and the strictures of the Employment Equity Act introduced in 1998. This act outlawed all forms of unfair discrimination at work and required all enterprises employing more than 50 employees to take affirmative action to bring about a representative spread of designated groups in all occupations and organisational levels within defined time periods.

Also in 1998, government created the National Empowerment Fund, a trust to hold equity stakes in state-owned enterprises and other private enterprises on behalf of historically disadvantaged persons. The NEF Corporation, established in terms of the NEF Act, 1998, was tasked with managing the trust in order to provide historically disadvantaged persons with the opportunity, directly and indirectly, to acquire shares; to encourage and promote savings, investment and meaningful economic participation by historically disadvantaged persons; and to promote and support business ventures pioneered and run by historically disadvantaged persons.

We must conclude from the short catalogue above, that the legislative interventions post-1994 are by no means unimpressive. The question that now comes to mind, though, is: What went wrong? Or in more positive terms, what is still lacking? Why, with all these wonderful legislative instruments and tools, have we still failed to turn the economy into a place for the broader participation of the masses as opposed to the very few who have become very wealthy as a result of the government's key economic transformation policy called BEE?

As a critic I must go beyond the rhetoric to soberly examine the areas of good performance and sharply critique the areas of non-performance.

Issues of national identity

On what basis can we and will we pull together as a nation? What is the core identity of the South African national team of citizens that will enable us to jointly conquer our problems? These are not easily resolved issues, as was demonstrated by the government's attempt to introduce into public schools a pledge of allegiance to be recited by all school children.

I suspect that the mere mention of a South African identity (be it personal or national) prickles the South African ear, especially if such an identity is not to be based on race.[6] At present, race-consciousness is all most of us know. Our entire society and history has been defined by race, notwithstanding the provisions and philosophy of non-racialism embedded in our Constitution.[7] The basis of the struggle against or defence of apartheid and colonial oppression is premised on race and the affirmation of blackness as equal to whiteness, or vice versa, depending on the racial point you wish to make.

My view, however, is that the ultimate struggle in South Africa was never really about race. Rather, it was about who controlled the money. Race was used as an instrument in the hands of the oppressor to achieve economic power and control. When one race conquers another, the winning racial group generally designs systems to benefit its own racial index and support base.

Fortunately, the constitutional framework of the new South Africa is premised on non-racialism, aimed at the improvement of the quality of life of all citizens and the freedom of each person.[8] However, the practical and everyday reality of life in South Africa is still governed by the geo-political and spatial politics of separate development. Thus, its everyday existence is based on multi-racialism, where the existence of race groups is acknowledged and socio-economic restructuring follows a hierarchy within this multi-racial framework. It is therefore no surprise that the entire economic policy framework of the new South Africa is premised on a racial index with verification agencies set up to police the entrenchment of a racial hierarchy and reward those who comply. In this regard, it is estimated that the BEE-verification industry is worth well over R2bn.

An additional issue is the open-ended timeline attached to the deracialisation of the economy through BEE. But is the absence of a fixed timeline not contrary to the intention and spirit of the vision of a non-racial nation? Put differently, at what point does BEE end? If it is intended to end at all? Was BEE intended to be a corrective short-term measure or a permanent entrenchment of economic entitlement based on race? What are the implications of the recent suggestion that BEE has failed?

The rewarding of a group based on a claim and verification of race as opposed to competence is dangerous and can prove deadly. Is it a coincidence that Chinese South Africans have recently been reclassified as black so that they can benefit from BEE in South Africa?[9] Is this a case of the power of money being able to determine one's racial identity? Who will be reclassified next? The Japanese? The French? The Greeks?

A lethal concoction

One must avoid being melodramatic about the crime and unemployment situation in South Africa. But the emerging choices facing South Africa and its citizens are simple. We have the option of using the bullet to kill each other as we compete for scarce resources. Alternatively, we can put in place management and leadership whom we will rigorously hold accountable by the power of the ballot.

It is evident and certainly no secret that the *new* South Africa (i.e. post-apartheid, post-liberated, post-1994) still faces many *old* and *inherited* problems and challenges. A survey conducted in the second quarter of 2008 revealed a large consensus among South Africans that the root cause of crime and violence is poverty. Logically, once poverty is decisively addressed, the levels of crime and unemployment will automatically decrease. So the real motivation and focus of any crime and unemployment solution, it seems, needs to take into account the challenge posed by poverty. Poverty reduction must therefore become a national obsession if we want to see lower levels of crime and unemployment.

There are two ways to reduce poverty. The easy method is through financial aid and charity. The difficult and more sustainable method is to teach the poor how to become rich and create their own "financial aid" – a kind of do-it-yourself method. Just consider how much money and financial aid (i.e. charity) is raised to feed and clothe the starving masses of "Africa". In South Africa we have resisted wholesale welfare and social grants, although the pressure is mounting to make more grants available to the masses of unemployed and unemployable alike. In terms of the international scene, it is unfortunate that the same level of charity-based financial assistance is not matched when funding the true empowerment of Africans by up-skilling them to solve their own poverty problems. Rich countries feel good that their money is going to a good humanitarian cause often defined as feeding the hungry African children.

There are huge global and ideological factors at play in any discussion on poverty in Africa. It seems as though it is better to keep Africans, who are mainly black, dependent on donor-funding, which is mainly white-sponsored. It is my view that there is very little intention to fundamentally assist in the true economic liberation of Africa from its woes of disease, crime and unemployment. Does the same apply to South Africa?

It is often the level of perceived seriousness of our problems that determines our line of action and the urgency we attach to finding and implementing solutions. This applies to both our personal as well as our public lives. Notwithstanding existing government solutions and their implementation (or lack thereof) under new police and industrial leadership, I have nevertheless, with this book, proposed a solution for consideration. I hold the view that the current solutions (i.e. B-BBEE-based solutions as one example) are deficient. I am ambivalent about whether or not the problem is solely implementation. But I would rather remain open-minded than be dogmatic. In other words, I am a pragmatist. If we have to live with B-BBEE, then we must find ways to make it accessible and beneficial to more than just the select few. For this to happen, a number of management-related interventions will be required over and above the political leadership.

Defining prosperity and industrial consciousness

My proposed solution to crime and unemployment is geared at shifting the nation from poverty to prosperity.

It may be useful at this point to pause and define prosperity and poverty so that we all share the same definitional base and subsequent picture of reality. R. Glenn Hubbard, author of *The Aid Trap, Hard Truths About Ending Poverty,* makes a useful distinction in his discussion on the pitfalls of charity and aid in addressing poverty in Africa. He says:

Prosperity and poverty are opposites. Poverty is the lack of prosperity, and prosperity is where you arrive when you rise out of poverty. Let's use the most basic definition of prosperity: a decent place to live, decent clothes, food on the table, and enough wealth of some kind – livestock, land, a building, money, jewellery, or other possessions – to survive setbacks like drought, sickness, economic crisis, or war.[10]

Nurturing aspirations to achieve prosperity as defined above cannot be seen to be unreasonable. For ease of debate and discussion, I will adopt Hubbard's definitional framework as a work space to interrogate and make sense of aspirations for prosperity and wealth and the move away from poverty.

In order to move in the direction of prosperity, we need to rapidly create a new national patriotism and identity premised on what I have called *industrial consciousness* as opposed to *race consciousness*. Industrial consciousness is here defined as:

> A fundamental inquisitiveness about how things are created, manufactured, maintained and repaired.

Harry Braverman, in a comment about the working class, points to three expressions of class consciousness worth quoting. He contends that:

> … it is only through consciousness that a class becomes an actor on the historic stage … Class consciousness is that state of social cohesion reflected in the understanding and activities of a class or a portion of a class. Its absolute expression is a pervasive and durable attitude on the part of a class toward its position in society. Its long-term relative expression is found in the slowly changing traditions, experiences, education, and organisation of the class. Its short-term relative expression is a dynamic complex of moods and sentiments affected by circumstances and changing with them … A class cannot exist in society without in some degree manifesting a consciousness of itself as a group with common problems, interests, and prospects …"[11]

Braverman's insight provides a valuable typology of consciousness. I wish to apply the theoretical apparatus of Braverman's discussion to the development of a national consciousness for South Africa where the shared consciousness serves as the basis for national unity rather than for purposes of pitting the working class against the ruling class, as was the original context of Braverman's analysis. Whether the Braverman purists will allow his thesis on class consciousness to serve as a basis for national unity and patriotism is quite another matter.

My proposed solution to South Africa's crime and unemployment challenges, and the creation of an economy that benefits the majority of the citizens rather than the minority, presupposes that every South African (and not just one particular class) must change his/her mindset from a race orientation to an industrial orientation. In this sense I am arguing that South Africa as a nation is in fact a broadly defined class, using the Braverman typology. Hence, the change of mindset of the entire nation (and not just one narrow class within the nation) is the magical key and the required first step towards full-blown economic liberation. History shows that wealthy classes don't readily or peacefully give up their gained wealth (regardless of how it was gained in the first instance). My proposal for a shared consciousness is therefore my attempt to promote change in terms of a consensual rather than a class-conflict index. The birth of the TRC is a visible example of how such a consensus can be developed. The alternative to this ballot is the bullet. So one must be sober about the gravity and implications of my proposal and its call for the development of a shared national consciousness and identity premised on what I have termed industrial consciousness.

I hold the view that an industrial consciousness which enjoys a national consensus and serves as a basis for a new South African patriotic identity, will unlock the potential for economic recovery, which will be a million times more powerful and empowering than the money that governments, charities or international donors may want to throw at our African and South African problems. It will also be more peaceful than any attempt on the part of the poor to dispossess the rich of their wealth.

Too much policy?

In South Africa our problem (at least from a government perspective) seems not to be a lack of public policy, but rather a lack of implementation. The same challenge faces the private sector. The difference is that the private sector can keep their problems out of the media whereas the public sector (i.e. government) does not enjoy this luxury. You can have the best policy framework and strategies in the world, including an anti-poverty strategy[12], but if your people do not have the required mindset, you might as well throw away your policies. All parties need to buy into the vision, mission and core values of the company, and the performance contracts of staff must reflect a commitment to achieving targets within this value-framework. Where there are skills deficiencies, these are developed specifically in order to achieve the central objective.

On the assumption that you have a clearly mapped-out grand plan, the logical next step is to ensure that your teams (i.e. workers, voters, supporters, etc) are on the proverbial "same page". It is my view that the first step in solving the crime and unemployment problems facing South Africa is changing the mindset of every South African. A change of mindset, of course, does not happen overnight. Race-consciousness has served its purpose and delivered the political freedom of 1994. But South Africa now needs a different consciousness to shift the economy and its benefits from a situation of near institutionalised poverty to one of wealth creation – before we die from the effects of the economic bullet which accompanied the achievement of the political ballot in 1994.

Industrial development as key

I agree with those who say that industrial development is the key to moving a country from poverty to wealth.[13] Kul Bhushan, former editor of the United Nations' *Africa Industry* said, "If Africa is ever to break the chains of poverty and move along the road to prosperity, it must industrialise."[14] Such thinking is not unfamiliar to our own politicians, as will be discussed in later chapters. It is worth quoting the newly appointed Minister of Trade and Industry Dr Rob Davies' address to the 13th General Conference of the United Nations Industrial Development Organisation (UNIDO) on 7 December 2009:

South Africa is firmly of the view that industrial development must be at the centre of efforts to overcome poverty and underdevelopment. We are well aware that there is no instance in economic history of any country, anywhere or at any time, overcoming poverty and underdevelopment without identifying and supporting economic activities capable of generating increasing, as opposed to diminishing, returns. Industrial activities have always been at the forefront of efforts to set out on such a growth path. [15]

But mere agreement with the industrialisation idea is not enough. Such agreement and sentiment needs to be translated into tangible and measurable action if it is going to bring about a trickle-down of wealth to the majority who are living in dire poverty. A well thought-out industrial policy position, for example, cannot remain a theory. The policy idea (e.g. industrial development) must be translated into measurable actions performed by the people themselves.

Perhaps it is too early to measure, but it may be instructive to note government's sober assessment four years into democratic freedom vis-à-vis industrial policy and action.

Certainly, it is evident that our current industrial policies are not having the desired impacts in particular areas – employment creation and SMME development, most notably. Indeed, some critics regard policy as significantly contributing to poor performance. In particular, trade liberalisation is seen as the source of employment loss. However, the empirical evidence is that employment creation through enhanced export growth has more than compensated for declines in employment due to increased imports – albeit, and this is of significance, employment growth has been very largely located in skills-intensive occupations.[16]

A similar lament can be heard emerging from the Expert Group Meeting on the Industrial Investment Policies in Africa held in Addis Ababa, Ethiopia on 8-9 July 2009 – organised by the African Union (AU) in collaboration with the United Nations Industrial Development Organisation (UNIDO). These experts make the point that:

Africa, with all its rich endowment of natural and mineral resources, is the least industrialised continent of the world. Decades after independence, the continent still depends on the export of raw materials to the industrialised world, which are processed and resold to Africa at much higher prices. The lack of industrialisation of the continent may be attributed to numerous factors, among them inappropriate industrial investment policies, problems associated with infrastructure, market size and lack of technology. Another dimension of the problem is the lack of information to support investment policy formulation due to weak partnership between the investment promotion stakeholders in both the public and private sector, which impacts negatively on evolvement of a common shared vision. More importantly, it is the lack of dynamism in investment promotion strategy design which is attributable to the fact that a constant and sustained outreach to the private sector is not given deserved priority.[17]

The gap between policy and action

The failure of implementation is caused by the gap that exists between policy and action. It is this "bridge" or "distance" or "space" that I call consciousness. This "consciousness space" is the critical bridge that joins policy with action. It is this bridge which is most often characterised by the "if only" discourse. In 1999 UNIDO's Director-General Carlos Magariños said:

> If Africa can process just half of its agricultural produce into finished and semi-finished exportable goods, it can do a great deal to increase its income and improve the standard of living of its peoples while creating employment. [18]

What is it that inhibits the kind of performance Magariños longs to see in Africa? Of course, the answers are complex and one must be careful not to blame the victim for an inability to perform when the victor has the victim tied up in chains. However, the Magariños comment is made in the context of Africa having received billions of dollars of assistance. So it appears that money is not the problem. Of course, as Hubbard rightly points out, aid-ism is no less dangerous than the other -isms (socialism, communism, capitalism and so forth).

Where does crime fit in?

Indications are that there is a growing level of despair regarding crime, which I suspect is beginning to engulf our entire nation (rich and poor alike). We are losing the war.

However, this is not unique to the black-led government of South Africa today. The white-led apartheid government faced similar problems and also failed to adequately deliver on the creation of jobs, safety and security for all.

What is the cause of South Africa's inability to deliver jobs and safety, and eliminate poverty as a result?

The magic-wand approach

If you could wave a magic wand, what would you change about South Africa? Its lethargic and largely incompetent and under-staffed civil service? The ruling party? Government? The over-promising and under-delivering politicians? The ruthless and greedy capitalist business sector? The lazy workforce always game for strike action? The religious leaders who too willingly bow to secular worldly standards and definitions of what it means to be good citizens and moral leaders of society? The plight of our youth? The lack of protection for our young children? So many problems! How does one begin to prioritise?

Many skilled and resourced people are leaving South Africa for greener pastures, notwithstanding government's efforts to retain or attract foreign nationals to South Africa. Skilled South Africans are being incentivised, motivated and encouraged to return home. For example, a daily newspaper recently carried a front-page article offering skilled South African expats generous deployment allowances to return to the country and join the civil service.[19] Those of us left behind and who desire positive change join the many others who similarly desire to change poverty into prosperity and crime into peace in South Africa in our lifetime. We justifiably desire more money in our pockets and we want to live in peace without the fear of senseless and violent crime constantly threatening our lives.

If I had a magic wand I would change the psyche of the entire nation. I would define our nation by what we are able to innovatively and ingeniously produce – black, white, pink and yellow – together as one.

History teaches us that industrial development has proven to be the only sustainable way a country and a nation moves from poverty and senseless violence to relative wealth for all citizens, while at the same time achieving a serious reduction in violent crime.[20] There are other ways to redistribute the wealth of a country. A popular and easy method is forcefully taking wealth (land, possessions, money) from the rich and giving it to the poor (i.e. redistribution of wealth). In the context of South Africa, there is almost justifiable emotional and moral support for this approach. "The whites, after all, have stolen the birthright and wealth from us blacks so we are justified to redress the situation," some might argue.

The targeted and vengeful dispossession of whites (all of whom are assumed to be wealthy) runs deep in the psyche of the black majority. The dispossession of whites will always be an option that enjoys private and tacit moral support. We can probably blame over 350 years of white domination for such a default consciousness. However there are better ways to fix crime and achieve peace and security.

Towards a green industrialisation

An editorial from the *Manila Bulletin* in 2005 is helpful in defining the concept of industrial development.

> Smoke-stack industrialisation may be a bit late … We are still far from that Utopia. In the meantime we have to get our act together. Our poverty is not that of Africa, whom we are unable to help, because of our own poverty. If we take industrialisation in a slightly different sense to mean productivity, organisation and efficiency, then we definitely have to industrialise. Even our agriculture has to be mechanised and information of the advances in microbiology transmitted to our farmers and fisherfolk.

Our South African Minister of Trade and Industry has not only refined his focus, but has innovatively contextualised and focused the industrialisation policy discussion to take account of environmental matters. In this regard, Davies talks about a "green industrialisation":

> While we talk of the potential of the manufacturing sector to contribute to economic revival, we also need to be aware of the imperative for all industrial activity to become greener and more energy-efficient. This is essential to avoid the catastrophic effects of climate change, but it also needs to be recognised that green industrialisation is a major source of opportunity for the development of new, medium-technology industries in the developing world in such areas as solar water heating, concentrated solar power production, wind and biomass energy production, and bio-fuels. [21]

The role of the state

One of the benefits of technology and scientific progress is the increased mechanisation of production processes. Of course, the downside is the redundancy of masses of labour. It is here that the tension is located. Do we pursue industrialisation knowing that a consequence will be increased unemployment and a situation where machines replace human beings? In this regard it may be instructive to note South Africa's national industrial policy framework, which says:

> Therefore our conceptualisation of industrialisation is not restricted to the manufacturing sector but involves a structural change in our growth path towards a more labour-absorbing, value-adding economy.[22]

The challenge we face in South Africa is to create work for millions of unemployed people. So the imperative can only be that of creating a labour-absorbing economy. But can such an economy be competitive or even productive?

A further and contentious policy debate pertains to the role of the state. It is true that the private sector and business in general is more efficient and productive than the state. The state is, after all, set up to govern and not to productively manage a business enterprise. The dismal performance of state-owned enterprises (SOEs) is a small window into this debate. An illuminating perspective on the mind of government and the rationale for what we commonly call the developmental state approach is a statement issued on the eve of the launch of the National Industrial Policy Framework:

> The government's approach to economic transformation is based on the understanding that the necessary changes in the economy will not emerge spontaneously from the invisible hand of the markets but from collective efforts aimed at shaping economic development, and such efforts should be championed by the state. This suggests a developmental state, and a developmental state is one that is capable of leading efficiently in the definition of a common national agenda, mobilising all society to take part in its implementation and directing society's resources towards this common goal.
>
> For the government to effectively play this leadership role it has to get the macroeconomic environment, skills development and industrial policy right. While the government plays this leadership role on one hand, the private sector on the other hand is the main engine of investment, growth and employment creation. [23]

Interim conclusion: So what's the missing element?

History teaches us that industrial development is the key catalyst for economic growth and sustained development.

If industrialisation is the key to eliminating poverty and consequently reducing crime, why is it not happening in Africa and South Africa?

Commentators such as Moeletsi Mbeki argue strongly that the exact opposite to industrialisation, namely deindustrialisation, is happening.[24] Mbeki points out that the manufacturing sector, which should be a key driver in the economy, is being replaced by ballooning imports, especially from Asia.

Whatever the debate, the reality on the ground is that the gap between rich and poor is growing and not narrowing.

If we accept that industrial development is the non-negotiable key that unlocks prosperity and wealth in the economy of South Africa, what would we need to do next given Mbeki's comment that industrialisation presupposes entrepreneurship, which in turn is considered to be a nuisance within the South African economic space? Perhaps a useful offset to Mbeki's comments is the large allocation of funds for youth and entrepreneurial development by the new Minister of Finance, Pravin Gordhan.[25] Too little too late? Or are we moving in the right direction?

Notes

1. See Mashigo P (2010) Socio-economic development and poverty reduction in South Africa In K Kondlo & M Maserumule (Eds) *The Zuma Administration: Critical Challenges*. Cape Town: HSRC Press, p.111.
2. Ibid p.121.
3. See Motlhabi M (1998) *Challenge to Apartheid: Toward a Moral National Resistance*. Grand Rapids: Eerdmans. Also, De Gruchy J & Villa Vicencio C (Eds) (1983) *Apartheid is a Heresy*. Grand Rapids: Eerdmans.
4. See DTI *South Africa's Economic Transformation: A strategy for broad-based black economic empowerment* http://www.thedti.gov.za/bee/bee.htm
5. A comprehensive resource for BEE and related legislation dealing with Employment Equity, Skills, Preferential Procurement as well as a range of supporting policy and strategy documents including Codes of Good Practice, Guide to the Codes, BEE Scorecards, Transformation Charters is the official website of Empowerdex (Economic Empowerment rating Agency) www.empowerdex.co.za, an agency which has been a pioneer in the field of BEE verification and auditing. See also the official website of the Department of Trade and Industry (www.thedti.gov.za).
6. Interestingly the issue of race and national identity as a challenge facing the Zuma administration is a glaring omission from the collection of essays which comprise the recent publication by Kondlo K & Maserumule M (Eds) (2010) *The Zuma Administration: Critical Challenges* Cape Town: HSRC Press. Professor Kondlo, in his Introduction: political and governance challenges (pp.9-10) does however make mention of race saying that "The democratic state, post-1994, despite the radical pretensions of the ruling ANC, cannot deal effectively with the challenge of poverty, as this challenge has implications for the reordering of socio-economic relations in South Africa…The change in socio-economic relations of power is the key project which goes beyond the removal of institutional racial oppression…The battle against poverty is largely a question of creating the circumstances that enable an individual or group to gain power and emerge from poverty on a longer-term basis". Notwithstanding Kondlo's comment in-passing, the almost explicit omission of the "race" question seems to reinforce the view that the Kondlo & Maserumule edited collection of essays does not consider race to be a critical issue facing the Zuma administration. The omission of this topic from the list of challenges facing the Zuma administration, in my view, is therefore most unfortunate. I argue strongly that issues of national identity and race still bedevil South Africa's psyche and

Dr Ruben Richards | 33

therefore it is of paramount importance that the Zuma administration addresses the matter if South Africa is to move towards a united and obsessive effort in combating crime and reducing unemployment.
7   See Appendix 1 below: Founding principles of the Constitution of South Africa.
8   See Appendix 2 below: Preamble to the Constitution of South Africa.
9   The Pretoria High Court made a landmark ruling on 18 June 2008 that South Africans of Chinese descent are to be reclassified as black people and therefore qualify for the benefits of South Africa's employment equity and black economic empowerment laws. The context of this ruling is the complaint by the Chinese Association of South Africa which took the South African government to court, saying its members had been discriminated against with reference to BEE and also claiming that their members often failed to qualify for business contracts and job promotions because they were regarded as whites. During the years of apartheid South African Chinese were classified as "coloured" but generally regarded as white today. See Mbola B (2008) *Chinese South Africans qualify for BEE* (18 June) http://www.southafrica.info/business/trends/empowerment/beechinese-180608.htm
10 See Hubbard RG and Duggan W (2009) *The Aid Trap: Hard Truths about ending poverty* (New York: Columbia University Press, pp3-4.
11 Braverman H (1974) *Labor and Monopoly Capital: The Degradation of Work in the Twentieth Century*. New York: Monthly Review Press, pp.29-30.
12 In 2008, under the leadership of Deputy President Mbete, government released a draft document for discussion called *Towards An Anti-Poverty Strategy for South Africa* – A Discussion Document – October 2008 http://www.info.gov.za/view/DownloadFileAction?id=92543 The proposed anti-poverty framework is anchored on nine pillars including (1) Creation of economic opportunities (2) Investment in human capital (3) Income security (4) Basic services and other non-financial services (5) Improving healthcare (6) Access to assets – particularly housing, land and capital, including public infrastructure (7). Social inclusion and social capital initiatives – combining programmes to ensure a more inclusive and integrated society, based on the development of more integrated structures and engagements across class and race, as well as community solidarity in communities and society as a whole. (8) Environmental sustainability (9) Good governance. Interestingly, this anti-poverty strategy does not problematise issues of national identity or patriotism nor issues relative to racial consciousness as having any impact on an anti-poverty strategy although its pillar dealing with social cohesion begins to address the issue; it locates such initiatives in the realm of arts and culture and family structure (See especially pp.42-43 of the anti-poverty strategy document).
13 A chief protagonist for the primacy of a pro-industrial development thesis for poor countries is Reinert ES (2007) *How Rich Countries Got Rich ... And Why Poor Countries Stay Poor.* London: Constable. The 20th celebrations of the UN sponsored observance of Africa Industrialisation Day created a renewed appreciation for the role of industrialisation. In this regard see the following statements: Kandeh K. Yumkella (2009) Industrialization key to Africa's full integration into global economy, says UNIDO Director-General, Tuesday, 17 November 2009 http://www.unido.org/index.php?id=7881&tx_ttnews%5Btt_news%5D=420&cHash=ecb7997713 Also see statements made by the United Nations General Secretary Ban Ki-Moon who said "The African continent must focus on industrialization as a critical engine of economic growth and development if it has to benefit from the world's recovery from the global economic downturn" (Ki-moon B (2009a) *Still not lived up to potential*, UN Secretary-General Ban Ki-moon's remarks at the 20th Africa Industrialization Day panel on "Industrialization Strategies and Policies: A Key to Economic Transformation of Africa", in New York, today, 20 November 2009. http://www.un.org/News/Press/docs/2009/sgsm12619.doc.htm and Ki-Moon (2009b) *Ban says Africa will benefit from economic recovery if it industrializes* (UN Secretary-General Ban Ki-moon's remarks at the 20th Africa Industrialization Day panel on "Industrialization Strategies and Policies: A Key to Economic Transformation of Africa" http://www.afriquejet.com/news/africa-news/ban-says-africa-will-benefit-from-economic-recovery-if-it-industrializes-2009112138657.html

14 *See* Bhushan K (1999) The industrialisation of Africa.(landmark conference on industrial partnerships and investment in Africa)(Cover Story) *African Business* (November 1, 1999) http://www.highbeam.com/doc/1G1-58169686.html http://www.highbeam.com/doc/1G1-58169686.html

15 *See* Davies R (2009) Statement by Dr Rob Davies, Minister of Trade and Industry during the 13th General Conference of the United Nations Industrial Development Organisation (UNIDO) 7 December 2009. Issued by: Department of Trade and Industry 7 December 2009. www.thedti.gov.za

16 *See* DTI (2001) Driving competitiveness: an integrated industrial strategy for sustainable employment and growth – Discussion Document Version 1.0 dated Monday, 21 May 2001. www.thedti.gov.za

17 *Concept Note*: Expert Group Meeting on the Industrial Investment Policies in Africa. Addis Ababa, Ethiopia 8-9 July 2009. Organized by the African Union (AU) in collaboration with the United Nations Industrial Development Organization (UNIDO).

18 *See* Bhushan K (1999) The industrialisation of Africa.(landmark conference on industrial partnerships and investment in Africa)(Cover Story) African Business (November 1, 1999) http://www.highbeam.com/doc/1G1-58169686.html http://www.highbeam.com/doc/1G1-58169686.htmhttp://www.highbeam.com/doc/1G1-58169686.html

19 *The Cape Times* (January 6th, 2010) featured a front page article "State offers 30% extra to skilled foreigners" written by Ciaphus Kgosana. See also www.homecomingrevolution.co.za.

20 cf. Reinert E (2007). *How rich countries got rich ... And why poor countries stay poor*. Constable: London.

21 Davies R (2009) Statement by Dr Rob Davies, Minister of Trade and Industry during the 13th General Conference of the United Nations Industrial Development Organisation (UNIDO) 7 December 2009. Issued by: Department of Trade and Industry 7 December 2009. htpp://www.thedti.gov.za

22 DTI National Industrial Policy Framework. (with the Executive Foreword by Minister of Trade and Industry *Mandisi Mpahlwa*). Published by Department of Trade and Industry, p.6.

23 DTI (2007) - Update on the process towards the launch of the National Industrial Policy Framework (NIPF) 19 April 2007 – The Developmental State. http://www.info.gov.za/speeches/2007/07041912451003.htm also http://www.dti.gov.za

24 Mbeki M (2009) *Architects of Poverty: Why African Capitalism Needs Changing*. Johannesburg: Picador Africa (See especially Ch 3 (pp.63-100) The Deindustrialisation of South Africa).

25 The maiden budget speech of the newly appointed Minister of Finance has clearly indicated that government's top priority is education and training as well as a focus on job creation particularly for young people. Wage subsidy schemes and the encouragement of employers to absorb youth without significant work experience as a vital part of the education and job creation drive with its focus mainly on the youth. *See* Gordhan P (2010) *Budget Speech 2010* – Minister of Finance. Pravin Gordhan 17 February 2010 www.treasury.gov.za See also a feature article by Chris Barron "Gordhan takes advice from a victim of red tap" (*Sunday Times Business Times*. February 21, 2010, p.10) where a young entrepreneur, Vuyisa Qabaka, is reported to be pleased that the minister acted on his advice to allocate a larger portion of the budget to youth development and entrepreneurship.

Appendix 1 – Founding principles

Founding provisions of the Constitution of South Africa
1. Republic of South Africa
The Republic of South Africa is one, sovereign, democratic state founded on the following values:
   a. Human dignity, the achievement of equality and the advancement of human rights and freedoms.
   b. Non-racialism and non-sexism.
   c. Supremacy of the Constitution and the rule of law.
   d. Universal adult suffrage, a national common voters roll, regular elections and a multi-party system of democratic government, to ensure accountability, responsiveness and openness.

2. Supremacy of Constitution
This Constitution is the supreme law of the Republic; law or conduct inconsistent with it is invalid, and the obligations imposed by it must be fulfilled.

3. Citizenship
1. There is a common South African citizenship.
2. All citizens are
   a. equally entitled to the rights, privileges and benefits of citizenship; and
   b. equally subject to the duties and responsibilities of citizenship.
3. National legislation must provide for the acquisition, loss and restoration of citizenship.

Appendix 2 – Preamble to the Constitution of South Africa

Preamble
We, the people of South Africa,
Recognise the injustices of our past;
Honour those who suffered for justice and freedom in our land;
Respect those who have worked to build and develop our country; and
Believe that South Africa belongs to all who live in it, united in our diversity.
We therefore, through our freely elected representatives, adopt this Constitution as the supreme law of the Republic so as to

> Heal the divisions of the past and establish a society based on democratic values, social justice and fundamental human rights;
> Lay the foundations for a democratic and open society in which government is based on the will of the people and every citizen is equally protected by law;
> Improve the quality of life of all citizens and free the potential of each person; and
> Build a united and democratic South Africa able to take its rightful place as a sovereign state in the family of nations.

May God protect our people.
Nkosi Sikelel' iAfrika. Morena boloka setjhaba sa heso.
God seën Suid-Afrika. God bless South Africa.
Mudzimu fhatutshedza Afurika. Hosi katekisa Afrika.

2 | Renewing the mind of the nation

Growing inequality serves only to erode the fragile unity which holds together the rainbow nation of South Africa.

This chapter discusses issues of patriotism, national unity, and a pledge of allegiance in the context of the call by President Jacob Zuma to build a nation mindful of its history. Notwithstanding this call for unity, the challenge presented by this chapter is its suggestion that instead of defining the nation by its past, we should consider defining ourselves by a vision of the future – an industrialised future and not a racial past. In spite of 16 years of sustained transformation and transition from apartheid, there remain a number of threats to our unity as a nation. The primary threat is poverty and the growing gap between the rich and the poor. Growing inequality serves only to erode the fragile unity which holds together the rainbow nation. A miracle is needed to ensure that the nation grows together rather than apart as South Africa continues to transform 16 years into its life as an emerging democracy and nation. This chapter therefore calls for a self-made and much-needed second nation-building miracle – which will require at least three parts: Part 1 – finding a new mind (i.e. a new basis for unity); Part 2 – living according to a new standard by which we measure nationhood and success; and Part 3 – getting our hands dirty as patriots of a new nation and meaningfully fighting poverty as a collective.

Of one mind

Patriotism and national unity
The worlds of sport and war teach us that a team functions best if all the players share the same vision of the future and of reality. Such a shared picture forms the basis of developing shared and common goals with the hope of developing a oneness of spirit. The same applies to the world of business and politics. Although the application and context may be different, the general principle holds true – your team, your workers, your nation need to be of one mind if you want to accomplish your goals and objectives.

Are South Africans of one mind? Do they share the same vision of the future and of the current challenges facing the country?

A pledge of allegiance
The most critical challenge facing the leadership of the "new" South Africa is to rebuild a nation that was bitterly divided by race. Research has shown that South Africans are among the most patriotic in the world,

according to a 2006 report from the National Opinion Research Center at the University of Chicago.[1] The survey results show that South Africa ranked fourth in terms of national pride, out of the 34 countries surveyed. The top five countries were USA, Venezuela, Ireland, South Africa and Australia. The bottom five were Latvia, Korea, Slovakia and Poland, and last on the list was Germany (East).[2]

People in the 34 countries surveyed were asked to rate how proud they were of their countries in 10 different areas: the workings of their democratic system; political influence in the world; economic success; social security; science and technological achievements; sports, arts and literature; the military; history; and fair treatment of all groups in society.

The report showed some general patterns: former colonies and new nations had high levels of pride, while nations in Asia and countries in Europe, especially those in Eastern Europe, had lower levels of pride.

Around the same time as this report, the Mbeki presidency released a report called *A Nation in the Making: A Discussion Document on Macro Social Trends in South Africa*, a continuation of work done on the government's Ten Year Review, bringing together surveys, census data and studies by a number of independent institutions. This comprehensive report paints a picture of dynamic change in South African society, with rapid social mobility and large improvements in both living conditions and race relations. The report stresses that although economic divisions within the country remain set along the racial fault-lines created by apartheid, South Africa is still a united nation, despite the divisions.

Early in 2008, after the ANC's historical conference in Polokwane but before Jacob Zuma took up office, the education department proposed the introduction of a national pledge to be recited every morning by all public school children. This proposal met with great resistance, notwithstanding the findings of the surveys indicated above. Why would a nation that seems miraculously to have overcome apartheid not be able to agree on a national pledge of allegiance which has as its intention to bind the nation? A confusing picture seems to emerge at the level of national consciousness.

The President's call for renewal

Since the advent of democracy in South Africa, there have been four presidents at the helm of the country. Even though they all emerged from the same political party and stable, their contributions and roles have been very different given the evolving challenges of transformation. Mandela will be remembered for his emphasis on reconciliation. Mbeki's driving vision was giving impetus to the African Renaissance and ensuring that the internal systems of the South African government were not only transformed but that they worked. Motlanthe was a caretaker president with a significant role during the transition from Mbeki to Zuma.

The overarching tone of the April 2009 inaugural speech and comments of South Africa's fourth democratically elected president, Jacob Zuma, was that of a call for renewal and unity. Speaking after being inaugurated as President at the Union Buildings in Pretoria, Zuma held out a hand to all South Africans, saying:

> Let us build a nation that remains forever mindful of its history ... of the many who put down their lives so we can be here today ... A nation filled with the laughter and joy of children. A nation filled with a hope born of the knowledge that, if we work together, we will achieve our dreams.[3]

In addition to the renewal theme, Zuma's speech also indicated a shift in focus and energy from complacency and cynicism towards a renewed energy and commitment to delivery and implementation. This was best illustrated by his personal pledge:

> I commit myself to the service of our nation with dedication, commitment, discipline, integrity, hard work and passion ... there is a lot to be done ... the dreams and hopes of all the people of our country must be fulfilled. There is no place for complacency, no place for cynicism, no place for excuses.

Zuma acknowledged that despite vastly different experiences, divergent interests and varying viewpoints, South Africans shared a common desire for a better life.

> We share a common conviction that never shall we return to a time of division and strife. From this common purpose we must forge a partnership for reconstruction, development and progress.

President Zuma's call and focus regarding government is refreshing, noting his emphasis that everything the government does must contribute directly and meaningfully to improving people's lives. To achieve this, government and civil society must hold themselves to the highest standards of service, probity and integrity.

Zuma urged South Africans to help the government build a society that values excellence and rewards effort while shunning laziness and incompetence; a society that draws on the capabilities, energy and promise of all its people.

A national crisis oddly restated

New priorities
The Zuma administration was elected into office in April 2009 after 16 years of active, deliberate and robust nation-building and societal transformation not seen on such a grand scale anywhere else in the world. Subsequently, the administration adopted the five key priority areas set out at the ANC's Polokwane conference. These are education, crime, unemployment, rural development and health. There seems to be consensus about the lack of public service delivery in general due to a managerial and implementation crisis. The lack of delivery is said to be both a skills and a systems problem. The assumption, then, is that with better managers we will see better delivery.

Two announcements made by the Zuma administration early in office provide useful insight into the critical challenges facing South Africa, as well as government's attitude and response to such challenges.

The first announcement came from the new Minister of Trade and Industry, Dr Rob Davies, who reported that there was no quick-fix solution available to recover the million jobs lost due to the recession.[4] The second announcement came from Bheki Cele, the newly appointed Chief of Police, with regard to the much-anticipated crime statistics. His comment to South Africa was brutally frank when he pointed out that no South African is safe in their own home. He further pointed out that the rapid and alarming increase in house-breakings with aggravating circumstances was a major concern.[5]

As a result of now more reliable and available crime statistics, a different policing discourse and strategy has emerged, constituting a paradigm shift. The current characterisation of police strategy is echoed by the quest of the police leadership to legitimise the "shoot to kill" approach. The debate was triggered by then Deputy Minister of Safety and Security, Susan Shabangu, famous for her words, "kill the bastards if they threaten you or the community", spoken during an anti-crime imbizo in Pretoria in April 2008.

Enhancing political management

It is my sense that much more has been said than actually done about crime reduction and job creation in South Africa. I further sense that the Zuma administration is obsessed with ensuring service delivery. All indications are that government is serious about performance.[6]

The only red flag I wish to raise here is the challenge of separating the roles of referee from that of player. One would have thought that a vibrant opposition would and should fulfil the function of providing a credible audit of performance on the part of the ruling party. It is even more concerning when the ruling party claims such a role for themselves vis-à-vis their own performance. A further feature of the Zuma administration, it seems, will be policy consistency. Zuma has indicated that there will be no fundamental policy shifts, but that the focus of government will be on implementation.

So what can we expect to change over the next five years? Is the lack of delivery purely a managerial and implementation issue, or are their policy problems as well?

I wish to build on President Zuma's political and managerial-leadership approach by proposing a new basis and standard to inform and support his call for renewal and national unity. My proposal is the creation of a new national industrial consciousness as well as a new standard by which to measure nationhood and the progress of South Africa's nation-building programme.[7]

The one competitive advantage we have as South Africans, it seems to me, is that we are all united in our desire for less crime (safety) and more jobs (money) – or as President Zuma said in his inaugural speech, a shared desire for a better life for all.

I believe this is therefore a basis from which to build a new platform, indeed a new national psyche together, with a new performance measure by which we can assess the success or failure of our nation-building programme. Failure to build on what unites us can only be seen as unpatriotic behaviour. In the context of our dire crime and unemployment situation, anything less should be viewed as an act of treason.

Competing realities and perception

The challenge facing South Africa's quest for a united nation is this: Whose interpretation of reality prevails? Whose sense of urgency about transformation and change is considered paramount? Whose view of the world becomes normative for a nation? By whose standards do we measure success?

If we don't have a shared and common understanding of the original target and the performance measure attached to such a target, we will never agree on performance outputs. Furthermore, we will never agree on what success or failure looks like as a nation. Perhaps the Olympic Games provides a useful analogy for our discussion on performance since it is, in the final instance, the global and final arbiter of excellence and performance in sport. The Olympics is the world stage at which the playing fields are assumed to be level. There is no preferential treatment granted for those athletes from disadvantaged backgrounds when competing with others who are considered more advantaged. When we compete against the best of the best in the world, none of our normal preferential excuses is relevant. We accept these conditions when competing globally. We enter the global arena according to the agreed rules of the game and if we lose we don't cry foul. Rather, we accept the results as being objective, fair and a true reflection of our ability.

Priorities: Lead and lag indicators

What constitutes the key priorities facing South Africa? We know that five priorities have been identified by the Zuma administration. In balanced score card and management lingo, we need to ask which of these priorities constitutes lead or lag indicators? If we were to apply the 80:20 rule, meaning 80% results from only 20% effort, what areas should be receiving the most critical attention from government?

Let us once again be helped by lessons from history. We learn from history that the only pathway to economic success and national prosperity is industrial development and the urgent development of a nation's manufacturing capability. There is no other sustainable way out of poverty. History also teaches us that the prosperous nations (old and modern) will invariably dictate to poorer nations how to manage and interpret reality. In a phrase, the wealthy nations of the world will forever be the economic necks that turn the political heads of the poorer nations. So the challenge, it appears, is to industrialise, get wealthy, be your own boss, and be the master and mistress of your own destiny, nationally speaking.

If this is the power of industrialisation, then why is South Africa not making industrial development the centrepiece of its nation-building programme and national identity? Indications are that South Africa hopes to re-industrialise the base of its economy through an infrastructure development stimulus package focusing on energy and transport, and with a budget in excess of R780bn. But does this constitute only one of many other competing policies, priorities and programmes on a cluttered nation-building agenda? I believe that industrial development should be the cornerstone of our economic recovery programme, not just in terms of political rhetoric but in every respect and aspect of the nation-building agenda.

Who must create the jobs?
My view is that the primary responsibility for creating new jobs is that of business and the private sector. Government's role should be to govern. My experience of the public service is that at a practical level, the state is ill-suited for the task of job creation.

It is in this context that the nationalisation of state assets must also be located. Countries that have enjoyed rapid economic recovery have shown a greater tendency to privatise than to nationalise.

The years ahead will no doubt be characterised by enormous tension between the emotional and nostalgic pull towards nationalisation as opposed to soberly assessing those economic recovery models which show an appreciation for privatisation. Government is certainly an enabler of job creation but, in my view, is limited in its ability to create and sustain decent employment.

An industrial consciousness?

Towards a definition
Is it appropriate to be talking about industrialisation for South Africa when the vast majority of its people are still living in rural areas and have

rural-agricultural-agrarian mindsets? Should we not rather talk about an agricultural consciousness? Should we not leave industrialisation to countries such as Japan, Korea, Germany and China? Of course, this is exactly where the fallacy resides. All industrialised countries were at some stage dominated by an agricultural mode of production, but did not stay in such a mode.

History demonstrates that through the centuries, countries, including those in the modern era, post-World War II (such as Germany in the 1940s and 1950s and the rise of the Asian Tigers (Hong Kong, Singapore, Taiwan, Korea) in the 1970s, 1980s and 1990s) have moved away from poverty towards wealth via the road called industrialisation. A review of the past 500 years of industrial development in Europe and the USA, and more recently in the Asian countries, confirms that this is the route from poverty to prosperity.

Korea, a major economic power today, was poorer than Kenya as recently as the 1950s. Germany today is among the wealthiest countries in the world and yet it was barely 50 years ago that Germany was reduced to ashes in the context of the Second World War. Of course, not only Germany, but the European continent as a whole, needed to be rebuilt after the war. How did these nations go from being destroyed by war into such economically powerful nations today? The short answer is: industrialisation.

The Secretary-General of the United Nations, Ban Ki-moon issued a statement on Africa Industrialisation Day which has been commemorated on 20 November for the past 20 years. He reminded his 2009 audience that "History teaches us that manufacturing acts as a stimulus for economic transformation in developing countries." He went on to bemoan the fact that 20 years after instituting an Africa Industrialisation Day, "Africa still accounts for just over 1% of world industry, and industrial development on the continent has lagged behind other developing countries."

I believe that the reason the African continent is as desperately poor and diseased as it has ever been, is because, while we have the correct words, our mindset is completely out of tune with the words and rhetoric of industrialisation. My assertion is that without an explicit linkage between theory and practice, one is likely to end up with 20 more years of industrial policy words, and absolutely no meaningful industrial action. The missing piece – the bridge – is what I call industrial consciousness.

Denialism and façades

South Africa remains a nation of contrasts in both its abilities and its economic status. We can't deliver basic services to the poor but we build world class sports stadiums and upgrade local airports to world class standards. It must be said that we may be able to buy time as a nation by hosting big parties like the soccer extravaganza FIFA 2010 World Cup, and enjoy watching those who can afford it take a ride in expensive toys such as the Gautrain, South Africa's first high-speed rail link operating between Johannesburg and Pretoria. These mega projects are vanity purchases made by the rich and the powerful – not completely necessary but flaunted for all to see. But once the novelty has worn off, we have to face some ugly realities which indicate that we are a nation in serious trouble. For example, the world class Cape Town International airport is located in an area with the highest murder rate per capita in the world. The airport is also adjacent to the second-largest sprawling township in South Africa with almost two million inhabitants, most of whom are living below the poverty line.

Instead of building magnificent façades such as the new hallway entrances to airports and world class sports stadiums so as to adequately impress the friends of the rich and the powerful, we should rather be uncompromisingly investing in and protecting our manufacturing industries.

Unfortunately, as a nation, we don't share the same priorities, and as a result, we are at risk of producing white elephants at worst, and at best purchasing toys which offer enjoyment for a limited and exclusive audience.

Cornerstone issues of nation building

Crime and unemployment are the cornerstone issues of any nation-building programme. If crime and safety issues were sorted out, many skilled people would choose to stay in South Africa. If unemployment was sorted out, poverty would be reduced.

Why has government not succeeded in reducing crime adequately or solving unemployment? I suggest that the primary reason, as indicated above, is that there is no unifying and all-inclusive nation-building principle that energises and propels the nation into collective and patriotic action.

Unfortunately the "better life for all" campaign has turned out to be a better life for some. The recent and innovative planning and performance-monitoring capacities in the Zuma presidency are to be applauded and if implemented as envisaged, will go a long way towards addressing some of the challenges facing government.

But more is needed than another commission. My view is that the Zuma-era intervention of planning and performance monitoring will not be enough. The planning and evaluation monitoring capacity will be limited and serve only to prioritise and monitor the performance of the players of the current game plan. The critical question is whether or not we in fact have a game plan in the first instance. And secondly, do we have the right players on the team to ensure victory?

What I am proposing goes beyond innovations such as the planning commission and the performance monitoring and evaluation ministry. The planning commission, at its core, intends to be that necessary internal management, prioritising and performance-enhancing watchdog, a long-overdue mechanism. But is this the sign of a totally new game plan or a minor adjustment to an existing plan? We learn from the private sector that an independent auditor or quality-assurance mechanism is considered far more reliable than the in-house capacity. In some instances, the law prescribes that such auditing should be completely independent and conducted by a third party.

What I am proposing is not the disbanding of initiatives such as the planning commission. The rules of conventional warfare teach us that for any army to win the war there has to be reliable intelligence and punctilious operational focus. With industrial consciousness, I propose a new intelligence base and focus – a non-divisive focus which goes beyond a party-political solution and one which has the power to energise and motivate an entire nation if correctly managed.

We need a paradigm shift

The rural-urban divide
A significant part of the problem and therefore challenge facing South Africa is that 80% of our population is still in the agrarian and agricultural mindset. The same could be said for a significant portion of the African continent. If we are to progress then we must change this mindset.

Perhaps the first step here is the rapid commercialisation of farming which could be a stimulus for industrial growth. However, given the sensitivities and unfinished apartheid land-claims issues, combined with the apartheid legacy which sees commercial farming still mainly in the hands of Afrikaner whites, the call for commercialisation of farming in general is likely to be a very politically charged matter.

A new dogma

The solution to our crime and unemployment problem starts with what you and I (i.e. the ordinary citizen) believe about ourselves in the first instance, and then what we collectively believe about our abilities as a nation united in purpose.

I don't believe that the mind of the ordinary South African has yet been fully liberated or properly educated with regard to the power and potency of industrial development. I also don't think that the ordinary South African has been properly educated or informed about the benefits of industrialisation and what is needed for our country to radically alter its crime and unemployment profile. I believe once we collectively understand these things, we will take a very different view of the performance of both government and private business.

I want *industrial consciousness* and *industrialisation* to be the new dogma, the new discourse, the new orthodoxy, the new DNA of the South African soul.

The bad things we tolerate!

I am astounded by the human capacity to get used to bad things and adapt to terrible circumstances rather than to change them for the better. I am amazed at how tolerant we as South Africans have become of the unacceptably high levels of crime and unemployment in our country. What is it about our South African psyche that makes us merely grin and bear our misery as a dispossessed people, country and continent?

I also suspect that we have become used to the fact that our national unemployment rate is somewhere between 25% and 35%. In any other country in the world, I suspect that such high levels of unemployment would be classified as a national disaster. This situation has the potential to escalate from criminal unrest to war – an internal war that will be characterised by a scramble for basic services and necessities. A starving person will not continue to starve to death if just across the railway line there is a house full of food.

As a nation we seem to have quietly accepted the recent finding that South Africa has the greatest disparity between the rich and poor class of any given society in the world. In the wake of such a finding, like water off a duck's back, we continue to live our daily lives as normal.

We have become used to non-delivery of even the most basic of services and the protests that occasionally bring this non-delivery to our attention. We have become used to corrupt and non-performing politicians and the myriad excuses provided to explain the abuse of public money. And we have become used to being unemployed and beaten up by criminals.

Change management

Adapt or die

It is my view that if all South Africans shift their thinking, their energies, and their emotions towards industrial consciousness, we will see the birth of a new and inspired nation – one that is determined and capable of ridding itself of the scourge of crippling poverty and debilitating crime; a nation that will successfully create its own wealth and prosperity; a nation that will not depend on handouts from rich countries or rich individuals in our own country.

The truth is that there is nothing stopping us, today, from achieving economic freedom. We have the resources, we have the skills, we have the people, we have the money, and we still have good international friends. But, unfortunately, we don't have the correct frame of mind that will direct our patriotic spirits and energies.

It is our "unwillingness to change" that accounts for why we as South Africans and we as the African continent are still in such a mess – politically and economically – in spite of all the rhetoric to the contrary. As they say, old habits die hard.

In order to change our way of thinking we must get behind the political and business rhetoric and unmask things. We need to go behind the veil and deal with what will at times be uncomfortable truths about ourselves as individual citizens and also as a nation.

Benchmarking and solutions

Characteristics of a solution
The best solution is not necessarily one that enjoys consensus or official support. In many instances the solution is wrapped up and to be found in visionary leadership surrounded by a team who trust their leader. Nevertheless, a solution to job creation and crime reduction must be all-embracing and one which all South Africans must be able to believe in.

I am bold enough to propose a solution, indeed a game plan, for consideration not only by the political and business leaders, but indeed for consideration and testing by the ordinary South African patriot.

My view is that if South Africa is to survive another 16 years, and deepen some of the gains of the previous 16, then something dramatic must happen at the level of job creation and crime reduction. As a nation we will only be able to live off the gains of the past for a short period – until the hunger pangs return. Levels of crime and unemployment have reached epic proportions and it is only a question of time before the ticking bomb explodes. We need a solution that welds together our nation with a singularity of purpose and vision.

Emulate success, not failure
We accept that the poor will always be among us and that there will always be a need for charity and humanitarian goodwill agencies. But when poverty is structurally orchestrated and institutionally dehumanising, a different approach and attitude is required.

The driving vision and desire of successful economies is the quest to achieve what is sometimes described as a "middle-income economy". The definition of such an economy needs to be carefully unpacked and can be both controversial and misunderstood. For example, South Africa is considered to be a middle-income economy occupying a space in the upper percentile with an average annual income of USD3,630 per person.[8] In current South African currency this equates to about R115.00 per day (approx USD 14.00 per day). In an advanced economy such as Singapore, for example, the average daily income per person is R 1,880.00 (approx USD 235.00 per day).

A middle-income economy is to be distinguished from a socio-economic environment where there are systemically orchestrated disparities and unacceptable gaps between the rich and the poor of the same country and economy, as revealed by the Gini coefficient analysis for South Africa. Middle-income economies are not characterised by grinding poverty, unemployment or destabilising levels of criminal activity. This interpretive framework helps to put matters into perspective when making comparisons of regional and global economies. The disparity between a wealthy First World and a poverty-stricken Third World economy is a case in point.

Strategic and multi-disciplinary interface

The bold proposal of this book is that the solution to crime and unemployment lies in the development of a national industrial (and not political) consciousness. My limited personal experience with regard to both government and private industry practices in terms of problem solving, is that there is a tendency to have a "silo" approach to matters. Rarely is a multi- or inter-disciplinary perspective brought to bear in terms of a theoretical solution. So, in the case of government, for example, crime problems are dealt with by the crime fighters, namely the police. When a cross-sectoral multi-disciplinary approach is adopted, it is generally in the arena of operational collaboration as opposed to methodological, theoretical or even ideological juxtapositioning.

The solution to crime and unemployment proposed here is based on the critical and strategic interplay between industrialisation on the one hand and a crime-prevention strategy on the other. Furthermore, the proposed solution as set out here is only valid if we accept that collaboration must go beyond operational efficiency and include a fundamental "ideological" restructuring of the psyche of the South African nation. This reordering of the psyche must go beyond party-political interests and must serve as the major motivator and driver of the masses as the primary driver for change.

It is only when the ordinary citizen embraces the solution, with a new mindset and a dogged determination to hold an entire society accountable; that we will see any real change in either crime or unemployment levels. A good reminder is that public servants must serve and not be served, all the way from the President to the municipal street sweeper. These are our paid employees who must realise that we pay their wages. We, the ordinary citizens, are their bosses.

A three-element solutions process

A self-made second miracle is required
What is needed, 16 years into democracy in South Africa, is a self-made second miracle which will provide a long-lasting solution to crime and unemployment. If the first South African miracle was political in nature, then the second miracle needed must surely be economic in orientation. In other words, South Africa desperately needs an economic miracle to complement the political miracle of the past 16 years. The creation of a middle-income economy with a vibrant and aspirant middle class is the real and ultimate goal that needs to be achieved if South Africa is to be a truly liberated country. This requires a change of mindset and the creation of a new basis for patriotic and national identity, the adoption of a new standard by which to measure nationhood, and collective action driven by patriotic self interest.

Element 1 – A new mind
The first step towards a solution is therefore the renewing of the mind and soul of South Africa – the creation of a new paradigm for patriotism using industrial consciousness as the foundation for such patriotism and national self-understanding.

Element 2 – A new standard as a precondition
The second aspect is the necessary adoption of an agreed-upon performance standard by which to measure nationhood and by which to assess the success or shortcomings of the South African nation-building programmes.

Element 3 – Get your hands dirty: A patriotic vested interest
The third step of the solutions process is a call for national action where every citizen is obsessively and positively contributing to the attainment of the agreed-upon goals set for the economy. In practice this means that the nation is abuzz with talk, activity, monitoring and reflection on achieving its goals – but not as spectators. We must all hold each other accountable for our actions and at the same time positively motivate each other to achieve the necessary targets. It must be as if the entire nation is on the edge of its seat cheering on its front runners in the race. In truth, many races are won by the sheer energy of the supporting crowd.

Concluding comments

Deepening existing solutions or finding a new way
I acknowledge that there may be many activities underway to solve an ever-deepening and desperate situation regarding crime and unemployment. Nevertheless, my intention is to propose a solution to crime and unemployment informed by my first-hand experiences, traumas and active-participant perspectives gained in the trenches of transformation and nation-building during the first 16 years of the new South Africa.

The solution-finding approach and premise adopted here is one which says that we sometimes already have the solution in our hands but we just don't see it until someone points it out to us. Thus, my approach is that of critically examining what is currently in the hands of South Africa to solve its problems, since it is likely that the magic may already be at our fingertips.

No holy cows allowed
There can be no holy cows regarding the current policy framework, regardless of who has formulated it. The type of economy required to stabilise democracy in South Africa is a matter that must constantly be reviewed taking cognisance of unique South African and contextual considerations such as levels of education, the national skills profile, work-ethic issues, cultural factors, belief systems and so forth. This, of course, raises fundamental macro-ideological issues around a social welfare state versus a free-market economy, or a government-regulated economy via the developmental state ideology. These matters will no doubt create a vociferous debate between the labour movement, business and the ruling party as to the type of economy best suited to help South Africa achieve a better life for all its citizens. But in the end, whatever the final policy decision, it will require a political and economic maturity to roll up one's sleeves and make a meaningful contribution to the solution, even if one's own policy suggestions are not translated into a mandate for implementation.

Let's have a war of words first
We need to find ways to weld together an increasingly fractured society. The issue of crime and unemployment is so serious that I believe the

President should call an official "state of emergency" and force the best brains to come up with a rescue plan for the nation. We are on the brink of disaster. The matter is so grave that we should all stop what we are doing and apply our minds to finding a solution. Let us, as a nation, engage in a war of words and ideas before we have a war of real bullets.

The new challenge

The renewal of our minds and souls begins with confronting some uncomfortable truths about ourselves – truths which we may initially deny and call baseless – and yet hidden deep in our psyche somewhere is a demon that must be exorcised.

As was often said during the anti-apartheid struggle days – *Aluta Continua* – the struggle continues.

Notes

1. *See* http://www.southafrica.info/about/people/nationalpride-norc.htm
2. *See* Appendix 3 – National Pride Rankings for 34 countries surveyed.
3. *See* Presidency (2009) Address by His Excellency Mr Jacob Zuma on the occasion of his Inauguration as fourth President of the Republic of South Africa - 09 May 2009 http://www.politicsweb.co.za/politicsweb/view/politicsweb/en/page71619?oid=128187&sn=Detail
4. *See* Samantha Enslin-Payne's article in the Business Report, Monday Nov 2nd, 2009, p.13 "No quick fix to recover a million jobs: Employment growth to lag economic revival"
5. *See* SAPS (2009) – *The Crime Situation in South Africa* (2008/09) – Annual Report (published on SAPS website – www.saps.gov.za). The report deals with the reported national serious crime figures and ratios for the 2008/2009 financial year (that is the period 1 April 2008 – 31 March 2009). These are compared to the figures recorded during the preceding financial years since 2003/2004. The provincial crime figures are also analysed in more detail and some findings based mainly on docket analysis of a number of contact crimes are discussed. More detailed crime figures are provided on the SAPS website. For example, the analysis for robbery shows that 59,5% of robberies occur in the public street, 15,2% robberies occur at residential properties and 11,5% of robberies occur at business premises (see p.16).
   As this book went to press the South African Police released its official report on the crime situation in South Africa for the period April 2009 – March 2010. All crime types show a decrease except for assault with the intent to inflict grievous bodily harm as well as common assault which when combined shows an increase of 3%. The decrease in crime overall provides a basis for cautious optimism. The sharp decrease in the murder rate is encouraging showing that 1,314 less murders were committed when compared to the figures for the previous reporting period namely 2008/09. This represents, a -7,2% decrease "... in real figures ... [and] is the single most significant decrease in the murder rate since the implementation of the 7-10% reduction target during January 2004." (page 8 of The Crime Situation in South Africa – 2009/2010 – For the full report See http://www.saps.gov.za/statistics/reports/crimestats/2010/crime_situation_sa.pdf
6. One of the first interventions of the Zuma administration was the creation of two new ministries located in the Presidency and designed to improve performance, monitoring and planning of government. *See* Chabane C (2010) Focus now on delivering the right stuff – Article in *Sunday Times* 14 February 2010, page 8. See also Boyle B (2010) Will Mr Delivery deliver? – Article in *Sunday Times* February 14, page 4

7   I share the view that performance measurement is the process by which businesses, governments and other organisations establish criteria for determining the quality of their activities, based on organisational goals. It involves creating a simple, but effective, system for determining whether organisations meet objectives. Effective performance measurement therefore requires quantitative evidence to determine organisational progress toward achieving its goals. For other useful and short definitions see http://www.ehow.com/about_5162691_definition-performance-measurement.html
8   *See* Economic Justice Network of FOCCISA Policy Series 3/2009, p.1. *See also* Income and Expenditure of Households 2005/2006 – Stats SA report http://www.statssa.gov.za/ies/Pamphlet.pdf which provides an annual income breakdown per population group as White (R280,870 USD 35,108); Indians (R134,543 USD 16,818); Coloured (R79,423 USD 9,928); African (R37,711 USD 4,714). Comparative statistics is always tricky but Singapore, for example, has an average annual income of USD 59,400 R 475,200) – *see* "Key Household income trends for 2008 – Department of Statistics, Singapore http://www.straitstimes.com/STI/STIMEDIA/pdf/20090120/op-s15.pdf

Appendix 3 – National Pride Rankings for 34 countries surveyed

As per 2006 National Opinion Research Center (NORC) at the University of Chicago in the US

Ranking for (area-specific) national pride:
1. United States
2. Venezuela
3. Ireland
4. South Africa
5. Australia
6. Canada
7. Philippines
8. Austria
9. New Zealand
10. Chile
11. Great Britain
12. Israel
13. Uruguay
14. Finland
15. Spain
16. Denmark
17. Switzerland
18. Japan
19. France
20. Portugal
21. Hungary
22. Bulgaria
23. Norway
24. Russia
25. Sweden
26. Slovenia
27. Germany (West)
28. Czech Republic
29. Taiwan
30. Latvia
31. Korea
32. Slovakia
33. Poland
34. Germany (East)

3 | The B-BBEE bombshell

Transformation is a hazardous business at the best of times.

This chapter discusses the alleged failure of South Africa's economic transformation policy and project, namely black economic empowerment (BEE), later refined to be more inclusive and subsequently renamed broad-based black economic empowerment (B-BBEE). My contention is that BEE has, in fact, worked brilliantly and as originally designed. BEE has created a new class of super-wealthy black aristocrats, as intended. It is now widely acknowledged that BEE has not benefited the masses, who, it seems, were under the impression that BEE would be the solution to the rampant economic inequalities inherited from past generations of colonial and apartheid white-minority economic protectionism.

In this chapter, a proposal is made regarding the creation of a wide-ranging middle class. Such a class not only serves to provide stability for an emerging (and also a mature) democracy, but also provides a level of risk mitigation where societal change and transformation management options tend to force the choice between the bullet and the ballot. In the final analysis, economic prosperity for the vast majority of citizens will only begin when there is an active attempt to improve the economy of the country. This is when the real battle for the heart and soul of the South African nation begins.

Unmasking South Africa's BEE psyche

BEE is not only part of our everyday vocabulary; it is part of the psyche of our nation.

BEE was designed to be the key solution in transforming South Africa's economy for the benefit of the masses, and thus solving the real problem of poverty. But as we are now learning, BEE has not worked as it was intended to. It has created an even wider chasm between the "have's" and the "have-not's". Our economy and our society is growing apart with two identifiable groups emerging – those "with" money and jobs, and those "without".

It is not true to say that BEE is the sole cause of this growing gulf. But what is being alluded to by many thought leaders is that BEE has become a major contributor to the growing divide between rich and poor.

After 16 years of transformation and nation building, South Africa's transition has brought with it not only the political ballot, but a fatal economic bullet, the effects of which we are only now beginning to feel.

Speaking on behalf of the President at the launch of the Presidential BEE Advisory Council on 4 February 2010, the Deputy President of South Africa, Kgalema Motlanthe, admitted that government's key policy intended to redress the economic wrongs of the past, namely BEE, has not worked as intended.

The economic transformation imperative

One of the most effective ways to address poverty is to create an economy that produces wealth and prosperity for all its citizens. BEE was intended to achieve this, we are told. Government defines BEE as:

> ... an integrated and coherent socio-economic process that will directly contribute to the economic transformation of South Africa and bring about significant increases in the numbers of black people that manage, own and control the country's economy, as well as significant decreases in income inequalities.[1]

At the launch of the Presidential BEE Advisory Council, the Deputy President said:[2]

> ... The speed of economic transformation, we have to admit, has been frustratingly slow at times ... We also have to admit that the "broad-based" part of BEE has seemed elusive. In the main, the story of black economic empowerment in the last 15 years has been a story dominated by a few individuals benefiting a lot ... Only a few benefit again and again from the bounty of black economic empowerment ... This state of affairs cannot be tolerated.

Motlanthe went on to call for creative solutions to one of South Africa's biggest policy setbacks. Motlanthe's challenge, directed at the BEE council, has a much broader audience as he quoted from the B-BBEE act to support his plea:

> We have to think creatively about ways in which ... we can increase "the extent to which communities, workers, co-operatives and other collective enterprises own and manage existing and new

enterprises and increase their access to economic activities, infrastructure and skills training".

Perhaps the most interesting and revealing comment concerns his view regarding a solution:

> We have to come up with strategies of "empowering rural and local communities by enabling [their] access to economic activities, land, infrastructure, ownership and skills" ... If we broaden the meaning of black economic empowerment in this way, the measure of success will also have to change. It can no longer be satisfactory only to count the number of black millionaires and billionaires, important as it is ... Fundamentally, we have to constantly strive towards making sure that more people are employed in decent jobs.

Similar sentiments were expressed by the Treasurer-General of the ANC, Mathews Phosa. More than a year before Motlanthe's speech quoted above, Phosa, himself a successful businessman and BEE beneficiary, delivered a lecture for MBA students at the University of the Free State. His view:

> I don't believe black economic empowerment (BEE) has worked in South Africa. It has created millionaires and superstars while our people should rather have been equipped with basic skills.[3]

The acknowledgement by the ruling party (i.e. the ANC) via its Treasurer-General,[4] and government's official acknowledgement via the Deputy President of the country that BEE has "failed" is sobering. The entire economic architecture of post-apartheid South African society and its economy was designed and premised on the assumptions and philosophical underpinnings of BEE. As a transformation imperative, BEE was intended to drive and facilitate the creation of an inclusive economy. It will, of course, remain a vociferous debate as to whether the policy of BEE has failed or whether it is merely a matter of poor implementation of an intrinsically and fundamentally good policy. The current government view is that it depends on effective implementation, with the solution being to curb its abuse. In this regard Motlanthe was clear, saying;

I would like to urge that because our collective future depends on the proper implementation of BEE, we should actively guard against its abuse. Moreover, we should ensure that as we criticise, we propose solutions to the problems we identify.

South Africa now needs to go back to the economic transformation drawing board and seek solutions to one of the most devastating consequences of apartheid ideology and Afrikaner nationalism, namely an economy that deliberately excluded the meaningful participation of the majority of its black citizens. This is second only to the devastation caused by apartheid education policies – the effects and after-shock of which we are also still feeling. The combination of a failed education policy coupled with the acknowledged failure of the BEE economic policy poses a serious challenge to the South African nation-building and transformation agenda.

What's the real problem?

Before one gets to solutions one must, of course, know what the problem is. In the case of our economy and BEE, is the problem that we have too few millionaires and billionaires? Or is the problem that we have a fundamentally flawed and failed economic strategy? Is the problem that there are too few black business owners and managers in the economy? Or is it that our economy continues to produce too many unemployed black people in our society?

A critique of BEE

In order to understand the real problem around BEE let us again lean on Motlanthe's sober commentary and analysis:

> Only a few benefit again and again from the bounty of black economic empowerment … this is a state of affairs that can no longer be tolerated … this may mean that we look at black economic empowerment beyond business deals and shareholding in companies.

The core thrust of BEE was, as Motlanthe says, about deals and shareholding. This was the way the economy was going to be arrested and transformed, namely by ensuring that we blacks got our hands on the current wealth in the South African economy, which was largely in white hands. We needed to get our piece of the pie through business deals and shareholding. The hope was that with blacks in charge and empowered with shareholding and management power, there would be a trickle-down of wealth to the black majority.

It is now evident that the shareholding transfer side of BEE has been a success. Those white-controlled businesses intending to benefit from government contracts were forced, by law, to create space for a black face on the board of shareholders as well as the management board. The fact that the community of black shareholders was limited and gave rise to what the media called the usual BEE suspects, is a natural consequence and combination of the design of BEE and the human condition of greed.

From a performance perspective, however, BEE has not failed. In fact, it has been a brilliant success. There has been superb delivery in terms of the core goal and objective of current BEE legislation, namely that of a change in ownership and management within the existing economy of South Africa.

A new solution is requested

The solution to a failed or underperforming economy involves a much deeper solution than fine-tuning existing policies such as BEE. Economic transformation, and recovery of our nation is dependent on the extent to which we develop a new national psyche – one which has an industrial as opposed to a racial flavour, as was the case with BEE. I do believe, however, that in order to fix the economy, formerly excluded citizens need to participate. But how? And at what level?

The BEE imperative, focus and hope was for participation at the level of ownership and management. And in this regard BEE has been extremely successful. One of the misleading elements and probably unintended consequences of the current BEE framework is its obsessive focus on ownership and management as opposed to, for example, entrepreneurship or the industrial competence of the workforce required for a growing economy. Not everyone can or should become a business owner, manager or entrepreneur. One school of thought states that the number of entrepreneurs required by any society is probably no more than 2% of the population. The entrepreneurs create jobs through their visionary and out-of-the-box approach to life. The managers get the job done by putting in place appropriate teams of people whose outputs are governed by tightly managed performance systems.

One must contrast the needs of entrepreneurs and managers with those of the masses. The vast majority of people simply want a decent job. We can't all be bosses and only some will ever be bosses and managers; the rest of us may be quite content to be ordinary workers.

In my experience, what matters most to workers is that their wages are decent, and that there is no exploitation. An absolute bonus is when the worker enjoys a level of job satisfaction as well. This does not mean that workers cannot be "owners" via a share-incentive scheme or a profit share or similar. But in the main, workers are driven by the need for decent work and pay.

A healthy economy is driven by a workforce that is emotionally and technically empowered. But how do you get a dehumanised, beaten-down, tired, depressed, unemployed and exhausted nation of citizens excited about work and economic revival? How do we revive a sense of patriotism and trust when the one policy that was meant to deliver the goods (BEE), is now acknowledged as having miserably failed the masses?

Nationhood and race relations

In South Africa one must be extremely cautious when talking of a shared national identity or consciousness. We come from a history saturated with racial conflict. Mandela's reconciliatory attitude and Archbishop Emeritus Desmond Tutu's notion of a rainbow nation have gone a long way to stabilise and capture a national unity within a context of cultural diversity and multiple ethnic origins. But tensions and uncertainty about our national identity remain.

So how is South Africa currently defined? Is it by race? This has important implications as we respond to the challenge of making a positive contribution to finding solutions to the shortcomings of BEE. The BEE intervention, as we have seen, is a deliberate attempt to deracialise the economy. So in the economic sense, race is still a factor. But, in theory, race is no longer a factor in terms of cultural identity. In short, we don't have race as a determinant of political and cultural identity – but we do have race as a determinant of economic identity and therefore, it can be argued, we need a race-based BEE economic policy.

So the thorny race-based question is this: What would be the difference if the economy remained in white hands? Given the outcome of BEE at present, let me put the question differently: What would be the difference if the economy remained in the hands of the wealthy class of our South African society – a class now not defined by race but rather by capital and asset accumulation? Let's ask one more heretical question: Was or is BEE a bounty-hunting exercise – a sophisticated dispossession exercise – or is it an attempt to create energy and entrepreneurship within the economy and thereby grow the economy? We have seen that a change of ownership and management control is no guarantee of a trickle-down. Greed, selfishness and nepotism, we are learning, are not racial characteristics. The unfortunate reality is that just because we have more black owners, this does not translate into a healthier economy. Regardless of who is in control of the economy, you would still need a battery of controls to ensure that exploitation and dehumanisation does not occur in the workplace. By the same token, you cannot afford economic entitlement based purely on colour to ensure the growth of the economy.

What is needed, in my view, is a total mindshift of all parties active in the economy. The owner wants to make as much as he or she can in terms of the bottom line. We live in a free and democratic country and after all, this is how the free-market works. Based on the current economic framework, workers also need to be able to sell their skills to the highest bidder and must be empowered to do so.

The problem arises when the managers and leaders of your society have produced a generation of citizens who, in the main, are unable to contribute meaningfully to the growth of the economy even where such a growth target is conservatively set at 4% to 6%. A country like Botswana, for example, has enjoyed sustained growth of 7% per annum for over 16 years. If Botswana can do it then why can't South Africa achieve the same, given that we have more resources than Botswana?

Where is the skills mismatch between where the leaders want to take the economy and where the people's skills are, as a result of the education policies of the very same leaders? How do we objectively performance-manage our nation and its leaders so that we all share the same picture of reality and understand the kind of performance outcomes we are anticipating? Too often the goal posts shift when people don't perform.

They just find another excuse for non-delivery. And the masses, like sheep to the slaughter, use the ballot to re-elect the same non-performing officials. Very soon, I fear, the bullet could replace the ballot. I hope we never get to that point in our beloved country.

The expectation gap between the rich ruling party and the poor masses who are allegedly part of the same ruling party is bound to create tension. This may be the basis of the alleged tensions within the current alliance partners of the ANC coalition. In addition to tension, this growing expectation gap is likely to cause performance anxiety. Up-skilling (i.e. education) is probably the answer. However, before we end up with another generation of post-apartheid mis-educated learners, we need to ask critical questions about the type of education and training that is required by our economy. And to do that we first need to agree on the type of economy we want to create – lest we end up with an even greater gap between the rich owners and managers in our economy on the one hand, and the poor and educationally misaligned impoverished masses on the other.[5]

The missing piece of the puzzle in South Africa is a vibrant middle class. A middle class emerges from the active and deliberate creation of a middle-income economy[6] with a punctilious industrial and manufacturing focus.[7] We need to refocus the mindset of our people to achieve that kind of economy where the predictable result must be jobs and decent pay for all, as opposed to shares and management control for a select few. If we don't create a middle class to offset the growing gap between rich and poor, we are headed for disaster.

Case study – The training risk: motivating workers to learn

Much continues to be said about the skills crisis in South Africa and much is being done to remedy the situation. This case study is a contribution to the discussion from the perspective of offering workers the opportunity to improve themselves through company-sponsored training.

The company was almost 90 years old and the largest in its industry sector, with a history of exclusive white ownership and management control. I put together a consortium and with the help of a visionary private financier staged a 100% black buy-out of the company. I was not able to convince the traditional BEE-funding agencies to put money behind my project. My consortium and consequently shareholders were therefore the first generation of owners who were not white in the 90-year history of the company. I was appointed as the first black CEO of the company, which enjoyed global brand recognition in its industrial sector. My board consisted of 80% black directors (three black males and one black female). We had one white male making up 20% of the board. He was a former shareholder whom we retained for purposes of skills transfer and institutional memory. He also provided a level of comfort to the client base of the company.

Many things were required to shift the company from the Stone Age into the Space Age, including installing a computer network and an email system. The change and transformation programme was extensive, robust and intensive, and constituted a major re-engineering of the company.

The company was unionised along predictable racial lines and as such had three active unions lobbying for membership. When we took over, an interesting shift took place. Certain members of management joined a union.

The company's services included marine and general engineering maintenance with a focus on heavy engineering, steel fabrication and electrical work. We offered clients a range of specialised services but, as I explained to my shop stewards, the way the company made money was not by repairing oilrigs and large ships; rather, it was by selling time coupled with services rendered in our massive workshops and with our on-the-move equipment.

The point I was making was this: we sold time and either made or lost money depending on the quality of labour and the level of productivity. It was for this reason that I did not want to hear about strikes or go-slows after the event. I needed to have an early warning system to alert me to potential labour disgruntlement, since the selling of labour hours was the basis of the company's economic and financial survival.

Fortunately, having worked on the shop floor I was well aware that labour disgruntlement is only ever about one thing – money. It's amazing how business owners tend to miss this point. People will work under the most horrendous conditions if the pay is right.

I called in my shop stewards to introduce myself and to set the tone for the new managerial-leadership. It was important to set new ground rules. I warned that I did not want anyone to come to me to ask me for an increase. I assured them that the company would pay the rate agreed as per the negotiated settlement at the bargaining council – the legitimised forum that sets the benchmark and standards by which we pay for labour. So if they did not like the rate, the appropriate place to fight it was not with me in my office, but at the bargaining council.

I also told my shop stewards that the only time I was willing to have a discussion with them about money would be in relation to a demand that I, the CEO, pay for their training and up-skilling – as shop stewards – and that of their members.

The shop stewards were justifiably suspicious of my commitment to training and skills improvement, since this was the one thing the workers had been denied by the former white owners and managers over the previous 10 to 15 years of the company's history. I told the shop stewards that they could guarantee to the workers that we would not deny them any opportunities to advance themselves in their trade or other areas of professional interest linked to the core business of the company. I asked them to trust me and to hold me to my word until we could sign off on a company-wide training plan.

My management-leadership style and mantra was simple: If your "work" life (i.e. skills) does not improve under my leadership then I will have failed you as a person. Of course, the flip side of this coin for me as the CEO, was a fundamentalist faith that says helping to improve the quality of learning and life for the workers would show a proportional increase in productivity, loyalty and commitment – which meant the bottom-line would be secured. If you want to motivate your workers to produce quality and productive work then afford them the opportunity to learn and improve themselves.

To my surprise, there was no mad scramble on the part of the workers to "up-skill" themselves. This might have been due to their enduring suspicion of management or it might have been an issue of timing – a case of too much too soon.

Although 90% of the former management team had been white, the majority of artisans were coloured, and the semi- and unskilled labourers were black. In the past, people had been promoted to positions based on their race. To break this entrenched and inherited apartheid labour legacy we contracted an independent company to conduct a skills and competency audit of the management and supervisory tier of the company.

I made it mandatory that the up-skilling needed to be preceded by a proper skills-gap analysis and competency audit, a right-sizing of hourly and monthly pay-rates, a re-alignment of the management structure of the company which took account of more than just race, and the introduction of technology to assist managers in tracking project performance, professionally forecasting project delays, cost implications, work-in-progress calculations and so forth. The change interventions sent out a signal that the new leadership of the company was serious about positive and focused change and transformation aimed at improving the bottom-line and not just about wanting to be "politically-correct".

I also implemented a managerial and supervisory assessment, which included an assessment of the manager by his immediate subordinates (i.e. a 360-degree process). The sense I got from the shop floor was that "justice" was now being done, since it was a known fact that race-protectionism was entrenched at the management levels. This all helped to contribute to a sense of calm rather than a frenzied scramble for skills empowerment as a way of getting ahead. Slowly but surely, things began to change.

A key challenge facing the turnaround of our economy is the much spoken-about skills crisis. The focus is often on the owner who is unwilling to spend more than the prescribed skills levy. In many instances, businesses are not set up to facilitate or enhance the training of their workers. Training is not the core business and businesses will often "buy-in" the skills required, as opposed to creating the skills.

The current emphasis in the artisanal training sector and environment, for example, is to convince businesses to train over and above their needs – and to incentivise such training. This is a matter discussed in more detail elsewhere in this book. The point I wish to make here, flowing from this short case study, is that even when workers were made the generous offer to improve their skills base – such an offer was not fully utilised.

What is illustrated above is that the greater challenge facing industry is to energise the workers – to make them thirsty for new knowledge and skills. The assumption is often made that workers are interested in up-skilling themselves. My experience is that this is not always the case. One needs to find a way of building trust and integrity in the work place. Both worker and owner need to get onto the same skills-development page, since the benefit of an empowered and skilled workforce is mutual.

Notes

1. *See* DTI *South Africa's Economic Transformation: A strategy for broad-based black economic empowerment* http://www.thedti.gov.za/bee/bee.htm
2. *See* Presidency (2010) *Opening remarks to the inaugural to the meeting of the President's broad based economic empowerment council* – 4 February, delivered by Deputy President Motlanthe at the Presidential Guest House.
3. Mathews Phosa is quoted in V Booysen's article (2008) 'BEE a failure' – http://www.fin24.com/articles/default/display_article.aspx?ArticleId=1518-1786_2395322
4. It is always difficult to know when an office bearer of any political party, particularly the ruling party, speaks in his/her private capacity or whether what he/she says expresses the views of the political party.
5. *See* Presidency (2008) *Towards An Anti-Poverty Strategy For South Africa – A Discussion Document* p.23 which states that "In 2000, the richest 10% of the population received around 45% of national income, while the poorest 40% received only 10%. This is comparable with Latin America, and is far more unequal than most of the fast-growing Asian economies."
6. Some argue that we are already a middle-income economy – I disagree. However, the point I wish to emphasise is that we need an economy that produces industrial jobs. This in my view is the key to success. If we are going to have a successful economy based on jobless growth, then the jobless people must, by definition, enjoy the bounty without the need to have "worked a job". If this is the economic philosophy (i.e. jobless growth) are we then not moving rapidly to a full blown socialist type state – or at least a welfare state where the majority of the population don't work but rather enjoy a liveable and decent income?
7. Some may justifiably argue that the manufacturing focus is already the case – or at least a priority. If this is the case then I am not asking for something that is different to what already seems to be policy. The remaining question is: So why is a 'cult of manufacturing' not happening? What's the missing piece if we already have the policy in place? My view is that the missing piece is that of the requisite mindset namely industrial consciousness.

4 | A new fulcrum for national identity

Judge me by what I want to become and not by the past I represent.

This chapter builds on the foregoing discussion and proposes that the basis of a South African identity should be industrial consciousness. It is this new kind of identity that stands the best chance of moving the South African nation from poverty to prosperity – for more than just a few. The new fulcrum will represent an explicit shift in the psyche of the South African nation, away from an embedded race-obsession and towards an explicitly and newly constructed industrial consciousness and obsession. One of the most significant advantages of industrial consciousness will be its ability to withstand a much greater degree of pressure and robust performance engagement than would a race-sensitive consciousness.

South Africa needs to clarify and redefine its national identity if it is to make significant headway in its fight against poverty, crime and unemployment. The solutions to these problems require all citizens to be united in their efforts. While this chapter lays the foundation and provides the initial parameters, a national debate around what South Africans deem to be an appropriate national identity and basis for nationhood and patriotism, is necessary. Finally, industrial development as a policy imperative can succeed only if it is premised on an industrial consciousness which is forward-looking and aspirational. But is the nation ready for a radical identity makeover?

A new national vision

What is our vision for the new South Africa of 2010 and beyond? How do we see South Africa in 15, 20 and even 30 years from now? Will we still be bickering about race and how apartheid has robbed black and white citizens of becoming a vibrant, all-embracing and prosperous nation? Will we still be plagued by the ghost of non-delivery of basic services to the poor and rich alike? Or will the rich make absolutely sure that the services are delivered – if not to the poor then at least to themselves.

In terms of the big picture, South Africa's big business sector, for example, has proposed a Vision 2040 in which it is envisaged that by 2040, South Africa will have graduated from an emerging to a fully developed nation and economy.[1] Perhaps small business and the citizens of the nation should also participate in a national strategic planning session expressing a long-term vision for the nation lest the rich again dictate the direction of the country.

It is not unreasonable to imagine a South Africa with significantly reduced crime and poverty levels, and where the majority of people are living in prosperity and comfort. In fact, it is hugely inspiring and positive to think of a crime-free and prosperous South Africa. It might seem like a pipe dream given our predisposition and experience of gloom and doom. However, I believe a prosperous future for South Africa is possible. But first we have to make a plausible case regarding how we are going to achieve that future. My proposed first step towards a prosperous future is to change our mindset and adopt industrial consciousness as the basis of a new national identity, which will inspire the nation to achieve a collective vision of health and wealth for all.

From race card to industrial card

We all desire to be part of a great nation. However, great nations are comprised of great people who are of the same mind and spirit with the same national aspirations, goals, vision and longings. Of course, the Constitution and our Bill of Rights reflect the ultimate goal. Our vision for a non-racial society has been applauded by the world. But the world also knows that the gap between vision and reality is sometimes very big. South Africa gets full marks for the vision we have for our society. What we now need are practical, achievable and measurable steps that help us determine and assess whether we are moving in the right direction in terms of reaching our ultimate vision.

It is vital that we unpack these kinds of issues every so often, if only to remind us that we are on the right track. It is my view that 16 years down the road in the new South Africa, we are realising that, in many respects, we have lost our way.

Our longings for a non-racial society are ironically race-card driven. In other words, in order to get to a non-racial and equal society we decided to use the racial past as a measure and an instrument to help us achieve the goals set out in our Constitution.

I envision a future where we exchange the race card for an industrial card and where the only debate is about what we are doing or not doing to make our country economically prosperous for the benefit of the majority of the citizens. In this regard I have no race preference regarding who controls the economy, as long as such control is to my benefit as a shareholder (i.e. as a citizen).

I accept the reality of differentiation of economic benefits across society. We can't all be millionaires. The reality is that some will make a lot of money and others won't. Some will have high income-generating jobs and other won't. But I do not accept that a singular society is morally justified to have grinding poverty and extreme wealth co-existing in the same economic space. I am also of the view that reparation entitlement, defined as "pay-me-for-my-sufferings-of-the-past" is a dead-end street. I am in favour of the principle of reparation but it must have a start and an end point. As painful as it may sound, there is a sense in which we must draw a line under our past and move on. As a society we need to reach a point at which we say the oppressors of our past have been forgiven and have sufficiently paid for their crimes and the benefits they have enjoyed at our expense as black people. In many respects, South Africa has moved beyond this point – or has it? Are the new oppressors the small group of elite BEE beneficiaries who are hogging the deal opportunities?

I do not wish to be regarded as an economically underprivileged person forever. I also long for a liberating and empowered feeling with regard to my finances and wealth aspirations. I realise that I may not achieve or reach the heights that someone else may. But I want to know that there is nothing in my society that structurally inhibits me from achieving whatever I set my heart on. We cannot afford to produce another generation of entitled and mis-educated youth. We must re-energise our entire society using positive reinforcement, and ride on the back of South Africa's entrepreneurial flair as we make a conscious decision to move from poverty to prosperity. The ever-recurring question is always: How do we get there?

Our demographic patterns will only change if we have complete integration of races (which is not practical). Without a migration and an intermingling of sorts, we will retain a race-based cultural index.

In the final analysis, we are a black-majority country. Our problem is not race, per se. Our challenge is economic mobility and the reduction of poverty which is essentially a black problem. So our challenge is to create an economic as opposed to a race migration. In this way, and if it is considered important, there will be a mingling of the races. But the primary objective should not be a desire to see white and black live side by side as though racial harmony is the goal. The goal must be an economic situation where people have the economic freedom to choose where to live, invest and create a social life for themselves.

The fundamental challenge in South Africa is therefore not to break down the race-based patterns designed by apartheid. This will automatically happen when enough black people have enough money to migrate to wherever their money can afford to take them. The struggle then becomes one of economics.

Very few people, if any, can afford to buy their way into a new economic stratum. In most societies, the people who can do this are the middle class. Tragically and dangerously, South Africa does not have a middle class that can structurally change these geo-spatial patterns in any fundamental way. It is perhaps this challenge that should be put to all South Africans, namely, to aspire to become part of the middle class – that class that provides stability and funding for a democracy to thrive; that class that provides the skills required for a society to function properly (e.g. nurses, artisans and teachers). The legacy of apartheid is not one of racial inequality, but rather a more fundamental economic disparity which is institutionalised.

My proposal is for every South African to demand to be judged by what they want to become and not by the pain of their past. The wounds of apartheid have the capacity to paralyse our nation by entrenching generations of fear, guilt and entitlement. Fortunately, the South African nation has agreed to put the past behind it and move forward.

My proposal is to build on our memory of the past by looking into the future for a solution. Of course, we need to understand the past in order to move into the future. But the question is: Do we move into the future with the past as our permanent baggage? Or do we release ourselves of the baggage imposed on us by our apartheid past and make a decision to define ourselves by the economic future we desire and define for ourselves and our children? The best way to move into that future is to adopt a new mindset – a mindset that is driven by a desire for large-scale prosperity for the nation – a mindset that will invigorate and excite the nation as opposed to depressing and angering the nation.

We need a new fulcrum on which to exert all the pressure that the debilitating poverty situation can and should exert on us as patriots and citizens of our country. Industrial consciousness is what is needed, not only to withstand the pressure, but to propel an army into action and win the economic war which will ultimately liberate us all.

FAQs

South Africa has the money to turn around our country and society as a whole. Money is not our main problem. Our problem is skills, we are told. I say, the even bigger problem is attitude (i.e. consciousness). But let's stay with the skills argument for now, using a question and answer methodology to support my case for industrial consciousness as a new fulcrum for national identity.

Question 1: *How do we create the skills which are in short supply?*
Standard response: What type of skills are required?
Smart answer to Q1: We should get people interested in wanting to learn the skill in the first place, otherwise you are throwing money away putting someone through a training course they don't need or want.

Question 2: *So do we need industrial skills as identified by Jipsa – those critical and scarce skills?*
Standard response: Yes, we need tens of thousands of artisans, for example, in order for our economy to grow.
Smart answer to Q2: We need two armies. An army of risk-taking and energetic entrepreneurs who create the industries, and an army of artisans who actually do the work. Both are needed in the economy.

Question 3: *So why are we not producing these skills? Why are people, especially young people, not interested in acquiring industrial artisanal skills if such skills are the key to our success?*
Standard response: We are projecting the wrong role models for our young people. We are telling them that the way to make money is not through hard work and dedicated service but rather through BEE deals where the primary criteria are the colour of your skin and your political connections, rather than honour and dignity, competence and skill.
Smart answer to Q3: There is a lack of interest because our society as a whole does not have an industrial consciousness – that inquisitiveness, curiosity and thirst for wanting to know how things are made and repaired. If we had this thirst, we would be unlikely to enjoy sitting around and being non-productive. We would be curiously pursuing our interests instead of hoping that the government will look after us. In short, our brains are not wired for industrial interests and that is why we are not seeing enough

young people desperately wanting to become artisans and tradesmen. There is also the prejudice thing – it's not cool to be a blue-collar worker – we have been programmed to aspire to becoming professionals – doctors, lawyers, accountants or engineers – not artisans.

Question 4: *So what is the solution? How then do we change this way of thinking?*
Standard response: We need to rewire the brain of the nation. We need to get a brand new consciousness.
Smart answer to Q4: The brain food required is maths and science and a good dose of self-esteem. Without this supplement we simply will not grow.

The ultimate solution: The country must direct all its efforts and energies into creating an army whose weaponry is maths and science geared towards a labour-absorbing industrial economy. So, for example, if we decide that we want to be a nation of ship builders, then the training of thousands of welders and related trades must become a national obsession. Every young person must end up believing that contributing to the building of a ship is much larger than just the ship-building process. The welder must feel that he/she is contributing to building the nation. Only once the ordinary citizen begins to feel a level of connection to the national cause, will there be a fundamental turnaround in the economy.

A must-win situation ... but what happens if we don't?

What happens if we don't create the much-needed jobs as per the AsgiSA or other growth strategy initiatives? What happens if our crime-reduction strategy is ineffectual? Is a Zimbabwe scenario looming?

Of course, a multi-faceted solution is required where we cannot afford to drop the baton at any point in the race. So, the education department, for example, must deliver the production of appropriately educated youth for absorption into the economy, and the police must find creative ways to contain a desperate crime situation. We all have our part to play to ensure that we succeed.

And the army?

What happens when millions take to the streets demanding social grants or jobs or food or the delivery of basic services? Will we have the luxury, then, to explain to the voting masses why another R3bn must be spent to replace the inferior quality houses which were built for the masses by BEE-compliant contractors, but have been found to be defective and not fit for human occupation? Or will the army be called in to ensure that the protests of the poor do not spill over into the living areas of the rich?

It is an interesting coincidence that the wealthy classes, both black and white, have bought private security to protect themselves and their property against the criminals who are generally assumed to come from the classes of the "poor". The wealthy classes, notwithstanding that their tax money funds the police and general state security, seem to have voted in favour of private security as opposed to depending on state-funded security. The private security industry, in the main managed by former "underpaid" security and police personnel, is said to have three times the capacity of the police in South Africa.

The elephant in the room

We have had momentous moments and achievements in just 15 short years of democracy in South Africa. These achievements are worthy of mention not only to show that we can, but to offset our lack of accomplishments in terms of defining our identity and impacting our national psyche.

Let's start the review by looking at the period between Nelson Mandela's release from political imprisonment and the first democratic elections held on 27 April 1994. It is this period that gave birth to the idea of a compromise settlement evidenced by the creation of a Truth and Reconciliation Commission (TRC). The fundamental basis of our miracle society was ostensibly a political compromise (as opposed to cultural or economic) reached during the Kempton Park negotiations, with particular reference to the need to tame the apartheid security forces. As a result of Mandela's leadership, we can safely say, as a nation, that we've done the "reconciliation thing" and created a new basis for a collective consciousness about our recent past. It is accepted that not all the TRC-related issues are resolved. But what can be said about the Mandela presidential legacy is that through the work of the TRC, South Africa was able to lay a foundation for the creation of a new national psyche.

As a nation we have managed to transform the police, for example, from an apartheid killing machine (i.e. an enforcement agency) to a protector of our rights enshrined in our Constitution and Bill of Rights (i.e. a custodial agency).

Furthermore, and in terms of the Scorpions and the recently formed Hawks, we can say that as a nation we are continually clarifying our specialised approach to organised and priority crime-combating. We also have a specialised unit called the Cobras – linked to the Asset Forfeiture Unit, and the Green Scorpions, focusing on environmental crime.

In terms of politics and performance we have also made an enormous paradigm shift. This is particularly evident when comparing South Africa's progress to that of the rest of the continent. The replacement of President Mbeki in 2008 was one of the greater tests faced by our new democracy. We have shown an amazing level of stability and maturity as a nation during this particular transition of political leadership.

In terms of the economy, it must be said that we are in the process of the necessary deracialisation of the economy through a range of black economic empowerment initiatives. Unfortunately, South Africa has the recent distinction of being a country with the widest gap between rich and poor. Also, it is unfortunate that certain BEE beneficiaries have been seen to be serial beneficiaries of tenders and contracts. And so, instead of a broadening of the BEE beneficiary pool, there has been the perception of a contraction of equity ownership, thus giving rise to a monied black aristocracy. In the main, however, we are in the process of structurally redesigning our economy away from racial capital towards what appears to be class capital.

In terms of youth leadership, the ANC Youth League (ANCYL) has anointed Julius Malema in spite of his sometimes too spontaneous commentary on a wide range of matters – in the process ruffling more than a few feathers on both sides of the political divide.

In terms of international cultural sentiment, the securing of the hosting and brag rights to the 2010 FIFA World Cup is a definite plus. The national psyche, I think, generally feels proud of the achievement.

The electricity and energy challenges facing a re-industrialising and urbanising South Africa are enormous. The ability of the country's power utility to raise foreign direct investment to assist in the upgrading of the electricity grid will have a huge impact on the pace of industrialisation and the realisation of job creation through massive industrial programmes such as Eskom's envisaged multiple power station building programme.

A final comment is reserved for the performance of the South African economy over the past 16 years. While overall the performance has been considered excellent, we are told that the economy has grown in a jobless manner. In other words, the economy has grown but the number of jobs has not grown to the same extent.

In spite of this litany of achievements, the elephant in the room remains unemployment and runaway crime. I have a penchant for the real and practical, and so I am attentive to the challenge facing our nation to create at least three million jobs in the next four years, now extended to ten years. And while we do this we also need to reduce crime significantly, so that South Africans shift from a feeling of being unsafe in their own homes to a state of feeling secure not just in their homes but also in public spaces, in which we are told 59% of all robberies take place in South Africa.

The last hope

Industrialisation for Africa in general and South Africa in particular has the potential it had for Europe through the Industrial Revolution more than two centuries ago, and for the Asian Tiger countries in the last quarter of the 20th century. In fact, South Africa, with its rich natural mineral strength and already partially developed industrial base, probably has the greatest potential of all African countries to effectively fight the scourge of crime and poverty. The challenge is to make wise and smart industrial choices.

Conclusion

In this chapter I have proposed a new fulcrum around which the new national identity and nationhood of South Africa can revolve. I have argued that such a fulcrum should be industrial consciousness. In the next chapter I propose a new standard or performance measure against which to measure the performance of our nation-building programme.

It is my view that the solution to our enduring problems rests with a change in the national psyche of South Africans and the adoption of a new performance measurement by which to assess the success or failure of our nation-building programme. I have argued for a paradigm shift in the national psyche from a retrospective to an aspirational and future-oriented mode of thinking and performance monitoring. The call is to measure the nation by what it desires and not by the extent to which it is being paid retributively for past crimes against it.

The South African government is in the throes of making industrial choices which will have a long-term bearing and effect on the quality of life for South Africans.

The remaining challenge is obsessively to find ways to create massive labour-absorbing industries. The benefit will be not only a reduction in crime, but a pathway out of poverty towards prosperity for our nation. The most important first step, however, is a change of mindset – and the subsequent development of a new national identity for the South African nation.

Notes

1. Well-respected and retired businessman Bobby Godsell is the chairperson and driving force behind the campaign initiated by big business in South Africa, loosely dubbed 'Vision 2040', which sets out as its overall goal the transformation of the country from a developing to a developed one over 30 years. To achieve this, a target of doubling the size of the economy over the period should be set, alongside objectives for reducing poverty and inequality. For more detail see T Cramer (2010) 'Big business wants doubling of SA economy by 2040 to be new national goal'. Article in *Engineering News*, 23 February 2010 http://www.engineeringnews.co.za/article/big-business-wants-doubling-of-sa-economy-by-2040-to-be-new-national-goal-2010-02-23

5 | A new performance standard for nationhood

If you want to cause war, murder and mayhem, then try to take away a man's wealth and money without good reason.

The central purpose of this chapter is to propose a new standard and performance measure by which to gauge the success of the South African nation-building programme and the "implementation" of the idea of nationhood. The chapter proposes that South Africans, as a nation (not as a political party – but as a collective nation), actively and explicitly agree on a standard by which to measure the success or failure of our nationhood and nation-building programme. Without an agreed-upon standard, the goal posts of performance will constantly shift, allowing functionaries and those involved in active nation building to wiggle their way out of being held accountable for performance or lack thereof. It is therefore imperative that we develop a national consensus on what we as citizens consider the hallmarks of a successful South African society.

By what standard?

A new bottom-line

If there's one thing I have learnt in business, it's the singular and punctilious focus on "the bottom line". Shareholders of a company have only one focus, namely "the bottom line". The bottom line is my proposal for a new performance measure by which to soberly assess our nation-building programme. The measure I propose says:

> *The level and nature of criminality in our South African society will be directly proportional to the pace and quality of the industrialisation programme of South Africa.*

In other words, I am suggesting that the longer we take to industrialise our country, the longer we will be burdened by the high levels of crime and violence in our society. Put differently, there is a link between the pace and quality of the industrialisation programme and the level and nature of criminality in society.

Very simply stated, we may cause more crime and violence if we choose the wrong industrial and growth strategy for the nation. If, for example, we decide to become a nation of ship builders and our education system produces a nation of potato farmers, then we have a crisis. Someone is not connecting the dots. We are aware that there are two economies functioning in South Africa. The first economy is essentially an industrialised First World economy and is functioning well. However, in the second economy we are confronted with unparalleled levels of poverty and degradation. The first economy feeds off the cheap labour of the second economy in order to buttress its economic advantage.

The split between these economies runs essentially along racial fault lines. So what is the growth plan and strategy that will ensure that the gap closes between these two economies? Newly elected Minister of Finance, Pravan Gordhan, has, for example, indicated government's intention to make a huge investment in entrepreneurial support for young people. We seem to be moving in an empowering direction, according to a frustrated young black entrepreneur named Vuyisa Qabaka.[1] However, there is always a great distance between policy and practice. In order to close this gap we need the bridge of industrial consciousness, which will close the divide between policy and action.

An aspirational formula for nationhood

I recognise that my proposed performance measure as indicated above may read more like a prophetic prediction than an actual performance measure. But what else is a performance measure, other than a predictive and preventative tool that identifies specific outputs – those desired and those not desired. A performance measure in my view is nothing other than a management tool used to obviate disaster or predetermine a desired outcome.

Importantly, and for our narrow purposes here, let me clarify that I am not using the industrialisation index of other emerging or established markets to determine the standards and measures by which we should be judging ourselves. Furthermore, the impact of globalisation and the volatility of our currency, in my view, are red herrings and excuses which legitimise the ongoing rape and mutilation of our economy by unscrupulous raw material and commodity traders. Undoubtedly these are matters for more extensive discussion and strategic policy direction debate. For the purposes of this chapter, I want to argue for a new benchmark for the South Africa nation-building performance using the index of our own industrial performance and capability. Such a benchmarking exercise is based on our mineral and raw material strength as opposed to the consumption needs of the first world. The blunt reality is that for centuries, the First World has been buying all our raw materials and selling it back to us at many times the price in the form of beneficiated goods such as cars, finished steel products and the like. Is it not time that South Africa beneficiated its own abundant supply of raw materials and sold it to the international world for ten times more, rather than the other way around?

Unmasking the new standard

The performance measure proposed (i.e. the new bottom line) can be restated, unmasked and reframed using different language and word configurations. This is necessary if we are to appreciate the full impact of the challenge facing us as a nation. We must strip away as many layers as required in order to get to a full understanding of the core argument being made here. In doing so I will unmask the performance measure using the scalpel of unemployment, crime, xenophobia and the skills crisis. In doing so I will conduct three unmaskings:

First unmasking – the size of the unemployment problem

The first unmasking is that of unemployment discourse. Let's ask a blunt and straightforward question: *What is the exact level of unemployment in South Africa?* The reality is that we don't actually know. But sufficient data is available to allow us to conclude that we have a massive unemployment problem – in the region of at least 25%. There is consensus in some circles that the levels are somewhere between 25% and 35%.

The next question: *What would we consider to be an acceptable level of unemployment, noting that there will never be 100% employment in any society?* I believe that any unemployment figure above 20% is a national disaster and should be the basis for the removal of the ruling party from office. However, what happens when the unemployed masses vote for the party that does not deliver the goods?

In South Africa we tend to adjust our minds and attitudes to the situation in which we find ourselves. This is more often than not a way of coping with our terrible circumstances as well as non-performance. Thus, we tend to be very pleased when there is a fractional movement in the unemployment figures. We engage in huge debates about a one or a half a percentage point movement in the unemployment figures. We are desperate for good news, so the slightest positive shift in the figures is interpreted as the economy being on a recovery path.

In terms of government's own targets, as per the AsgiSA goals and objectives, South Africa needs to create in excess of two million new jobs in the next four years – or should that be three million jobs? Dr

Rob Davies, Minister of Trade and Industry, has already indicated that recreating the almost one million jobs lost during the recession is going to be a challenge. We need to remind ourselves that there are still at least an additional two million new jobs that need to be created over and above the one million lost due to the recession, if we want to make a serious dent in the unemployment and poverty figures. Interestingly, the newly revised IPAP 2 now projects a less ambitious figure of just over two million jobs to be created by the economy – but only by 2020 (i.e. over a ten-year period) – and not by 2014 as projected by AsgiSA. The IPAP 2 is silent on the AsgiSA targets and the growth trajectory outlined therein. What this means is that we are projecting the creation of much less than what we said we would deliver by 2014 and we are saying that it will take double the time to achieve half the target originally set for the economic liberation of our country.

The reason I rehearse the IPAP 2 and AsgiSA issue here, is to show the potential disjuncture between the envisaged growth trajectory desired and the reality of the skills of the citizenry on whom we are dependent to get us there. Simply stated, and as per my proposed performance measure indicated above, the pace of growth will fundamentally impact the level and nature of crime. The longer we take to get loitering young people off the streets into productive employment, the longer it will take us to deal with social fabric crime, for example. The devil finds work for idle hands.

The issue around creating labour-absorbing industries is pertinent since it is quite possible to have an economy that is considered successful, productive and efficient with the use of mechanised and automated industrial industries to boost our GDP growth. This is not dissimilar to the discussion concerning the alienation of labour in a capitalist economy – an increase in automation and a decrease in the need for specific tradecraft skills.[2] Increased mechanisation and automation will not, however, solve the problem that we have – namely millions of unemployed youth loitering in our streets.

But here's the big issue. The education system has not prepared the youth to take up jobs in the economy in which their education has taken place. The reality is that the youth are ill-prepared for the South African job market. Do we blame the designers of the education system that has produced these defects or do we blame the learners themselves? If we link this kind of thinking and questioning to the days of the TRC, the issue is this: Do you blame the soldiers who did the torturing or do you blame the general who gave the instructions?

Second unmasking – crime out of control

The second unmasking of the proposed new performance standard (i.e. the new bottom line) is the acknowledgement that crime is out of control, or put differently, has stabilised at unacceptably high levels.

The policing strategy cannot be properly appreciated if it is not located within the broader context of the challenges faced by the criminal justice system. In this regard the prisons are overcrowded and the court roll is jammed with a backlog of at least three years. So even if the police were to increase their efficiencies by 10% to 15%, through crackdown operations and so forth, the reality is that there is no place to house any more awaiting-trial prisoners or any others who are arrested as a result of police efficiency.

Does this mean that crime-reduction strategies will have to exclude the arresting of suspects? It may need to explicitly exclude arresting any more of the already six million illegal immigrants inside our borders and who are the easy, though not exclusive targets of xenophobic violence. Are refugee camps the alternative places of incarceration, given the more visible xenophobia in our poorer areas in particular? Perhaps our challenge is to contain rather than arrest illegal immigrants.

Third unmasking – the nature of the skills shortage

My sense is that government has realised that a sustainable solution to both crime and unemployment is the creation of an industrialised economy[3]. It has certainly identified transport and energy infrastructure (e.g. rail, road, sea, airports, power stations) as a critical cross-functional capacity that will stimulate and hopefully facilitate a revival of economic activity across a range of sectors. And so government's approximately R780bn (and growing) public expenditure programme is directed at building transport infrastructure as opposed to subsidising selected industries.[4]

However, along with allocating the budget for infrastructure growth came the realisation that the ongoing lack of available skills would be a serious impediment. This is dealt with later under industrial terrorism. The bottom line here, though, is that we barely have the skills base to build the required infrastructure. We certainly don't have the skills base to maximise the post-infrastructure period through macro-industrial labour-absorbing industrial growth and entrepreneurial programmes. Our skills crisis is severe.

So, we would appear to have the money, the vision and the policy, but we don't have the abundance of local skills. The lack of technical (i.e. artisanal) skills is compounded by a lack of managerial skills. The current municipal crisis in South Africa is indicative of the fact that we do not have the management capacity to responsibly manage either budgets or programmes. Much has been said about these shortages and to this end a government-funded entity called Jipsa[5] was designed to unblock those systems unnecessarily inhibiting training and development of scarce skills required for AsgiSA.

The litany of challenges and problems outlined above has the potential to cause analytical paralysis and cause a state of deep national depression and anger. However, denying the gravity of our problems is not a solution either.

Case study 1 – Defining a 1000 to 1 standard

Close the inequality gap

One of the explicit performance indicators for nationhood proposed here is the narrowing of the gap between rich and poor within our society. The explicit performance standard and measure by which to gauge success or failure of the performance indicator should be a widely consulted and agreed-upon formula. For example, as a nation, and not just a group of stuffy economists, we should agree that the gap between the wealthiest and the poorest must not exceed a ratio of 1000:1, for example – where the wealthiest person is not allowed to be more than 1000 times wealthier than the poorest person. The nation's economists must be instructed to guide the nation as to what an appropriate ratio should be, given the variables in the economy. We don't want to kill the entrepreneurial spirit but we also cannot condone, in ignorance, the further entrenchment of the inequalities in our society.

The point I am making is simply that we need a new standard against which to measure our nation's performance. If we don't have such a standard, we are likely to simply shrug our shoulders and condemn the poor and praise the rich, perpetuating an unequal society until a destructive civil war levels the playing fields.

There are at least three elements and issues that affect the selection of a performance standard. These are: a consensus of the standard, the need to inject morality (explicitly) into the debate, and the need for the standard to be explicit.

Morality and economics

Any discussion focusing on the inequalities in our society is a moral one. Is it morally acceptable that South Africa has a growing gap between rich and poor? If it is not, then we need to be practical and define the standard by which we propose to measure and ensure that the gap between rich and poor is lessened.

The explicit standard

I refuse to accept that economic inequalities are simply a function of the market. Market forces are not governed by some other-worldly power. Certain structural interventions need to be made in the economy in order to address the legacy of structurally designed inequality within South African society. The critical question is: What is the standard by which to measure the closing of the inequality gap in our society.

My suggestion of a 1000:1 ratio is an example of how we can begin to think practically with regard to measuring performance. It is not simply a matter of taking from the rich and giving to the poor. And it is not a matter of the poor sitting on their backsides and waiting for handouts from the rich. The energy of nationhood must cause movement in both directions. I am not suggesting a radical equalisation of economic wealth through forced redistribution. This would spell death for any economy. A level of inequality will always exist. Our South African problem is that the level of inequality was structurally enforced along racial lines. The inequality was not a function of market forces. The deracialisation of the economy through BEE was an attempt to rectify this situation. This strategy has not worked either.

The challenge

The level of difficulty and sensitivity of the task of "closing the gap between rich and poor" is not a good enough reason for us as a nation to avoid having this very sensitive nationhood discussion, and not merely an ideological war between business and labour, or a divergence between the alliance partners of the ruling party. We need to find those things that will cause us to move collectively in a positive direction as we try to narrow the gap between the "have's" and the "have-not's". We may agree as a nation to give ourselves 15 more years to reduce the inequality gap from what it is at present to an agreed-upon ratio.

Benefit of 1000:1 approach
This proposal is guaranteed to send shivers down the spines of those who have accumulated enormous wealth over many generations in an economy that until recently was legislatively racist and oppressive. The same shivers will be felt by the "nouveaux riches".

A discussion on performance standards such as the 1000:1 ratio has the potential to cause a war – hopefully of words only. The real liberation struggle and victory, as we have noted elsewhere, was not the ballot of 27 April 1994. The real freedom to be won is economic and not political.

Case study 2 – Weighing up the priorities

Prioritising and selecting the indicators
What are the performance indicators of a successful nation? Is it the abundance of a wonderful philosophy called ubuntu? Being a forgiving rainbow nation? Being a God-loving nation?

Should the performance of the economy be an indicator? How else are we to judge the success of the economy? Is the success of an economy judged by jobless growth or the extent to which the economy is labour absorbing? Norway, for example, has a negative unemployment rate.

Should another measure be the gap between rich and poor? What should that gap be? Should it be limited to a 1000:1 ratio as discussed above – a target which becomes invalid after the playing fields have reached a certain level?

Should crime statistics be an indicator? If so, what statistical data becomes the normative measure for success? Is it considered a national crisis if one's country has one of the highest murder rates in the world? How do we mobilise the positive energy of the nation to effectively address the crime problem?

Should maths and science literacy be a performance measure? Should we make the appointment of a Minister of Education dependent on the nation's performance in maths and science?

Are these the performance indicators by which we can measure the

South African nation-building project as a success or failure? Or are they just pieces of information whose actual numbers (i.e. statistics) have no consequence for those in charge of the portfolios being described. Statistics are merely facts and figures. However, if these facts and figures are placed within a performance framework to which a measure is attached – for example, target reduction of 15% in the murder rate over the next 12 months – then the numbers begin to become meaningful. They become even more meaningful when someone is held accountable for achieving those targets. In many respects this is what the Zuma administration has introduced. This is a first for government and must be applauded. However, the critical question is: Who sets the performance targets? Who decides what is reasonable and achievable?

It remains to be seen if government and the Presidency will have the kind of private sector courage to rid itself of under-performing employees and buy in the best brains and talent in order to achieve the set targets.

I am not interested in singling out the performance of individual politicians or business persons or political parties. What I am interested in is establishing our national, collective and shared sense of achievement or lack thereof.

Practical application: Five priorities – one goal

How would you rank government's five priority areas in order of importance? Management experts will, for example, begin a process of identifying and differentiating "lead" indicators from "lag" indicators. They will try to establish which of the priorities will have the greatest impact if they are successfully to be implemented.

In terms of the five priorities stated above, let's ask some questions. First, what is the most important of the five priorities? Does government have a clear, focused and inspiring vision that all South Africans can rally around? Is there a vision for which every South African is prepared to sacrifice (and if necessary, die)?

My own list, for example, would have the following ranking:

First priority = Jobs
Second priority = Education
Third priority = Crime
Fourth priority = Rural development
Fifth priority = Healthcare

Once we have ranked our priorities, the next question is: how will we know that we have achieved our vision. From a balanced score-card perspective, what will our success look like from the four classical score-card perspectives, namely:

Perspective 1 – Financial performance
Perspective 2 - Growth and innovation
Perspective 3 – Internal operations
Perspective 4 – Customer (voter) satisfaction

I now wish to introduce and suggest an objective measure against which to judge the health and well-being of our nation. Assuming the overall vision of our country is to be a healthy and wealthy nation – the slogan might read "health and wealth for all".

The most objective measuring instrument to measure "health and wealth for all" should be the extent to which we collectively address poverty and unemployment. I hear some of you say: But that's nothing new. And I agree. What is new, and indeed the central thrust of my argument, is my insistence on a different configuration of performance measures which juxtaposes two critical sectors affecting our nation, but which seem to live in their own silos. My proposed performance measure for South African nation building is therefore as follows:

> The level and nature of criminality in our South African society is directly proportional to the pace and quality of the industrialisation programme of South Africa.

The longer we take to industrialise our economy the longer it will take us to solve the crime problem.

I am not aware that the juxtapositioning of a crime-reduction strategy and the concept of industrialisation, in South Africa at least, has informed public and policy debate or discourse with respect to how we plan to rebuild our nation.

I am arguing for the creation of a nation-building framework that gets the criminologist and the economist to sing from the same song sheet. In short, I am proposing a radical juxtapositioning of policing strategy on the one hand and industrial strategy on the other. And let's see what comes out in the wash. Hopefully a cleaner sheet.

Issues impacting the debate

The picture in 2010
Despite our best efforts to rebuild South Africa over the past 16 years, crime in my view is out of control, unemployment on the increase, with a global recession factor now negatively affecting South Africa.

By the time this book is published, the FIFA 2010 World Cup soccer extravaganza will be behind us. The postmortems of its economic and other success with be driven by different considerations and figures. However, for our purposes we will confine ourselves to the business case motivating for the event to take place in South Africa, and the benefits such an event will hold for our country.

Those who have written the business case for South Africa's hosting of FIFA 2010 tell us that it will be good for our economy. The anticipated headline numbers read as follows: *The event will lead to direct expenditure of R12,7bn and will contribute R21,3bn to GDP. It will also generate the equivalent of 159 000 annual jobs and an additional R7,2bn will be paid to the government in taxes.*

In more tangible and practical terms, what we are being told is that at the end of the 2010 soccer extravaganza we will have gained the following: *12 state-of-the-art stadiums, an overhauled transport system, a brand spanking new infrastructure and the international exposure and recognition that will be received as a result.*[6]

Was the soccer extravaganza a stimulus for real economic growth or is it merely a smoke screen to mask the aspirations and desires of a monied aristocracy whose vanity is satisfied and supported through big "industrial" projects such as Gautrain and modernised airports? Are the poor, for example, the real beneficiaries of the 12 new stadiums and a high-speed rail link between the wealthy suburbs and business centres of Johannesburg and its international airport?

I sometimes wonder what the poor would have chosen to purchase if they were confronted, for example, with the option of staging a soccer extravaganza, or the creation of a mega-factory that builds train coaches for export and where thousands of workers are employed.

Notes

1. Vuyisa Qabaka's budget tip was taken seriously by the new Minister of Finance. "His tip to Gordhan was to allocate a larger portion of the budget to youth development and entrepreneurship, and was the result of ten years of banging his head against a wall in a futile attempt to source enough funding to help him start and run his own business" – quote taken from Chris Barron's article, *Gordhan takes advice from victim of red tape* – Article in *Sunday Times Business Times* February 21, 2010 page 10.

    A further innovation within Gordhan's budget reflecting a significant emerging synergy between the ruling party and the opposition is the introduction of the "wage subsidy" for young people. The aim, according to the minister, is to raise employment of school-leavers by a further 500,000 by 2013. For a useful and quick multi-sectoral analysis of the 2010 Budget Speech see the special supplement to the Business Report issued on Thursday February 18, 2010 titled "The Budget Report 2010".

2. The merits of automation and mass production versus the tradecraft of the worker will need to be seriously debated in South Africa given that the South African challenge is to create labour-absorbing industries for the millions of unemployed. The bias of a high-performance free-market capitalist economy would be toward mechanization and its consequential deskilling of the base of the workforce. In this regard the groundbreaking classic by Harry Braveman (1974) *Labor and Monopoly Capital: The Degradation of Work in the Twentieth Century*. New York: Monthly Review Press, provides a point of reference for debate and discussion. The heart of Braveman's criticism of capitalism was his view that capitalism was a "crime against humanity" because it deskilled the craft workers by splitting their traditional crafts into many small parts, and redesigned the work such that anyone could do any number of the small parts. This had the consequence of removing craft pride, and the sense of oneself as a worker trained in an ancient skill. It also had the political consequence of weakening working-class consciousness. Put differently, Braveman pointed out that the separation of hand and brain is the most decisive single step in the division of labour taken by the capitalist mode of production. He further pointed out that the skill is taken out of work and thus a fragmentation of tasks and deskilling of production occurs, making a lesser requirement for skilled workers. Braveman more than any other modern Marxist theorist has poignantly observed that the consequences of deskilling are very profound. They go hand-in-hand with bringing the worker away from home and subjecting him or her to factory discipline in the Industrial Revolution. Where once workers could control days and hours of work, manner and pace of construction and even, in some cases, what to make and its shape and decoration, these areas of idiosyncrasy, skill, pride and creativity were progressively removed by capitalist manufacture. The more work is centralised, the more items are mass-produced, and the more science and technology get built into the machines and procedures, the more interchangeable workers become and the less control they have. Ultimately, workers (i.e. warm bodies) will not be needed. Machines, however, become indispensable and this, in Braveman's view, is beyond degradation and becomes a crime against humanity.

3. DTI (2007) *Implementaiton of Government's National Industrial Policy Framework : Industrial Policy Action Plan*, August 2007.

4. See Trevor Manuel's speech delivered at the Gordon Institute of Business Leadership, Johannesburg, *Economic Policy And South Africa's Growth Strategy*, Republic of South Africa GIBS-HSF 'New Growth Paths' 19 March 2007.

5. "Jipsa was established by Cabinet two years ago to support AsgiSA. AsgiSA's objectives are to reduce the unemployment rate from 30% to 15% by 2014, reduce poverty from one-third to one-sixth of the population by 2014 and to increase the annual GDP growth rate from an average of 3% to 4,5% per annum for the period 2005 to 2009 and to 6% for the period 2010 to 2014. Jipsa has rightly seen skills acquisition as an economic and labour market issue, as well as a problem of education and training – meaning that the resolution of these issues is dependent on the social partners, as well as on government ... Jipsa was thus established in March 2006 with the following mandate: lead the implementation of a joint initiative of government, business and organised labour to accelerate the provision of priority skills to meet the AsgiSA objectives;

give momentum and support to the implementation of AsgiSA; prioritise key skills and develop appropriate human resource development strategies to address these in the short to medium term; mobilise senior leadership in business, government, organised labour and institutions concerned with education and training and science and technology to address national priorities in a more co-ordinated and targeted way; promote greater relevance and responsiveness in the education and training system and strengthen the employability of graduates; lay the foundations for more co-ordinated and effective human resources development strategies; report to the AsgiSA Task Team and Cabinet on progress made towards agreed objectives; identify blockages and obstacles within the system of education and training that stand in the way of the achievement of Jipsa's objectives; lead an effective programme to communicate Jipsa's objectives and consult with stakeholders. (Taken from Presidency (2008) *Jipsa – Report on activities in 2007*. Issued by the office of the Deputy President of South Africa (April 2008), pp7-8.)
6 *See* http://www.sagoodnews.co.za/newsletter_archive/the_2010_soccer_world_cup_will_south_africa_score_.html

Part 2.
The emergency rescue plan

6 | Six components of a rescue plan

A crisis becomes an emergency when enough people say, "Let's fix it now!"

This chapter provides an outline of the components that make up the rescue plan required to address crime and unemployment in South Africa. Each component will be discussed in more detail in its own dedicated chapter. The emergency rescue plan section is deliberately practical in orientation and includes case studies, presentation slides and exercises. The components identified have been specifically selected to trigger matters of consciousness. The selected component parts as described below are therefore designed to help achieve the goal of facilitating a shift in consciousness. The abiding question is: *How do you change the consciousness of a person or a nation?*

Beyond the "paralysis of analysis" trap

It is easy to fall into the trap of forever criticising and consulting – also known as "the paralysis of analysis". The alternative is equally easy, namely the provision of a "to do" list aimed at fixing our crime and unemployment problem. However, the approach taken by this book is to address our crime and unemployment problems at their very deepest causal root, namely the level of consciousness – a not-so-easy task.

It is commonly said that we don't need more government and public policy. We need implementation. We don't need more analysis. We need action. One recognises that there will never be a 100% correct solution, so to analyse until we reach the perfect solution is also not viable. We need to act and reflect at the same time.

The challenge is robustly to reach a decision and then to implement it, warts and all. In this regard I define implementation as "strategy plus action". It takes courage to implement, especially when there are many unpredictable variables. As managers, we are left with no option but to combine strategy and action in the hope that implementation happens in the way we envisioned. As we implement, we need to regularly assess our progress against the standards we have chosen to use to measure our success or failure in reaching our desired goal or target.

We may be disappointed with the results of the BEE-oriented solution proposed for the economic turnaround of an apartheid-designed racial economy. But what must be applauded is the fact the ANC-led government eventually made a decision based on the models and information it had at the time, not forgetting its ideological bias, and drove it by way of policy direction, legislation and regulations. The recent acknowledgment by the highest political authority in the land is that BEE has been found wanting. The envisaged trickle-down of wealth to the masses has not happened.

The important point to note is that if we don't leave the comfort of ivory tower analysis and engage in implementation in the trenches, we are unlikely to find out whether what we designed on paper actually works on the ground. It is in this context and spirit that the six component parts of the rescue plan are recommended for consideration.

This section is designed to recommend explicit action steps aimed at reorienting the psyche of the South African nation towards industrial consciousness.

BULLETS OR BALLOTS
THE EMERGENCY RESCUE PLAN

How to Build a New Industrial Consciousness, Create Jobs and Reduce Crime

- **SIX COMPONENTS OF THE PLAN**
  - Structural change: 9 "what if" scenarios
  - Personal change: 4 steps to victory
  - Find your voice: Say the unspeakable
  - Confront your prejudices: 8 uncomfortable truths
  - Performance morality: Racial and voter abuse
  - New ground rules: 10 do's and don'ts

Figure 1: Six components of a rescue plan

The six components of the emergency rescue plan

The proposed emergency rescue plan has six inter-related components:
(1) Changing systems by considering nine "what if" situations
(2) Changing individuals by proposing a four-step change process

(3) Finding and empowering your voice to say the unspeakable – developing the courage to honestly and humbly speak "our" truth as we see it
(4) Confronting eight hard and uncomfortable truths embedded deep in our psyche
(5) Confronting three moral issues which impact our performance
(6) Proposing ten new ground rules – the do's and don'ts of industrial consciousness

Each of these components will be explored in the following chapters. The diagram below illustrates the connectedness of each component of the rescue plan.

Figure 2: The connectedness of the six components of the rescue plan

The bridge between theory and action

The central call of this book is for a new industrial mindset. Perhaps I am suggesting the impossible. Our psyches are "hard"-wired and rarely shift – unless something dramatic occurs and forces a shift to take place.

When individuals undergo a mindset change (i.e. a shift in their consciousness), it invariably results from a "Damascus Road" type of experience – a life-altering moment or series of moments. For societies and nations, it's no different. Some or other big event or moment triggers a shift in the thinking of the nation (i.e. the thinking of the people). In most instances, such events are an integral part of leadership. We have witnessed and experienced the power of great leaders such as Mandela, for example.

In addition to the influence of leadership, we must rightfully ask what factors, structurally, legislatively and systemically, will facilitate a shift in the thinking and consciousness of South Africa's masses. For example, South African citizens spoke differently to and about each other after the TRC moment. Altering the state of consciousness of a nation is not a small or insignificant exercise. We are talking about fundamentally changing the psyche of the nation – not something you do every day.

It is no different regarding my argument concerning industrial consciousness. We are not talking about a small insignificant intervention. We are talking about the need to fundamentally shift the way in which the nation thinks about and sees itself and its programme of action regarding poverty alleviation through industrial development. But we need to remind ourselves why we are even considering such a shift, namely, the desperate need to find solutions to the crime, unemployment and poverty challenges we face as a nation.

7 | Nine "what if" scenarios

People do not share their money as easily as their time.

Changing systems

This chapter explores nine hypothetical "what if" scenarios to illustrate that it is possible to awaken the nation's consciousness and cause a shift in its thinking, bearing in mind that there will be enormous resistance to this shift. The invitation is to visualise and hypothesise, just for a moment, and see what reaction it causes within the inner recesses of our minds and hearts.

My objective is to create an atmosphere where we begin to think differently about ourselves as a nation. We need to ask what will serve as a catalyst for such a shift in our thinking. In this regard, I propose that we allow our minds to explore nine scenarios (i.e. what ifs) that are likely to cause a massive shift in awareness and hopefully result in the emergence of a new consciousness. Such an exercise is also likely to cause anger. I anticipate a highly emotive response to my "what if" scenarios. But I am confident that when the various layers attached to each scenario

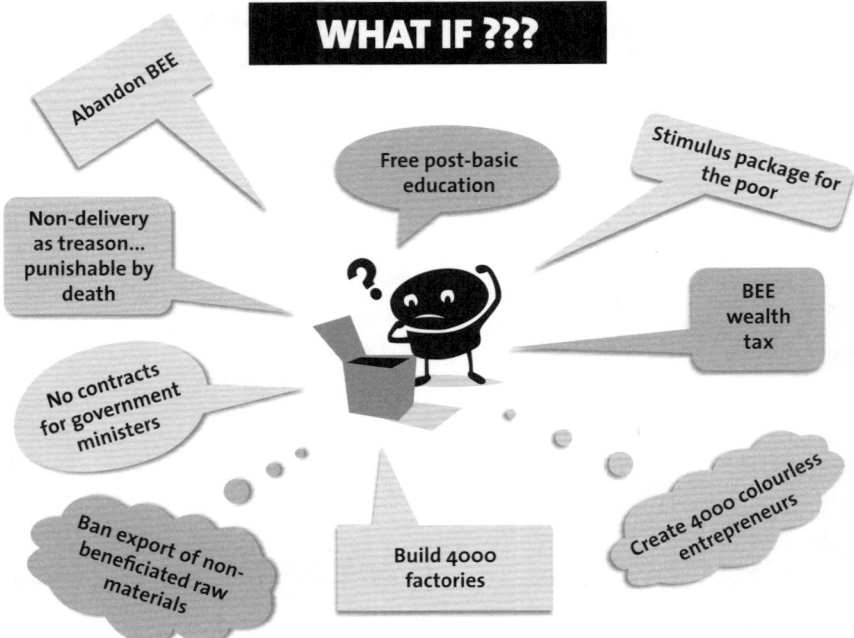

Figure 3: Nine "what if" scenarios

are peeled back, a level of consciousness will emerge that can weld the nation together.

With these provisos, let's get practical and walk along the bridge which takes us from theory to action – the bridge called industrial consciousness.

Nine macro-social "what ifs" to consider

Abandon BEE and create colourless entrepreneurial millionaires

What if we abandoned BEE as a policy? What if we told the still 90% white-controlled business sector of South Africa that BEE as a government policy no longer applied and that they, as white business, could continue to hold onto ownership and management of their companies. Instead, to revive the economy, all government support would be redirected to an entrepreneurial fund to support the creation of a 3000-strong army of South African entrepreneurs of all races and colours. Let's call this fund the EMF-SA – the Entrepreneurial Millionaires Fund of South Africa. These entrepreneurs would be tasked with creating massive new labour-absorbing manufacturing businesses and factories each employing 500 to 1000 employees earning decent wages. These entrepreneurs would be massively incentivised with bold assistance from government and the private sector. Such entrepreneurs would receive "generous golden handshakes" from government and the private sector once they had achieved their goals. These entrepreneurs would be the nation's ultimate rescuers and the people's heroes and heroines. Furthermore, what if, as a society, we unashamedly celebrated and generously rewarded such innovation, courage and determination?

It is often said that economic recovery is driven by entrepreneurial flair and freedom rather than prescriptive governmental policy and regulations. This first "what if" proposal not only taps into positive entrepreneurial energy but also directs energy towards the industrial and manufacturing space.

I wonder how many traditional BEE beneficiaries would jump at this opportunity given that there is no free ride here?

Abandoning BEE may be a radical step, but BEE and racial redress eventually becomes entrenched racial protectionism when such redress goes beyond a certain point. What is that "certain point" for the new South Africa, given that we are a black majority country? What standard should we use to define that point and what indicators should we use to measure whether we are achieving our objectives?

We risk entrenching an attitude of racial entitlement as opposed to an attitude of industriousness and innovation if we do not define the boundaries of the racial redress designed to enable black participation in the economy of the country. This is the problem with the current BEE framework. It would appear to be an entrenched system of racial-economic redress with no defined end target. It may well be that the target is relative to the number of black directors on the JSE. However, the improvement of such a target does not translate, structurally, into the creation of a massive labour-absorbing economy. What we need in our economy is an army of entrepreneurs who, with their out-the-box solutions, will propel the economy along a sustainable growth path.

If we can find just 3000 entrepreneurs who each create manufacturing businesses of 1000 employees each, suddenly we have three million new jobs. Of course, we need to couple the creation of these entrepreneurs with the ongoing challenge of creating an army of artisans and other blue-collar skills flowing from the AsgiSA and Jipsa initiatives. For now, the assumption made by this "what if" scenario, is that innovative manufacturing businesses need to be created and this is likely to create a skills appetite lower down the "food-chain". The one energy source (i.e. entrepreneur) can feed off or energise other energy sources, namely the training of artisans.

No contracts for government officials and politicians

Secondly, what if we passed a law which said that no government employee or politician, while in office, may acquire shares or have active interests in companies benefiting from government contracts? What if we took this position one step further, making the penalty for being found guilty of such an offence, the loss of a person's entire personal wealth. Consequently, their entire personal wealth and estate would be confiscated by the state and the proceeds placed into a private sector-driven entrepreneurial funding agency, the EMF-SA, to finance the kind of entrepreneur that we identified above.

Declare non-delivery as treasonable offence

A third "what if" scenario says: What if incompetent, non-delivering government employees as well as lying and cheating politicians as well as those found guilty of non-delivery were fired and publicly shamed for their non-performance? In fact, what if the act of over-promising and under-delivery was considered a treasonable offence? Non-delivery should at least be considered morally repugnant in a context where the aspirations and hopes of the poor are too easily abused by under-performing public officials. In short, what if we criminalised the non-delivery of public officials? Imagine a public service that served the public and not the public official!

A once-off BEE amnesty wealth tax

Fourthly, what if we said that all those who have benefited from BEE over the past 16 years, black and white alike, must make a once-off donation to the EMF-SA (i.e. the entrepreneurial funding agency) identified above. The criterion would be that if your net asset value were over an agreed-upon amount (let's say R10 million or more) or if you had accumulated cash in excess of R10m over the past 16 years as a result of BEE deals and restructuring, then you would be required to donate 10% of that wealth to the EMF-SA. (Perhaps the 10% "BEE tax" could be a once-off amnesty tax and not just a voluntary donation?) One does not want to scare away investors, but neither does one want to kill the capital accumulation freedom required to drive the economy.

A critical success factor for the EMF-SA idea is that the fund must not be managed by government or any of its parastatal agencies. The fund must be accountable to government and its voting citizens, but it must be managed by the private sector. The management of the fund would be at the behest of private sector individuals who have a track record of driving an industrial development agenda for South Africa and who would have no financial interest in any of the ventures being financed by the funding body. This has echoes of the post-war Marshall Plan and we could learn a great deal from a customisation of this development plan which actually worked.[1] The idea is that all the money collected by the EMF-SA would eventually be paid back to government, but via the profits of the successful labour-absorbing entrepreneurial enterprises which have a minimum of 500 employees, as described above. The EMF-SA would allocate an interest-free loan to innovative and high-risk entrepreneurs. The business proposal of the entrepreneur would be evaluated by a panel of business experts and private industrialists and not by government administrative bureaucrats. The risk profile and appetite of the EMF-SA would be biased towards high-risk and greenfield projects. The bottom line is that if the entrepreneur is successful, then government will benefit by way of loan repayments and, of course, the community will benefit through the creation of hundreds of decent jobs.

A crucial aspect of this plan is that the entrepreneur must be highly incentivised. A proviso must be that the entrepreneur may hold 100% equity but the business must be structured on at least a 70:30 profit share, with 30% net profit after tax shared among the employees. Any entrepreneur with a little savvy will realise that a major incentive for employees may well include shareholding in the company. But this must be the call of the entrepreneur exclusively.

An economic stimulus package for the poor[2]

Fifthly, what if every citizen earning less than the poverty dictum of $2 per day were given a once-off cash payment spread over six months – e.g. R 1000 per month over six months to be used for consumables and daily living costs – an economic stimulus package, as it were. The same kind of administrative system used for the current social grant system could be used to achieve this once-off stimulus "goodwill" gesture. The proviso is that the beneficiaries need to be "banked" persons. In this way, we allow for the creation of community banking infrastructure – forming an infrastructure which later becomes absolutely necessary as we industrialise the economy. It is this infrastructure that could serve as a basis for implementation of lessons of success from successful development financing programmes such as the Grameen Bank founded by the 2006 Nobel Peace Laureate Muhammad Yunus.[3]

Creation of industrial zones

A sixth "what if" relates to the creation of industrial zones. What if we said that for every township (broadly defined as a residential space occupied by residents – formal and informal) that has more than 200 000 people, there must, by law, be at least two major labour-absorbing businesses created by the EMF-SA entrepreneurs. In other words, from a town-planning point of view, we must not and will not allow the growth of human settlements where there is no industry to sustain such a settlement. In fact, the reverse is generally true. People migrate to the city (which by definition is more industrialised than the rural countryside) because of better work opportunities. The existing and sprawling human settlements must be demolished, relocated or upgraded by way of creating industry close by, which will provide the kind of support required to sustain the human settlement.

Ban the export of non-beneficiated raw materials

A seventh "what if" scenario relates to the sensitive issue of the export of raw materials and needs to be discussed at some length. What if we placed a ban on the export of all non-beneficiated South African raw materials? Furthermore, what if, as was proposed some 300 years ago for England by the English economist John Carey, we punished exporters by death if it were found that raw materials were being exported without being beneficiated by a South African industry. Interestingly, it was this approach that laid the foundations of Europe's wealth in the 17th and 18th centuries and what was coined as Carey's "cult of manufacturing".[4]

Let's contextualise what may be considered an inhumane and archaic practice as espoused by Carey and later practised by Britain in respect of British economic policy in the colonies. In the modern era, we need to ask why we (i.e. South Africa) are exporting/selling our raw materials to foreigners only to buy them back in a different form and at a higher price. Who benefits from such a transaction? Certainly not the country exporting the raw materials!

The issue of exporting raw materials is not a modern economic problem. As far back as 1558, the Spanish Minister of Finance made a similar observation and wrote a memorandum to the King of Spain saying that "by buying back their own [Spanish] raw materials at an exorbitant price, the Spaniards are made the laughing stock of all Europe."[5]

A lesson from history (and indeed of our own experience) is that a finished product will sell for ten to 100 times more than the price of the raw material. The diamond ring that we buy from Europe at 100 times the price that was paid for the raw diamond taken from our soil is a case in point. Economic logic thus dictates that it makes more sense to beneficiate your own raw material and to sell it or export it at 100 times the price of the raw material. Reinert aptly makes the point that:

> Between raw materials and the finished product lies a multiplier: an industrial process demanding and creating knowledge,

mechanisation, technology, division of labour, increasing returns and – above all – employment for the masses of underemployed and unemployed that always characterise poor countries.[6]

South Africa's economy is a raw materials export-driven economy. Sixty percent of our exports take the form of raw materials exported out of our economy, including gold, diamonds, platinum, chromium, vanadium, manganese, uranium, iron ore and coal. What if South Africa created massive industrial complexes to beneficiate every raw mineral that came from its soil and oceans? What if this became a national obsession and a mark of patriotic service to the nation? What if our artisanal class became more than just an army of blue-collar workers, but indeed the ultimate rescuers of the nation through their artisan skills, considered by the nation the highest act of patriotism in South Africa?

The gold mining industry makes for a fascinating case study. Forty percent of the world's gold reserves are in the Witwatersrand area of South Africa. For over 100 years the economy of South Africa has been built on its gold mining reserves and its raw materials export industry. Yet, there has been no serious industrial investment geared at creating beneficiating industries that maximise this raw material. There is no reason why South Africa should not be a nation without poverty given its huge reserves of raw materials. So why is poverty still the major problem facing South Africa?

The challenge and solution is to shift away from our image as a raw materials exporter towards a semi-finished and finished products market. To achieve this one needs capital-intensive modernisation of the industrial structures which became outdated during apartheid's isolation. In addition, we need to ignite that flame of industrial curiosity among the population of South Africa so that an energy and desire is created within the psyche of the nation regarding the benefits of industrialisation – and in this instance, the creation of beneficiation industries.

The revised industrial strategy (IPAC 2), on paper at least, notes the need for manufactured goods to be exported. So the policy atmosphere is halfway conducive to promoting the beneficiation of raw materials. However, this needs to become the new industrial dogma of a new South Africa, namely "no export of any raw material will be allowed unless it has been beneficiated by a South Africa industry". In short, South Africa needs not only to create manufacturing and beneficiating industries, but it also needs to provide the protection possible for such an industry to flourish. This is exactly what England did to its American and later, its African colonies. England built up its own manufacturing industries buying in cheap raw materials from its colonies and then selling back finished products to its supplier of raw materials at 100 times the price. The prohibition of manufacturing industries in the American colonies is what gave rise to the American war of independence. Africa seems to have accepted and internalised its economic exploitation. The USA, on the other hand, went to war, and after independence, interestingly, followed the same practice as England, building its manufacturing sector which gave rise to its wealth, with particular reference to the US industrial development plan between 1820 and 1900.

Let's not fool ourselves into thinking we are dealing with non-explosive issues when talking about raw materials and what happens to them relative to the economy. Fortunately, South Africa is half-way down the road in this regard, and its revised industrial strategy captures some of the sentiment expressed above.

Free post-basic education based on merit not entitlement

The eighth "what if" scenario relates to education and training; what if all post-basic (i.e. university and college) education were to be free and the entry-level requirements were based on merit and not racial quotas or entitlement? This would certainly create a different energy earlier along in the process, with the demand by parents for better quality early learning for their children. The denial of access to good quality education has been the most effective weapon used by oppressive regimes to maintain power and privilege. Apartheid was no different.

If there was one thing that should have been a top priority in the immediate post-apartheid period, it should have been education. Many will argue that this was in fact the case. But the pathetic literacy and numeracy levels of South African children 16 years after 1994 is evidence enough to show that either education was not a priority, or the educational leaders were completely incompetent and have effectively colluded with apartheid forces to keep the masses of South Africans ill-educated and therefore useless to the economy, other than as a cheap labour resource.

If post-basic education were to be made free, based on merit, would whites, for example, still dominate the number of people being trained at post-basic educational institutions? Is a quota system and structural redress of admission numbers to post-basic schooling institutions still required? If the current education system continues to produce a generation of educationally dysfunctional and skills-deficient (i.e. mismatched) students, then where do we locate the responsibility for this mess? And for how long will there need to be redress? We need to ask if we are redressing the incompetence of the education leaders and system, or whether we are arguing that blacks are intellectually inferior and will forever need to be compensated for their inadequacies.

It is only a matter of time before race is no longer a factor, given the racial demographics and profile of the South African population. Why then the obsession to ensure that quotas are fulfilled? I can live with the quotas in the short term but I can't and refuse to compensate for incompetence, especially when this is structurally caused by an educational leadership that is out of tune with managing the nation's education system.

Create middle-class heroes for our children

A final "what if" scenario relates to how our society identifies and projects role models to be emulated by the rest of us. In the context of our discussion above, what if we actively created a different set of heroes and heroines for our society – a generation of middle-class, wholesome and accessible role models rather than the glamorous, irreverant fashion and media moguls.

The missing link in the South African economy is the proverbial middle class. South Africa needs to find a way to create a middle class which is a buffer between the rich and poor, but also provides a level of stability and sanity across all sectors of society.[7] The middle class typically comprises people with buying power (albeit limited), but it is not necessarily a propertied class. They can afford housing, schooling and medical aid with some cash left over for entertainment. This is typically the stratum of teachers, doctors, artisans and engineers – the very areas in which the scarce skills have been identified.

The question is how to create this substantial middle class. This is also the question posed by government's AsgiSA-based growth strategy. We need this stratum of society in order for the economy to grow. However, how will we achieve this, given the skills shortage?

My proposal is very simple: Create new heroes and heroines (i.e.

new role models). For example, double the salary of a primary school teacher. Actively create and affirm the army of artisans and other skilled manufacturing workers required by the economy, and turn them into the heroes and heroines of South Africa. Make them feel that without their contribution, South Africa will fail.

In other words, we need to create an atmosphere of aspiration so that the contributions of our teachers and artisans are the real role models for our society. These are role models that are touchable and reachable, unlike the entrepreneurial stratum of EMF-SA which is by definition an exclusive club. The teacher-artisan stratum is a place that masses of people can reach with some effort on their part; and the benefits will speak for themselves. This new middle class will be able to afford housing and a better standard of living than a shack dweller with no technical or professional skill to sell into the market.

An affirmed and aspirant middle class that is premised on hard work and not on entitlement is hugely energising and empowering. People will see that their rewards are based on their hard work. And this is far more satisfying than living off handouts from the state. It is this stratum of society that has the best chance of displaying a new patriotism and a new sense of belonging.

Commentary

The nine "what ifs" serve to merely jog the mind and heart as we grapple with the big issues facing our nation relative to crime reduction and job creation. They represent the kind of "out-of-the-box" brainstorming required if we want to unleash positive energy and a solutions-finding momentum for the country.

The motivation and rationale underpinning the "what-ifs" is not to be punitive or restrictive. We need an economy that is energised by risk-taking entrepreneurs who are handsomely rewarded for their efforts. We should not be restrictive in this sense, lest we blunt the sharp edge of pursuit of personal gain and adventure which are the twin sides of the entrepreneurial coin. Nobody is motivated to create wealth for someone else if there is no personal gain and incentive involved. Human beings are not altruistic by nature and so one must be realistic in this regard.

Put in a different context, taxpayerss are happy to pay tax if they get the services their taxes are meant to pay for. But when those administering the tax (i.e. government) squander and abuse public funds, there is no incentive on the part of the taxpayer to be more than just legally compliant. Scandinavian countries, for example, have an incredibly high tax rate, but they receive good government services in return. It's a quid pro quo situation. The withholding of tax is an offence in South Africa. Tax evasion is a crime; tax efficiency an art. Smart business people strive to pay as little tax as possible where government is seen as not adequately delivering or abusing taxpayers' money.

The nation-building needs of an emerging South Africa are enormous. The apartheid government's lack of investment in adequate infrastructure for the entire population is now costing the country dearly. The constant raising of tariffs and taxes to fund such infrastructure investment is always a sensitive subject. However, when there is a perception that those who hold public office are corrupt, greedy and incompetent, the trust-base of the tax-paying public diminishes dramatically.

There will be no easily reached consensus position, especially when it comes to issues of money – be it private or public money. People do not share their money as easily as they do their time or any other commodity, especially with those who are deemed to be undeserving.

Conclusion

These nine "what if" scenarios are intended to free up the imagination – our very futures depend on it.

This chapter also aims to demonstrate that regardless of how difficult or impossible a situation may seem, there are always solutions. It may require a super-human effort to bring those solutions to the surface and an even greater effort to ensure that one's solutions become part of the mainstream. But how can we fail to try?

Notes
1   Hubbard RG & Duggan W, the authors of the 2009 publication, *The Aid Trap: Hard Truths About Ending Poverty*. New York: Columbia University Press make the point that the Marshall Plan which guided the post-war reconstruction of Europe was a masterful success and, given some contextual modifications could well be applied to Africa. It is the Marshall Plan that inspired the former Prime Minister of England, Gordon Brown, to propose a similar plan for Africa. Hubbard

and Duggan, however, critique the Brown proposal arguing that it will plunge Africa into a deeper crisis since the proposal is not premised on properly empowering the business sector, which according to Hubbard and Duggan, holds the key to a successful reconstruction of Africa using the principle of the Marshall Plan that worked for post-war Europe.

2 BIG – Basic Income Grant – Council of Churches has called for a universal income grant http://www.africafocus.org/docs04/big0411.php 3 July 2001 Poverty and inequality pose the greatest threat to the success of South Africa's young democracy. A bold initiative is urgently needed to confront this challenge.

We, the undersigned organisations, call for the introduction of a universal Basic Income Grant as a key intervention to combat poverty and to improve the lives of the majority of South Africans. At least 22 million people in South Africa – well over half the population – live in poverty. On average, they survive on R144 per person per month. A Basic Income Grant would provide rapid and sustained relief to all South Africans by:

- providing everyone with a minimum level of income,
- enabling the nation's poorest households to better meet their basic needs,
- stimulating equitable economic development,
- promoting family and community stability, and
- affirming and supporting the inherent dignity of all.

The Basic Income Grant should be founded on the following fundamental principles:

- Universal Coverage: It should be available to everyone, from cradle to grave, and should not be subject to a means test.
- Relationship to existing grants: It should expand the social security net. No individual should receive less in social and assistance grants than before the introduction of the Basic Income Grant.
- Amount: The grant should be no less than R100 per person per month on introduction and should be inflation indexed.
- Delivery Mechanisms: Payments should be facilitated through public institutions. Using community Post Banks would have the additional benefit of enhancing community access to much-needed banking services.
- Financing: A substantial portion of the cost of the grant should be recovered progressively through the tax system. This would demonstrate solidarity by all South Africans in efforts to eliminate poverty. The remaining cost should be borne by the fiscus. A range of new measures should be introduced to increase revenue so that the additional cost can be accommodated without squeezing out other social expenditure.

In recent weeks, the following organisations have come together to endorse this basic platform and to commit ourselves to working with government to make the Basic Income Grant a reality. We call on all South Africans to join us in this campaign and invite them to add their endorsement to this platform.

Signed by – Alliance for Children's Entitlement to Social Security (ACESS); Black Sash; Child Health Policy Institute; Congress of South African Trade Unions; Development Resources Centre; Ecumenical Service for Socio-Economic Transformation; Gender Advocacy Programme; Community Law Centre, University of the Western Cape; South African Council of Churches; South African National NGO Coalition; Southern African Catholic Bishops' Conference; Treatment Action Campaign.

3 Muhammad Yunus is the visionary and founder of what is today called the Grameen Bank. Bangladesh, with a population of over 120 million people, is the home of Grameen Bank and came about as the result of the inspiration of economist Yunus, Bangladesh-born and US-trained. Instead of spending his life as a university economics professor, Yunus decided in the mid-1970s to develop a micro-lending programme to help the poorest people of his country. Yunus based the programme on his strong belief that the very poor do not need complicated training programmes to improve their economic lot. They need money, in the form of loans. This programme has empowered thousands of people – many of them women – and surprised experts in economic development who never believed that the very poor would find the

initiative and ability to repay even the smallest (R175.00 – R 3,500.00) loans. Grameen ("of the village") Bank has developed into an internationally acclaimed and replicated method for assisting the impoverished in Malaysia, the Philippines, Nepal with worldwide applicability and relevance.
4   Reinert ES (2007) *How Rich Countries Got Rich ... And Why Poor Countries Stay Poor.* London: Constable, p.7
5   Ibid p.87
6   Ibid p.87
7   Mbeki M (2009) *Architects of Poverty: Why African Capitalism Needs Changing.* Johannesburg: Picador Africa, p.36 makes the point that the ideal is the creation of a middle-income independent middle class.

8 | Four steps to personal victory

Be inspired by a visionary and positive future and not a broken and unchangeable past.

Changing the individual

This chapter outlines a four-step process leading to the creation of jobs and consequently destroying crime and poverty in our South African society. These steps are:

Step 1 – Change your mindset (i.e. consciousness)
Step 2 – Change your skills profile (i.e. ability)
Step 3 – Buy a bullet-proof vest (i.e. protect yourself)
Step 4 – Be a patriot (i.e. join and celebrate with others)

Figure 4: 4 Steps to Success

It's time to declare war

How do we create an economy where we can all share in the wealth of that economy? I jump to this question because we all acknowledge that if we solve poverty, which is the root cause of the problem, then we will effectively have solved a host of our problems including the crime problem. But how?

A sustainable solution to the poverty problem, in my view, is through the creation of a wealthier economy which produces decent-paying jobs, which in turn creates a series of different life chances for people. Simply creating *any* type of job is not a lasting solution. At the most basic level, given the high levels of unemployment, we tend to grab at straws and are satisfied with the creation of any type of job. However, this is where the danger lurks.

Poverty is not eradicated by simply creating any kind or type of job. It is a particular type of job in a particular type of economy that is required to break the back of poverty. And those types of jobs, as we have shown, are jobs that help to build an industrial base for our economy so that our economy can grow.

Fortunately, South Africa has identified the type of economy that it requires, and the type of jobs as well. The economy required is one that has a manufacturing bias, and the jobs needed are those generally described as artisanal or tradesman-type jobs. We have seen that South Africa has gone a step further by putting in place mechanisms to try to unblock all training initiatives designed to create the kind of artisan base required for the South African economy to grow at a rate of between 4% and 6%. So if we have done all this, why do we still have an unemployment and crime problem? Why are we not producing the type and the number of artisans we need? These are the compelling questions which have prompted me to go in search of answers, especially since I was once an artisan myself. At the time, I never thought of my job as being important to the overall economy.

In the course of my search for answers, I have discovered that there is a huge gap between desire and action; policy and implementation. It is this gap which is the missing link. And it is this link that I have labelled *industrial consciousness*.

The short answer is this: We need to make a mindshift at both an individual and a national level – and that mindshift is one that will move us from racial consciousness to industrial consciousness.

Of course, only a small segment of the millions of currently unemployed people will become the artisans required by the economy. What about the rest? At one level, one could argue that it's not the quantity but the quality of jobs that will eventually remedy the poverty situation. But in the meantime, we have millions of people in need of any job they can lay their hands on.

In short, it's a specific type of job, and the specific kinds of skills required that are important if we are to truly break the poverty cycle and trap. The jobs and skills in question are industrially oriented jobs and skills.

Step by step to victory

We will now unpack the four-step process for the creation of jobs:
Step 1 – Change your mindset (i.e. consciousness)
Step 2 – Change your skills profile (i.e. ability)
Step 3 – Buy a bullet-proof vest (i.e. protect yourself)
Step 4 – Be a patriot (i.e. join and celebrate with others)

Consciousness
The first step to creating or finding a job in the new South Africa is to change your (job-seeker) mindset. Take care not to confuse mindset with skills. Before you acquire skills, you must first change your attitude so that you are ready to learn a new skill or apply a skill which you may already have mastered.

Changing your mindset does not cost any money. It requires willpower. It's the most important change in your life that money cannot buy. You alone can decide to change or to stay the same. Of course, I can always bribe (i.e. financially incentivise) you to change, but such change will never be long-lasting or permanent. The bottom line is that anyone can afford the first step that is required in creating or finding a job. Everyone can afford it because it does not cost any money. What it costs is emotional investment and brain power.

It is this first step that this book is about. I am trying to convince you to adopt industrial consciousness as opposed to race consciousness as a basis for your new South African identity. This new identity goes as follows: *I want to be known for what I can change about the future and not for what I cannot change about my past.* In other words, I want to be known by what I aspire to become, and not by what I cannot change in my past.

The change required at a personal level is also required at the level of the national psyche. We can wait for a sufficient number of individuals to share the same mindset and then "hope" that there will be a critical mass to impact the direction of the economy.

Alternatively, as a nation, we can collectively re-energise our entire society towards a new awareness of national self via industrial consciousness. As a society, we can agree to construct all sorts of rewards for supporting the new focus as people prepare to partake in an economy from which they have been actively excluded for many centuries. I am not calling for a blindly nationalist and state-orchestrated programme unless the carrot is that every South African stands to benefit. In a sense I am calling for a new nationalism of sorts, but one that is aimed at creating an economy in which millions of South Africans can participate either through being employed in decent jobs, or becoming owners and managers of businesses within that economy. The bottom line is that accomplishing this first step, with the necessary buy-in from the whole of South Africa, will require serious effort and will not happen overnight.

Ability

Let's move to Step 2 of the process. Once you have decided to change your mindset, then you must *want, demand, desire,* and have an *appetite* for skills acquisition, because it is your skills that people generally want to know about, rather than your mindset. So let's get the order correct – first change your mindset, then focus on the issue of skills.

You may already have an appropriate set of skills, in which case you are ahead of the pack. If you don't have the necessary skills, then you need to be desperately hungry for the training and education needed to acquire those skills. Skills acquisition is the twin sibling to a changed mindset. Or put differently, attitude (i.e. mindset) and skills (i.e. ability) are two sides of the same coin. You must believe that the skills you learn or already have will get you a job in the economy. Of course, there must be a high level of alignment. It's pointless qualifying as a potato farmer when the economy is looking for nuclear scientists.

Self Protection

Then comes Step 3 – also a big step. Somehow we, the citizens of South Africa, together, must change our economy. The economy belongs to us, for goodness sake. Maybe you have never thought of yourself as owning the economy or having much power. Well, the fact is that we have the power in our hands. It's a choice between using your bullets or your ballots. We can no longer have an economy in South Africa that benefits only a few people who are either the right colour or the right religion or whatever. We need an economy that benefits all South Africans and in which there are decent jobs for all.

My vision for the new South Africa is simple: *A healthier and wealthier country for all.* What's the point of having won our political freedom in 1994 (via the political ballot) if the vast majority of our people are now economically poorer and less educated than they were during the apartheid years (i.e. because of an economic bullet)?

We voted in 1994 for a better life for all. But it turns out there is only a better life for some – the chosen few.

I believe that we *can* change the economy of South Africa so that it benefits us all and not just a few select people. But it starts with adopting industrial consciousness as the new mindset.

Once you have changed your mindset and are clear about the skills you need or already have, you must then buy yourself the proverbial bullet-proof vest (i.e. step 3), because the rich and powerful are not going to simply let go of an economy that is making them rich – and keeping the masses poor. So, Step 3 is linked to self preservation. In the new South Africa, there is a class of rich people, both black and white, who are making lots of money. Much of this is made through legitimate means. However, the large gap between the rich and the poor is also explained, in part, by the fact that the rich get richer by exploiting (directly and indirectly) the masses who are poor, under-educated and growing angrier and hungrier by the day.

In terms of the idea of buying a bullet-proof vest, let me say this: People are not always employed because they are competent. They are employed, among other things, because there is some or other level of trust or "payback" involved. Rarely are people appointed purely on the basis of their competence. It therefore stands to reason that incompetent people are generally threatened by a competent person and will find ways to undermine the competent person who simply wants to get the job done well. Your bullet-proof vest will be needed to protect you against mediocrity, where there is very little reward for competence and much reward for entitlement.

It is hard and painful to absorb these kinds of bullets which damage where it hurts most – deep in one's soul and psyche. So we need to buy that bullet-proof vest to protect ourselves against those who worship the gods of incompetence, nepotism and corruption. Expect to be attacked.

But you will not be alone. There is a whole army of us in your position and this brings me to the next step.

Solidarity

Step 4 is all about patriotic solidarity with like-minded people – that army of loyal South African patriots. We need to adopt Nelson Mandela's mantra of resisting white domination and black domination alike. The only way to do this is collectively – we need to be of one mind, body and soul. If we, as a nation, adopt industrial consciousness as the basis of a new South African identity, without minimising or discarding our cultural roots and heritage, then we will have a new non-racial platform that binds us.

We therefore need to find new ways to relate to each other as "industrial" South Africans. The way to do this is to adopt industrial consciousness which has, as its sole aim, the creation of a South Africa where there is health and wealth for all. We don't want to be a country living on handouts or foreign aid. We want to be a proud people who together can turn our economy into the wealthiest in the world, and in which all our citizens share in creating and ultimately enjoying that wealth.

There are many examples of countries with fewer resources than us, who have shifted from poverty towards relative wealth and indeed a middle-income economy. These include countries such as Georgia, Vietnam, Costa Rica, El Salvador, Morocco, India and even Columbia, to name just a few.

We too have the ingredients to make it happen – a wonderfully diverse population, the raw minerals, the basic industrial infrastructure, a government that on paper is committed to wanting a better life for all, a Constitution and a Bill of Rights that guarantees our hard-earned freedom, and a people that proved the world wrong on 27 April 1994.

An industrial consciousness will ensure that the appropriate "wealth-generating" skill is spread around so that more of us can access more opportunities. We are all members of the same army – an injury to one is an injury to all.

It is the spirit of togetherness and "*helpmekaar*" (help each other) that we need to nurture and build upon in the new South Africa. We need to love our country. But we have to love each other first, warts and all. The best way to start is to define ourselves by the collective future we want to share, rather than defining ourselves by the broken past we come from.

Conclusion

The four steps to victory are neither magical nor easy. What starts off as a very personal journey ends up as an act of community where like-minded people reinforce and encourage one another. The call for a shift of the mindset of all South Africans is an ambitious and somewhat arrogant call to make. However, as is argued throughout the book, it all starts with the individual who thinks and believes differently, and sooner or later the little spark develops into a raging fire. There are already many little sparks trying to ignite a new approach to our country's problems. It all starts with brave individuals who are prepared to risk examining the way they think and are prepared to make a change – for the good of all.

9 | How much truth can a nation tolerate?

Is truth not like beauty; faultless, pure and desirable to the eye of the beholder?

How often do we express the real truth about what we feel and think, especially when it comes to sensitive issues such as race, religion and morality? In this regard there are two extreme positions: one is dogmatic and fundamentalist, and the other is accommodating and liberal in the extreme.

Invariably we only express and display our vulnerabilities and uncertainties in a context of safety. And yet, we all have a set of beliefs and truths we hold dear. Rarely do we critically examine these truths and beliefs until someone tries to convince us otherwise.

This chapter explores the thinking and deep-seated emotions behind the words we sometimes say in our minds but do not verbalise – especially regarding issues of prejudice, be they racial, gender-related, religious or otherwise.

Of course, certain things are best left unsaid. However, in the context of trying to forge a new psyche, we need to be explicit, honest and truthful without being vengeful, and without intending to harm the next person. This would constitute arrogance and reflect our unwillingness to listen carefully to the honest views of another – even if we vehemently disagreed. The challenge is to find a happy medium without stifling honest reflection.

Figure 5: Jewish and Rwandan Holocaust

The pictures in Figure 5 are a horrifying reminder of what can happen when we enforce our dogma and version of the truth, as opposed to jealously guarding a society in which freedom of conscience and speech is allowed to flourish and where there is respect for alternative views.

Speaking truth to power

The truth is generally costly

An internationally respected organisational consultant introduced me to the concept of "speaking truth to power". It sounded great, until I tried to implement it. I discovered that bosses and one's superiors in general do not want to hear the truth about things. Telling your boss the real truth (i.e. speaking truth to power) is most often a career-limiting exercise. You need to tell them the things they want to hear. When I merrily proceeded to share truthfully with my boss my thoughts and critique of the company, what happened to me is what often happens to whistle-blowers, prophets and other "truth-tellers". I got blown away.

I learnt very quickly that speaking truth to power needs the right conditions and protection, and if possible, the right kind of economic (i.e. personal financial) buffer so that if your boss does not take too kindly to your wonderful wisdom and truthful advice, you can at least survive once you are fired, demoted or marginalised, or charged with insubordination. I also learnt, through my TRC experience, to ask the question: How much truth can a nation tolerate?

Saying the unspeakable is no different from trying to be truthful and honest about what one observes or senses. The trick is to be able to say it, test it, and if one finds it to be an erroneous belief, to change it. But to do this we must first find a way to say what we are thinking. We think and hold stuff in our minds but we don't dare say it for fear of being misinterpreted. So invariably we simply "shut-up", grin and bear it, and hope someone else says what we are thinking!

Truth and heresy

Truth and heresy are two sides of the same coin. What makes something truthful and something else false? The "truth" topic remains controversial and over the centuries has been the basis of more destruction of human life than its preservation. I therefore approach this topic with caution and as sensitively as I can. Strangely, though, what is true today, may not be true tomorrow and may be seen as heresy. In modern times, South Africa's experience with apartheid is a case in point. These days it is hard to find someone who ardently believes in what came to be called, in theological circles, the Heresy of Apartheid.[1]

In addition to the many other philosophical and religious considerations when discussing the notion of truth, I wish to highlight at least two things that we must bear in mind when talking about truth. These are the differences between fact and opinion, and the role of power in determining what is true or false.

Truth, like beauty, is in the eye of the beholder. It's a matter of perspective. Or is something true regardless of the view of the beholder?

Our own experiences as a South African nation concerning what it true or false is still fresh in our memories. Most people believe something to be true because an authoritative figure such as a teacher, parent, religious leader or politician asserts it to be so. But as we know from our own experience in South Africa, truth can change depending on the power dynamics. Few people in South Africa still believe that the white race was ordained by God to be the superior race of the universe, as well as the custodians and supervisors of the black race. No-one believes any longer that blacks are subordinate to whites simply by virtue of race.

Perception as truth

A common way of expressing oneself is to assert that the content of one's communication is factually true. This is often done expressively by raising the volume of one's oral communication so as to give credence to what one is saying. Of course, the level of loudness (i.e. volume) does not necessarily translate into deeper truth for that which we may be asserting.

Very rarely do ordinary people engage in detailed discourse about the nature of truth and whether or not truths are self-evident regardless of the context in which they are expressed. Invariably our ordinary perceptions of truth are emotionally and intuitively based. Interestingly, as our economic status changes, so does the intensity with which we express our notions and views of truth or falsity.[2]

It seems to me that issues of truth, morality and religious belief are more important when one is poor. As one moves into the categories of prosperity and wealth, issues of truth and religious belief become matters of private concern (or no concern at all). Furthermore, issues of truth or falsity tend to become issues only when our economic well-being or interests are affected. I may be stereotyping unfairly, but it seems to me that when people's financial status is secure, they couldn't care what others think or believe about them. Neither do they care much about their religious beliefs. Issues of self-esteem are largely taken care of when one does not need to beg, borrow or steal to ensure one's financial livelihood.

An example closer to home may be easier to grasp. A truth now familiar and held by most South Africans is that of the equality of race, and more accurately the equality of human beings regardless of race. At least that is what the new South African Constitution and its Bill of Rights hold to be true for South African society. Whether all South Africans accept this to be true is a different matter. I, for one, *want* to believe that few today would argue for a truth which claims that blacks are morally and genetically inferior to whites, or vice versa.

Then there is the matter of who is allowed to say what about race. Racial sensitivities are such that only blacks or whites, for example, are allowed to describe themselves using certain words. If whites were to use the same words to describe blacks, and vice versa, they would be considered racist. Therefore, in a race-imbued society such as ours, discussions about race remain explosive, especially when there is radical economic inequality between the races.

The truths I wish to highlight in this chapter have their roots in the racial history of our country. Many prefer the ostrich approach and would rather hide their heads in the sand or remain silent with regard to emerging social trends, especially when it involves race. I am fully aware that I am treading on dangerous ground.

The truth of the matter

The truth of the matter, in my opinion, is that, despite external appearances, South Africa is on the brink of a formal civil rebellion. The prisons are full, the police are not coping with the crime situation, and unemployment figures are alarmingly high.

Crime statistics suggest that there is already a low-intensity urban and rural war taking place in South Africa, with particular reference to public reaction to the lack of service delivery. How else could one describe the murder of a public official who is considered by the community to be corrupt, a poor performer and an impediment to service delivery?[3]

If we don't do something dramatic about crime and unemployment, then we can expect violence and anarchy to erupt in our streets. As a result, we risk losing all the miraculous gains that have led to South Africa's liberation from apartheid and minority rule.

There are enough doomsday prophets predicting that South Africa will go the way of Zimbabwe and the rest of Africa. I say, "Let's prove them wrong."

Expressing the unspeakable

How is truth or heresy determined, particularly in the context of political and racial discourse? Is it the power of the bullet or the power of the bank balance that determines truth? Is truth a fact verified via scientific experimentation or is it an act of faith?

Saying the unspeakable is not unlike what, in management theory, we call "having difficult conversations". One must confront one's own prejudices in order to deal with them. For example, how would it be received if I were to argue for a truth which says that life under racial apartheid and white minority rule was better than life under black majority rule over the past 16 years of democracy in South Africa? Such a statement would probably be considered heresy rather than the truth.

In more specific management and performance language, for example, could it be said that education management during apartheid produced better results than education management at the hands of the newly elected black government since 1994? Would such a statement be true or false? Heresy or orthodoxy? Is this statement a plain and simple distortion of the facts?

Sometimes it is safer to keep one's thoughts to oneself. In the context of the observations to be made about uncomfortable truths, and the questions just posed about education and political management, one can already sense the explosiveness, and possibly heretical nature of the discussion at hand. Some assertions, observations and questions will have somewhat predictable responses depending on one's ideological and racial predisposition and heritage. But this does not mean that the difficult questions should not be asked.

The fact that such questions can be raised in a context of freedom of thought and expression, illustrates that South Africa has moved rapidly from being a closed and insular apartheid society to a free-thinking and open society where critical questions can be asked of any institution or person, regardless of political sensitivities and the discomfort caused by asking the question.

While private institutions may find protection in terms of the laws of privacy, public institutions do not enjoy such protection and must publicly account for their activities and face very difficult and robust questions and comments from the public. The balance must, however, be that in questioning, one seeks not to destroy but to build. Criticism for the sake of it is destructive and not intended to improve current circumstances.

In the context of the change of leadership from Mbeki to Zuma, the General Secretary of the ANC, Gwede Mantashe, has often described the ANC as a movement akin to an ocean that cleanses itself, which suggests a kind of self regulation by reverting to what is normative for the party. It is true that we have an emerging culture of robust critique and debate emerging in South Africa, even though, in many instances, those providing the critique of the ruling party come from within the ranks of the ruling party itself.

Nevertheless, the question is this: *Under what conditions is one allowed to ask awkward questions about the delivery or non-delivery of the governing party without being condemned as disloyal or racist?* The race-card still lies very close to the top of the conversational deck of cards in South Africa. One naturally expects opposition political parties to be somewhat disingenuous when assessing the performance of the ruling party. This is the nature of politics. And in Parliament there is the luxury of parliamentary privilege and protection. Fortunately, after stripping away the political jeering and rhetoric of cheap politicking and political point-scoring, it is possible to develop a picture of the true realities and challenges facing South Africa. It is only then that one can soberly and objectively ask some probing questions based on observations or detailed analysis.

The enduring sensitivity and the challenge is the following: *Who has the legitimacy to raise awkward questions and make critical observations about the performance of our society as a whole, especially when such observations involve race-sensitive matters?* Have white people lost the moral legitimacy to be critical of a black government given their overt and covert collusion as a race with apartheid forces and ideology? Of course, this is a broad and sweeping generalisation but it does help to make the point. A new-generation white Afrikaner recently said: "I am tired of apologising for what my ancestors did to black people."

Allow me to ask the question differently: *Do white South African patriots enjoy the same moral credibility as black South African patriots?* Does the ruling party have hegemonic control of performance standards and critical discourse in South Africa to the extent that no one other than the ruling party may be critical of its performance? Where is the voice of civil society?[4] What – and who – determines the truth of the situation and the gravity of the problems facing our country?

Comparing apples with apples

Is the critical questioning of the performance of the ruling party and government in general the sole purview of the insiders to the ruling party, and a largely tolerated but discredited white, race-based opposition party? I suspect that we are sufficiently far down the road in the new dispensation to be able to make some comparative notes and comments regarding the performance of the ruling party and its management of the nation's rebuilding programme. Unfortunately, 16 years does not provide a long enough case history. As managers would say – we need to compare apples with apples. Most adult South Africans have a "before" and an "after" perspective – before and after apartheid, or before and after democracy. The choice of comparative framework itself is also reflective of a particular consciousness and is not incidental to one's analysis and perspective. Right here we have our first challenge, namely the issue of comparative analysis.

What should be the comparative basis of black-managed nation building under democracy versus white-managed nation building under apartheid? Is a comparison of ANC government performance with that of the National Party's not an act of analytical heresy in the first instance? How dare one compare the governance of an illegitimate regime with the governance of a democratically elected political party? Should we even be comparing these two moments as if one were a benchmark for the other?

Political truth, of course, must always be tested. Fortunately, as a nation we do this every four years. The most recent test results have given the ANC a mandate to govern – and that is the truth. Or, was the overwhelming vote which the ANC received in the 2009 general elections rather a reflection of the aspiration of the masses who are giving the ANC one last chance to deliver on basic services and a better life for all?

The central thrust of this book is a call for industrial consciousness as the basis and fulcrum of a new national identity for South Africa. I wish to make my observations, and later discuss what I consider to be some "uncomfortable home-truths" in the context of this theme, namely industrial consciousness.

Different words ... same reality

There are many ways to say the same thing. My parents taught me that it is often not what you say but how you say it that matters most. The challenge, they said, is to find a way to tell someone to go to hell in such a way that they look forward to the journey! I was always taught that diplomacy is generally the desired mode of communication. However, sometimes it's best to call a spade a spade, especially in a crisis.

If the lingering problems of crime and unemployment in South Africa did not carry with them such dire consequences, I would probably concede to a more diplomatic approach to the topic. But the situation is desperate, in my view. Neither freedom from apartheid nor post-apartheid multi-party democracy has yet delivered for the vast majority of South Africans, either in the area of a reduction in poverty or in the area of reducing unemployment. The discussions throughout this book are premised on two major assumptions. The first is that crime and unemployment are the two most critical challenges facing post-apartheid South Africa. The second is that failure to adequately address these twin challenges places at risk all the gains of the first 16 years of nation building and democracy in South Africa.

Stated positively and in *management* lingo, the problems posed by crime and unemployment are the challenges of crime reduction and job creation. Stated strategically, these are police and/or internal security strategy issues and industrial strategy issues. Stated *politically*, these are "legacy of apartheid" issues which are difficult to overcome, says the ruling party. We are in serious trouble.

One last chance

Notwithstanding efforts by the government to address the twin challenges of crime and unemployment, the primary focus and purpose throughout our discussion is to unmask the interplay between crime-reduction strategies (i.e. police strategy) on the one hand, and job-creation strategies (industrial strategy) on the other. It is my interpretation and understanding that South Africa's drive to re-industrialise the base of its economy is a euphemistic way of saying that South Africa has one last chance to save itself from destruction caused by grinding poverty and a country permanently disabled by its social grant system.

Neither poverty nor a permanent social grant system is desirable or sustainable, especially not with a dwindling tax-collection base and rising unemployment. However, given a different set of assumptions and motives, there may well be ideological forces afoot that desire a state of social grant dependency and a lack of progress in terms of poverty reduction. Free market philosophy is not necessarily based on the upliftment of the poor and the oppressed, or on the spirit of spreading wealth. Capitalism is about wealth accumulation, often with scant regard for ethics and morality. Socialism, on the other hand, has proven to be a failure. And yet, truth be told, even the most capitalistic of nations have a socialist underbelly that cares for its citizens. The recent First World bail-out packages for failed business, as was the case with the USA; and the economic stimulus packages of other countries as a way to offset the impact of the global recession (as was the case with Australia), provide enough evidence that in the final analysis, nations generally look after their own first, even if it means providing socialist-oriented care with a capitalist label.

Conclusion

What is truth? Many times the basis of what people believe is not blind faith but tangible evidence. Furthermore, how does one distinguish between truth, opinion, attitude, and unfounded opinion and conjecture? Is legal truth, which is based on provable fact, more reliable that religious truth, which has its roots in faith? These kinds of questions become relevant when we talk about truths which make us uncomfortable, but for which we can't really provide factual evidence.

Notes
1   *See* De Gruchy JW & Villa-Vicencio C (Eds.) (1983) *Apartheid is a heresy*. Grand Rapids: Eerdmans.
2   To take this one step further and at the risk of stereotyping, issues of truth and falsity are more intense in contexts of poverty than they are among the rich and wealthy classes. A similar

pattern is observable in relation to levels of religiosity. It seems that poorer folk are inclined to be much more religious than wealthier folk who tend to move towards agnosticism. The predisposition of a socio-economic stratum of society to particular forms and expressions of belief with its accompanying moral and ethical codes are for another discussion. However, as is raised in the Postscript of this book, we should not too easily disregard the power of religious belief and its impact on the industrialisation project. An interesting question and juxtapositioning would be that which has come to be called the Protestant work ethic in contrast to the work ethic undergirded by ubuntu, for example. Is there a discernable difference? And what has been the impact of the belief systems and worldview on productivity.

3   http://www.news24.com/Content/SouthAfrica/News/1059/9b73541f10d54a73830c5575d55fa4a2/15-03-2009-08-23/Councillor_killed_outside_home

4   Pinky Khoabane, a *Sunday Times* columnist, recently expressed the sentiment from a dream she had that "...this country had a robust and vibrant civil society movement that looked after the interests of all citizens ... [and] whose membership profile traverses racial and gender boundaries and is made up of a cross section of people and institutions, including labour unions, business, religious groupings, non-governmental organisations and the broader public working for a common vision we could all be proud of."

10 | Eight uncomfortable truths

During apartheid the coloureds were not white enough. Now they are not black enough.

Facing our demons

This chapter identifies eight uncomfortable truths about the new South Africa which I believe we must confront if our nation is to effectively develop a new national psyche – an industrial consciousness which I argue must serve as the new paradigm for dealing with and thinking through job-creation and crime-reduction strategies. The ultimate motivation for risking a discussion of such an explosive nature is the desire to change things for the better. In this chapter we confront what I consider to be some destructive demons within the psyche of our nation, with the intention that healing of the mind, body and soul will ensue. We cannot build a prosperous and industrious nation when, lurking not far below the surface of our national psyche, are unresolved race-related issues with a propensity to divide rather than unite.

Testing the waters

I tested some of my observations concerning "uncomfortable truths" on some trusted friends. Their response can be summed up as follows: *"Ruben, you can think these things but you are not supposed to say them. In fact you dare not say them. You will be labelled as all sorts of negative things and you will be misunderstood. This is South Africa after all."*

The reaction I encountered is precisely the reason that we need to confront these demons. My central argument in this book is the call for a paradigm shift within our psyche as a nation, from a race-based psyche to an industrial consciousness. I am not saying that the race-based psyche is racist in orientation. We all need to feel fully comfortable in our skins. We need to feel culturally affirmed and liberated in respect of our racial and cultural roots.

My argument for industrial consciousness is premised on the fact that race consciousness has limitations and inherent dangers, and is unlikely to move us to the level of industrial and economic development that is required to rid the country of its ongoing unemployment and crime crisis.

In short, we need to find a safe and affirming environment in which to locate the issue that most bedevils our progress, namely an unbridled race consciousness coupled with a huge dose of entitlement. We need to find a way to express (i.e. exhale) the bad air, in the hope of taking in some fresh air.

Perhaps the xenophobic incidents in the townships and squatter camps around South Africa which peaked in 2008/09 serve as a window into the reality of racism and the national psyche. The brazenness of the response of the seemingly unsophisticated poor people towards their fellow township dwellers who happened to come from other parts of Africa reflects brutal honesty. The economically less fortunate seem unfettered by sophisticated forms of intellectual camouflage or rationalisation, and revealed their true thoughts which manifested in acts of xenophobic violence. The poor and less sophisticated "do" what many of us only "think" – yet we will never own up to thinking this way about foreigners or "the others". These thoughts remain the deep secrets of our supposed non-racial South African heart.

South Africa is lauded for its miraculous transition from a race-torn society to what Desmond Tutu termed a rainbow nation. The bloodless transfer of political power from white hands to black is often held up as a miracle. There has been a series of post-1994 miracles and transformation successes. We need to applaud ourselves as a nation for accomplishing what many doomsday prophets said was not possible. However, there are significant challenges which remain. There is a disturbing growth of negative racial attitudes, opinions, facts and beliefs which are at present too sensitive to deal with publicly or even privately. We prefer to internalise our feelings in the hope that things will get better.

What often triggers racial emotions are events such as the recent xenophobic attacks, or a senior manager taking her employer to the Equality Courts arguing for a promotion in spite of her "whiteness".[1] The unspoken issue here is that most whites are not likely to be promoted in a context of BEE and affirmative action.

The list of truths below is my subjective list. The eight truths I identify could quite easily be denied or dismissed as groundless speculation. Yet, I suspect that many people will acknowledge these assertions to be true for them too. My only hope is that in facing these attitudinal observations, we are ultimately driven by a desire to change things for the better. The ultimate aim should be the healing of the mind, body and soul so that we can, as a new nation, be united in our efforts to fight poverty, crime and violence in our society – and to build an economy from which we can all benefit and become more prosperous.

8 Uncomfortable Truths

1. White opinion is no opinion
2. Money can buy a race card
3. Non-racialism's racial hierarchy
4. Performance is NOT colour-blind
5. Coloured people remain the ham in the sandwich
6. White is right because it's white
7. B-BBEE has failed the masses
8. Black spirituality is heretical

Figure 6: 8 Uncomfortable Truths

White opinion is no opinion
In South Africa, white opinion no longer enjoys the same legitimacy as black opinion, particularly when it comes to race-based matters. Put in the form of a question let me ask the following: *Are whites considered to have equal moral integrity to blacks in SA?*

The flip side of this coin reflects a different nuance on the same matter: *Is black opinion about whites more easily tolerated than vice versa, even if such opinions border on being racist?*

I have been privy to many discussions with white people where, after a certain level of comfort has been reached in the relationship, the discussion goes something like this: "I don't mean to be racist but ..."

On the other hand, I have engaged in many conversations with black people where white opinion is not sought and is rejected simply because it is white. In other words, as far as a black attitude is concerned, whites have lost the legitimacy to offer an opinion. What we seem to have here is a situation where we do not separate the message from the messenger. Whether whites accept this level of disempowerment because of apartheid guilt or whatever other reason, is a matter to be explored. And whether blacks are justified to hold the higher moral ground because of their experience at the hands of white racism is a matter not easily resolved.

Money can buy race: Just ask the Chinese!
Is money neutral or does it have a race? The recent Pretoria High

Court ruling allowing for the reclassification of the Chinese as black, suggests that money can determine race. The primary purpose for the reclassification of Chinese people as "black" was to enable them to become beneficiaries of B-BBEE opportunities in South Africa. The torturous and tenuous history of the Chinese in South Africa is not to be down-played. The Chinese fell into the proverbial apartheid cracks, to the extent that the apartheid government could never place the Chinese into a neat apartheid race category. At one stage the Chinese were classified as "white" and at another "coloured". I always wondered about the Chinese store located in our community, with the owners living on site (i.e. in a coloured area).

If China was of no consequence, economically speaking, would we even be having this discussion? Does a powerful economic base and global ideological and expansionist interests qualify one to be a beneficiary of an economic policy that was intended to benefit the poor of South Africa?

An uncomfortable truth is captured in the proverbial expressions "money talks" and "money makes the world go round". The best intentions in the world require money and resources for implementation and execution. The critical question is: "Whose money rules South Africa?" Is it white money? Black money? South African money? Chinese money?

These intrusive questions have the potential to spark another war when people realise that South Africa is in fact not economically free, in spite of Freedom Day celebrated on 27 April each year. It could be said that the political freedom and victory as per the 1994 miracle of democracy moment constitutes, let's say, only 20% of the battle. The real and ultimate struggle to be fought and won should be nothing short of full-blown and total economic control and power.

The current reality is that the economy of South Africa is still white-controlled with an emerging class of ultra-wealthy black elites joining the ranks of the already wealthy white elites. The Chinese have now been officially invited to join these ranks, it seems. The creation of the wealthy black class, in the main, has been facilitated by the policy of black economic empowerment, and the intention of accommodating the Chinese is so that they too can benefit from black economic empowerment. Where does this leave the poor?

One cannot help asking who will be the next to buy blackness. Will it be the Japanese? The Greeks? Or are the "not obviously black" entities and groupings such as the Brazilians, Spanish or Italians, for example, already benefiting from B-BBEE to the extent that they do not need to be reclassified to be awarded South African government contracts or benefit from the preferential procurement system underpinning B-BBEE?

A non-racial society with a racial hierarchy

A third uncomfortable truth is that the new non-racial South African society is based on a racial hierarchy where a disabled black female is now the most valued in the BEE scorecard hierarchy, and a white male the least valued. Apartheid society was based on an explicit racial hierarchy. There was a pecking order and there was a system in place to allow for mobility within the system. People could present a case to the apartheid racial reclassification board if they wished to be reclassified. Every year, the apartheid system reported on how many coloureds became white, how many Indians became coloured and so forth.[2] This sounds too terrible to be true and yet it was a system that not too long ago dominated the national psyche and identity of South Africa.

Since 1994, South Africa has reordered its society and adopted a non-racial democratic order where race is not meant to matter. The uncomfortable truth is that while there may be no laws to legislate it, there is a new racial hierarchy and pecking order that governs the psyche of South Africa. This is best captured in the expression used by many coloureds in the new dispensation: "During apartheid we were not white enough. Now we are not black enough".

The fact of the matter is that tenders and business deal proposals are more often than not scored and allocated points based on the different levels of racial and suffering hierarchy resulting from apartheid.

The greatest anomaly is that a racial hierarchy governs the non-racial societal order in South Africa. The practical question is: How else do you deracialise the economy if you don't actually count the racial numbers. My question is: *Who said that deracialising the economy was the best way to ensure an economic revolution which benefits the majority of the people of the country?*

Performance is not colour-blind

The fourth uncomfortable truth is that performance is not colour-blind. It appears that our society has become tolerant of the underperformance of blacks. In the political arena and the civil service this is most visible and explicit. Certain non-performing public officials are not only tolerated, but are paid handsomely. It is often said in jest that one of the quickest ways to become a millionaire is to be appointed as the top dog at one of the parastatals, underperform and get yourself suspended – with full pay and benefits, and await the outcome of the investigation into your alleged non-performance which you, of course, will have contested. Eventually, a golden handshake does the trick and the next transformation appointee stands in line to take up the vacated post and repeat the cycle.

The private sector is no less guilty. Racial window-dressing is an art form in many private sector environments. I have personal experience in this regard. I was appointed to the board of a company as the only black non-executive director. There were subsequently two problems that emerged as a result of the appointment. First, my surname was not obviously black and second, my mouth was active during board meetings. Having read and studied my board packs, I asked some awkward questions during board meetings. I thought that honest and robust engagement with the contents of the board pack was a decent way to earn my board fees – and besides, was it not the responsible thing to do? The response I got from more seasoned black directors in later "support group" discussions when I complained of my dismissal from the board was: "Welcome to the real world my brother – you are not supposed to talk – just nod, collect your pay cheque, smile and be grateful." I did learn the hard way that the boardroom was a very different place to that of the robust academic environment where freedom of thought and expression are cornerstone values. And yet, even here I am learning that academic freedom is not quite as free as one would like to believe. Speaking truth to power – even as a nutty professor – can be a hazardous exercise.

There is no doubt that performance issues continue to be plagued by race issues in the new South Africa. I have previously challenged an audience of predominantly white educators by asking the following question: "When was the last time you refused to pass a black student because he/she had not performed to the required standard?" My question was not meant to be unnecessarily controversial yet it sparked what became a raging mountain fire around performance issues in education and training. The general response from white educators was that insistence on certain standards would be misinterpreted as a racial issue. I chastised my audience for colluding with racial sensitivities at the expense of quality performance which we demand from the learner. I begged the educators not to accommodate poor performance just because the student happens to be black. This is not only a disservice to the student, but a crippling disservice to the future of the country.

A different perspective emerges when considering non-blacks who are performing but are demotivated because transformation has come to mean that no matter how competent you are as a non-black, every job or post will be filled first by a black person.

The uncomfortable truth here is that performance is not colour-blind in South Africa. Often, just the opposite seems to be the case.

Coloureds remain the ham in the sandwich

Alan Boesak in his recent book, *Running with Horses*, laments the prevalence of the old adage among coloured people, namely that they feel they are still the ham in the South African racial sandwich. As the foremost proponent of non-racialism as the organising principle for the political activism of the United Democratic Front (UDF) in the early 1980s, Boesak reflects a tone of resignation to the reality of coloured folk nurturing the ham-in-the-sandwich syndrome. It used to be politically correct to distance oneself from this kind of thinking and to dismiss these "coloured" fears as unfounded and a product of a coloured inferiority complex. [3]

Unfortunately, the apartheid chickens have come home to roost. Coloureds were never as brutally and harshly treated as blacks. Coloureds were to serve as the economic buffer between the whites who "had" and the blacks who "had not". The coincidence of race and economics thus gave rise to preferential treatment for coloureds at both a legislative and societal level during apartheid. The creation of an economic buffer (i.e. a "not-so-bad-off" class of people of colour) was complicated by the fact that culturally, ethnically and historically, the birth of a mixed-race nation resulted from union between black and white. The product was labelled "coloured" which, depending on the shade of the skin, either leaned towards the adoption of black ancestry or white. In the harshest racial terms, coloureds thus became the unwanted bastards of society – a visible reminder of what was not supposed to be, namely a union of white and black.

A few centuries of mixing between black and white, local and international and all shades in between, logically gave rise to a community of people for whom a narrow concept of race could not apply. The apartheid ideologues understood this and engineered a racial identity to suit the economic purposes of racial apartheid capitalism.

It was therefore no coincidence that apartheid created seven different sub-categories for coloureds. A person like myself, born in Cape Town, was classified as "Cape coloured". My very dark skin tone raises other considerations, while my Tswana friend has a much lighter complexion than me as well as sharper facial features. Messy and crazy!

It is understandable that blacks would feel that coloureds got a better deal than they did during apartheid. The consequential thinking is that coloureds therefore should be second in line for the spoils of the democratic gains of war. The new South Africa, it would appear, must first reward the most damaged victims of apartheid and then move down the hierarchical ladder of pain and suffering. The somewhat passive bystander in this discussion is the Indian community who, not withstanding the experience of Gandhi, for example, also experienced their fair share of suffering, pain and humiliation at the hands of the apartheid state.

The TRC process tried to show the equality of pain and suffering. In discussions around reparation policy, these issues came into sharp relief. How would we compensate someone who had lost a limb compared with someone who had lost a life? And how would one take into consideration the depth of pain, suffering and humiliation linked to the racial classification system? Did a black person who was tortured suffer any less pain that a coloured who was tortured? Surely the issue had to do with scale and volume rather than anything intrinsically racial? How do you begin to repair the pain of the past, structurally orchestrated, but personally experienced, if your measure of pain is driven by a racial measure and standard?

Are coloureds justified in their unspoken paranoia and feelings that in the new dispensation they are not black enough to benefit from the spoils of war while during the apartheid era they were not white enough? The ham-sandwich syndrome is all-pervasive; unfortunately an uncomfortable reality.

White is considered competent by virtue of being white

A sixth uncomfortable truth is that apartheid ideology created a racial default drive within our psyche which automatically equates whiteness with competence. This default consciousness runs deep in the psyche and surfaces especially when black non-performance is evident. Rarely does white non-performance get any attention.

Furthermore, an additional default drive of apartheid ideology is that white management engenders a level of trust and confidence disproportionate to the actual job being done. Is competence a white/black thing, is it a function of social class, or is it a skills and opportunity issue that is void of race?

I encountered the preference for and assumption of white competence when negotiating an engineering contract with an international company in France. This was the first time the company had dealt with a black South African CEO of an engineering company. Strategically, it made sense for me to be accompanied by a senior engineering consultant, who happened to be white. The presence of this engineer seemed to bring a certain level of comfort and relief to the matter at hand, even though the negotiations were not primarily about the nitty-gritty engineering aspects but rather the commercial structuring and timing of the deal. In short, my engineering consultant was not "technically" necessary, but his presence was an "emotional" imperative.

B-BBEE has failed the masses

We have dedicated an entire chapter to the issues of B-BBEE and its limitations. However, a few headline issues need repeating here. The recent acknowledgement by the Presidency that BEE has not created the trickle-down for the masses as was originally envisaged, goes a long way to relieve some of the discomfort expressed in the corridors concerning BEE.

A cursory glance at the number of black directors appointed to JSE-listed companies is an index on transformation (or lack thereof) in the economic sector.[4] The conclusion drawn from these statistics is that the South African economy in general is still, in the main, white-controlled. The transfer of economic power from white into black hands has not happened, notwithstanding the imperatives of black economic empowerment as a politically motivated policy to deracialise the economy of South Africa. Significant economic wealth has been transferred from white to black hands, but only a few black hands.

Is a legislated deracialisation of the economy the solution, given that by sheer numbers, we as blacks outnumber whites by an almost 11 to one ratio? Is the management, revival and growth of the South African economy not an issue of competence and entrepreneurial flair rather than reparations for past injustices experienced by the black majority of the country?

Assuming all whites were to leave the country tomorrow, would we "blacks" be able to manage the country and its economy? Put differently, do we still need whites in this country, given that we, as blacks, racially outnumber them? What then is the obsession with BEE and its ownership and management emphasis? Should we not be creating future generations of patriotic and skilled entrepreneurs, regardless of colour, in order to grow the economy and fundamentally address the unemployment and crime problems facing the country? Or must we stay locked into a race formula as a means to shift the new South Africa away from the strictures and ideological bondage of the old?

Black spirituality is too tolerant of abuse

What is it about black spirituality that has enabled us to tolerate the levels of abuse over the centuries. From slavery to apartheid, a common theme is the morally superior levels of forgiveness shown by blacks towards their oppressors. What is it about black culture, if there is such a notion, that turns it into a sponge that soaks up pain and trauma inflicted upon it by the greed of ostensibly the white world?

A useful yet contentious contrast in response to dehumanisation is to compare the African response to slavery with the international response to the Jewish holocaust of Nazi Germany. Six million Jews were brutally slaughtered and gassed to death by Hitler's Nazi Germany. The sensitivities of the Western world are such that the horrors of Nazi Germany will never be repeated. Days of remembrance occur on a global scale to ensure that the world remembers the pain and suffering of the Jewish people. In a similar vein, Chika Onyeani in his book *Capitalist Nigger* reminds us that:

> In the 17th century, more than 36 million African men and women were taken into slavery and brought to the shores of America. Of that 36 million, more than 18 million died in the Trans-Atlantic crossings ... We are talking of over 36 million African men and women who were rounded up by a handful of Caucasians, and our ancestors could not do much to stop the onslaught. This is just a small group of Caucasian men coming into our midst and we ran helter-skelter, without any much defence to stop the rape and incarceration of our Kings and Queens. Am I supposed to take

delight in telling this story, which we as a people have nothing to stop from happening again, and which is in fact even happening at a greater frightening speed than in the 17th century ... The black race is a slave – pure and simple – an economic slave.[5]

Of course, blacks colluded with white slave traders and owners. In modern times, could one say that blacks continue to collude with white traders and owners of the South African economy, which has left the vast majority of blacks impoverished and living in conditions which white people wouldn't allow their animals to live in? What is it that quietens the rage which should drive the black person to better his/her life and the lives of those around them?

Is there something within the index of black spirituality that finds it acceptable to be treated like second-class citizens and be reduced to living in conditions that are totally unacceptable for any human being to endure? Is ours a spirituality of docility and tolerance of abuse rather than one of empowerment and entrepreneurial flare? Onyeani laments the plight of the black person:

> I am not ashamed to say that I am also purely motivated by the same greed that motivates Caucasians with "killer instincts" and "devil-may-care" convictions. I see myself as an Economic Warrior for my people, and not a victim. As a predator and not a victim, I have decided to confront the truth of my misfortune and when I look in the mirror, I see the culprit standing right in front of me – it is me.[6]

Conclusion

The contention of this book is that South Africa needs to nurture a new consciousness (i.e. an industrial consciousness) as the basis for its new national identity. A significant step in that direction is to exorcise from our spirits those negative forces which inhibit the development of a wholesome new South African self-identity. My contention is that we need to move beyond race towards an industrial consciousness if we are to make significant progress in the ultimate struggle, namely the economic liberation of South Africa, where all, and not just a select few, benefit from a prosperous economy.

Notes

1. Employment equity cases are generally racially explosive even though the labour courts have to weigh up the twin imperatives of representivity (i.e. race) on the one hand and efficiency (i.e. effectiveness) on the other hand. In the case of Solidarity obo Barnard and Another v South African Police Services (JS455/07) [2010] ZALC 10 (24 February 2010) In The Labour Court of South Africa (Held at Johannesburg) Case No: JS455/07 In the matter between Solidarity obo Mrs R M Barnard Applicant and South African Police Services Respondent, the presiding officer ruled that "(1) The Respondent is directed to promote the Applicant to the post of Superintendent with effect from 27 July 2006. (2) The Respondent is ordered to pay the Applicant's costs.
2. The apartheid classification system made provision for racial migration. For example, as recent as 1984, the Minister of Home Affairs reported to Parliament that 795 South Africans were reclassified. They included 518 former coloureds who became white; 2 whites became Chinese; 1 White became Indian; 89 Africans become coloured and 5 coloureds became African (See Roger Ormond (1985) *The Apartheid Handbook: A Guide to South Africa's Everyday Racial Policies*, England: Penguin Books, pp.24-29).
3. See Boesak A (2009) *Running with Horses: Reflections of an Accidental Politician* (Cape Town: Joho Books)
4. According to a survey conducted by Business Unity SA relative to the demographic and age profile of the top management echelons of all 295 listed companies during April and July 2009, blacks and women in particular were found to be unrepresented. Some of the study's major findings show that of the 269 chief executive positions, Africans occupied 4 percent, coloureds 3 percent, Indians 2 percent and whites 91 percent. Women accounted for 3 percent and men 97 percent. For more detail see Khuzwayo W (2010) Too few black and women directors – March 3, 2010 http://www.busrep.co.za/index.php?fSectionId=552&fArticleId=5375264
5. Onyeani C (2006) *Capitalist Nigger: the Road to Success – A Spider Web Doctrine*. Johannesburg & Cape Town: Jonathan Ball Publishers. (Originally 2000, Tibuktu Publishers), p.5.
6. Ibid, p.xvii-xviii.

11 Performance morality and the poisoned well

What ultimately matters is the performance and not the colour of those in power.

This chapter offers a practical discussion of performance morality. Three thorny issues impact South African society: racial morality, voter morality and the morality of democracy as a system. This chapter is illustrative rather than exhaustive and uses a case study, "The poisoned well", to elicit and enable us to apply our views on personal and societal ethics to an everyday situation.

What is worse?

Four short scenarios follow, aimed to serve as triggers to enable us to contextualise what can otherwise be a very theoretical discussion on the topic of morality and ethics. The objective is to link the issue of morality to performance in an attempt to understand what motivates and drives people to perform well or to tolerate poor performance.

Scenario one
What is worse?
- Living under white minority apartheid rule and its clearly defined moral order, however repulsive we may have thought it to be?

Or:
- Living under black majority democratic rule and its failure to deliver basic services, even though they have been promised?

Scenario two
What is worse?
- Living under a system (i.e. apartheid) that is explicitly racist and geared to ensure that a minority of people benefit?

Or:
- Living under a system that proclaims to be non-racial and democratic but fails to deliver basic services for that majority?

Scenario three
What is worse?
- Winning your democratic freedom but being denied the opportunity to prosper and enjoy complete well-being?

Or:
- Being told that you have won freedom but in reality you are still in bondage – this time under democracy as opposed to apartheid?

Scenario four

We have won our freedom from apartheid and embark on a programme to rebuild the country and its people. But when we go to drink from the fountain from which we draw our nation-building strength, we discover that the well has been poisoned or, to put it more mildly, the water is polluted and needs to be purified. What do we do? Drink what we have or purify it first?

Morality and performance assessments

One of the challenges of any performance assessment is the moral value which those being assessed attach to what they do – or don't do. People are motivated to do things primarily by a sense of duty, a sense which arises from personal and societal ethics. We need to consider whether we have removed moral considerations from our public and political discourse, and reframed our lack of performance as purely a function of management, divorced from ethics.

Core values should underpin management's performance framework; they form the value proposition that supports a company's vision and mission. The sanctions and rewards we attach to performance are probably the most revealing window into the extent to which we value or devalue moral behaviour and performance.

In the context of assessing nationhood and nation building, we therefore cannot avoid discussing perceptions and practices of morality.

Racial and class morality

A pervasive assumption that existed in the context of the struggle against apartheid is that black morality was superior to white morality. And yet we know, instinctively and theoretically, that morality knows no racial or class boundaries or preference. Another assumption is that the leadership of post-apartheid South Africa is driven by a moral imperative to ensure that the standard of living of the vast majority of people will improve from what it was under white rule. The implicit assumption is that our black leaders will be more morally upright than the explicitly racist apartheid politicians.

Another generally held assumption is that those who seek and fight for political control have the intention, once in power, to exercise economic control for the greater good. They invariably promise that the benefits that will flow as a result of the new "political" ownership will be greater than those from the incumbent; they themselves may have been previously economically disadvantaged by their status quo and hence the quest to take over political control of the state, its institutions and resources in the first instance.

Experience, however, shows that political independence is rarely sought for purely altruistic purposes. For our purposes here, it could be argued that the primary motivation of all political struggles is the quest to control the means of production of an economy. Even in established and wealthy nations such as the USA, the election of Barack Obama was not devoid of promises of better economic policy and benefits for those voting him into power. The alternative motivation is, of course, to preserve the economic privileges of the status quo. In Africa, where the state exercises enormous control over the economy, this battle is even more pronounced. The matter is exacerbated when there are stark contrasts between the "have's" and the "have not's".

In this regard, Moeletsi Mbeki, brother of former South African President Thabo Mbeki, points out that the titanic South African battle is about control of the huge mineral resources and wealth which have been at the heart of many of the battles in South Africa's history and its colonial past.[1] Strangely, and unique to South Africa, ownership and control of these mineral resources is mainly in private hands as opposed to the state. Of course, the surest way to ensure that these resources remain in the hands of the current incumbents is to make certain that those in political control do not change the rules of ownership and engagement, and in the process dispossess those who currently own the much-desired mineral assets of the country. It is in this context that we begin to locate the policy debates and tensions between nationalisation versus privatisation and the imperatives of BEE.

The bottom line is that after almost 350 years of white colonial domination in South Africa, the country's mineral wealth still remains firmly in white minority hands. However, we cannot assume that an exchange of mineral wealth from white to black hands will necessarily result in a better economic dispensation for the majority of black people. Or is there a silent assumption that black rule and control of the economy will bring with it a higher level of morality and a determination to reduce crime and create a better life for the masses of poor people?

Ultimately, it is the performance of those in power and not the colour of their skin that matters. It is therefore imperative that there is an agreed-upon performance measure to assess progress and dispense discipline where there is a lack of performance. And if such a measure is agreed upon and serves as a mandate from the electorate to govern, then by the same token, failure to deliver on the mandate must result in the removal from office of those elected to deliver on that mandate. This is after all what democracy is about – the expression of the will of the people through a ballot and not the expression of the whims of the leaders through the bullet.

The solution to crime and unemployment that I propose does not assume that black economic hands are any more moral than white economic hands, although there is a view to the contrary.[2] The solution goes beyond race. What South Africa ultimately needs is an industrial revolution which will create millions of decent jobs. Failure to do this will only result in more crime and violence as the masses begin to compete for and fight over dwindling resources while the racial finger-pointing continues. The moral imperative for such a revolution is a necessity rather than a "nice-to-have".

This discussion should enable us to make sense of the interplay between the character and manifestation of crime in South Africa against the backdrop of unemployment resulting from the structure of the economy. We can begin to understand the current unacceptably high levels of crime in South Africa. What is required are bold and innovative solutions if a second miracle is to dawn on the South African horizon and dissipate the low-hanging dark clouds of doom already forming.

Could it be said that regardless of who is in control of the economy, the important thing is that the economy must be designed to create decent employment with the concomitant reduction in crime? Or is the critical performance indicator the identity of who is in control of the economy as opposed to the quality of the outputs of such control? In other words, does it matter what race is in political and economic control in South Africa? We need to examine for whom these control issues are important and why.

South Africa has come through a history of white political and economic control and a limited period of black political control. The black quest for economic control is still in its infancy. However, thus far the black economic gains have created a small black moneyed elite rather than widespread wealth and prosperity for the masses. Nevertheless, be it previous white or current black political control, the twin issues of crime and unemployment still plague the nation. Fairness dictates that one cannot compare more than 350 years of white domination with only 16 years of black rule. What can be said, though, is that if creative solutions are not implemented in the near future, the miraculous gains of the first 16 years of black rule and post-apartheid nation building are likely to be reversed, possibly forever.

The prickly issue remains: Is black morality deemed to be superior to white morality? As a result, do we tolerate more easily the shortcomings of a black government than we would those of a white government? If we were to look at the situation as a business manager, we would need to look at outputs and then either reward or sanction performance. At what point then would the black majority government no longer enjoy its implicit moral authority and the support of its electorate?

Voter abuse and political morality

A second big issue in the context of social morality relates to voter apathy and the abuse of voter support. In mature democracies, politicians have developed a reputation for overselling and under-delivering. In a context where the issues are not a matter of life and death, it is easier to tolerate the overselling and under-delivering paradigm. But in a context of human dignity versus human degradation resulting from non-delivery, political promises to the voters carry an ethical imperative. Non-performance in this context becomes a moral issue as opposed to just a management and performance issue.

South Africa has been called a miracle nation because of the unexpectedly smooth transition of political power from apartheid to democracy. Despite a range of successes and milestones achieved during the first 16 years of democracy, crime and unemployment remain. In fact, the problem is worsening for two reasons. The first is the impact of globalisation and the global economic recession on a previously isolated South Africa. By choice, South Africa is part of the global village and participates in the global economy. As a result, it is not exempt from the tribulations experienced by global economic giants who constitute the various groupings of wealthy nations (i.e. the G-7, -8, -11 nations, for example).

A second reason that crime and unemployment continue to be problematic in South Africa can be attributed to the "expectation gap". In the absence of service delivery, the poor and marginalised continue (as during apartheid) to vocalise their rejection of abuse by the state and its insensitivity to their plight. In fact, this is precisely the political mobilisation ticket that was used to re-elect the ANC government led by Jacob Zuma in 2009. The focus on Jacob Zuma as a victim versus the abuse of state machinery (with special reference to the Scorpion's investigation of Zuma) at the hands of his rival and comrade, Thabo Mbeki, was effectively used to show an alignment and close affinity between Jacob Zuma and the people of South Africa. This, as former President Mbeki's brother points out, is a very powerful and persuasive cocktail.[3] What remains interesting to observe is that the vast majority still direct their hopes at a black government as opposed to a white-led opposition. However, the emergence of a limited black opposition to the ANC has begun to change the political landscape and has created more options for South Africa's electorate.

The point being made here is that the underprivileged masses have a fundamentally racial- and moral-based expectation that the black-led ANC government will bring about Utopia without necessarily fully appreciating the complexities of governing a democracy.

Black voters not only expect the government to solve the unemployment and crime problems: they also believe that the leaders will feel more obliged to deliver for the poor as they have the same culture of being black. This expectation is furthermore linked to a rising attitude of entitlement, driven by the Constitution of South Africa, which may make us feel entitled to receive certain things as citizens of the republic. This sense is not always accompanied by the prerequisite attitude of "I must work hard for it". For some, there is a very thin line between inalienable human rights and socio-economic rights such as the right to work.

Black people understood that the former government was not interested in improving their quality of life beyond a certain level. Racial capitalism in general, and Afrikaner nationalism in particular, meant that the wealth of South Africa was to be the preserve of the whites, with blacks being relegated to second-class citizenship. These racial and ideological lines were clearly drawn and the then ruling National Party were experts at communicating and enforcing the rules of engagement. On the other hand, the majority of blacks in South Africa now expect the ANC-led government to solve their problems. But are those in power doing enough or, more importantly, are they doing the right things, to adequately address issues of crime and unemployment?

These kinds of matters are debated just before and around the time of general elections, when candidates subject the voting masses to their often undeliverable promises. A useful fallback position is the policy framework of the ruling party. In this instance, voters and investors alike have been assured that there will be no fundamental policy shifts to the foregoing 16 years of ANC-led rule in South Africa. Notwithstanding the ANC's professed openness to review policy, we must assume that the industrialisation approach (in other words the public expenditure programme) together with the crime-fighting strategy, and poverty- and unemployment-alleviation policies, will ostensibly remain the same. If this is the case, we must ask if South Africa is to brace itself for more of the same as experienced in the previous 16 years – that is, increased levels of both crime and unemployment.

The limits of democratic morality

Has democracy delivered the goods for the vast majority of the citizens of South Africa? Was life better under apartheid? Would life be better under full-blown socialism, for example?

The characteristic feature of the modern-day South African political miracle is its relatively peaceful transition from apartheid to democracy. However, South Africa's change to democracy is not unique. Other countries have undergone similar transitions accompanied by enormous economic and social turmoil. Ursula Beek's *Democracy under Construction* is a useful and cautionary reminder that countries such as Poland, East Germany, South Korea and Chile all offer lessons which South Africa would do well to learn from.[4] Another point of difference is that South Africa's transition, as Patrick Bond points out in his *Elite Transition: From Apartheid to Neoliberalism in South Africa*, was not from apartheid to democratic Utopia. In fact, as the title of his book reflects, it was an elite transition from apartheid to neoliberalism.[5]

A useful and cautionary reminder is that in global political and democratic terms, South Africa is an infant, miraculously still alive despite the negativity of the prophets of doom. Some longer-standing democracies have yet to surpass South Africa's recent gains in many respects. The South African Constitution, for example, is often cited as the most progressive and forward-thinking Constitution in the world. Contrasted with this is South Africa's inability to deliver basic services or adequately deal with issues of crime and unemployment. Some of these contradictions can be explained theoretically. However, the populist voter often finds it convenient to blame apartheid and use the past as an excuse and a crutch.

On the eve of his assisted departure from office, former President Thabo Mbeki provided the South African nation with a performance report card outlining the gains and losses of governance in a new democratic dispensation.[6] In spite of all the gains, problems remain. Is this the result of a flawed policy or the failure to implement a policy, flawed or otherwise? Many competing priorities face the South African nation-building project. The Zuma administration has identified five key priority areas, namely job creation, education and skills, healthcare, rural development, and the fight against crime and corruption. But these priorities emerge from the policy fabric of an evolutionary failure of policy frameworks. Bond explained it by saying the ANC were talking left but acting right.[7] So the pertinent question is: are we trapped in a flawed policy framework or is it simply a matter of implementation?

The economic inertia of the vast majority of the population awaiting their entitlement from government – be it a social grant or a job – is a recipe for disaster. We need to change this mindset of "we will wait for government to do it for us".

The erosion of the trust of ordinary citizens in the security machinery of the state, and a nation-building policy and programme that is not designed to provide a safe place for its citizens to live and an environment in which people can be gainfully employed, is not worth the paper it is written on. The ruling party has a vision of "a better life for all". The challenge is how to improve life for all and not just for the fortunate few.

The well-fed think ... the hungry act

Our beliefs greatly influence our actions. The moral value we attach to things influences the intensity with which we label an action as either a success or a failure. This is particularly true of South Africa where the entire basis of white oppression and the black liberation struggle has been steeped in a particular sense of morality. Despite the new social, political and economic morality agreed in 1994 as a framework for the building of a new South African society – as enshrined in the Constitution – the immorality of poverty and human degradation seems to continue and be further entrenched.

The anti-apartheid struggle and anti-National Party government protest was largely an ideological battle waged and driven by intelligentsia (i.e. clerics, academics, leftist ideologues, artists). By contrast, the current anti-government protests, commonly called service-delivery protests, are the result of a groundswell of discontentment among the poorest of the poor. The protests are practical and implementation-focused rather than consisting of public oratory or high-level intellectual discourse. The message communicated by the protests is moral in tone and simply says to government: "You promised to deliver but we see nothing". They see politicians and councillors earning enough money and living well but who have no moral compulsion to drive delivery and transformation for the benefit of the masses. It is this level of blatant honesty that the policy-makers need to connect with if there is to be a serious review of the genesis of the service-delivery problem.

Case study – The poisoned well

The balanced scorecard (BSC) model in context: A poisoned well

The vision and mission of our nation can be likened to that of a well of water from which the nation drinks in order to draw inspiration for its activities. The water in the well must give life to four perspectives, namely customer, growth, operational and financial perspectives.

At the moment the water in the well is poisoned. The nation drinking from this well is getting sick. We therefore need to change the water – not the well. To expand the analogy, the infrastructure of the well is fine. It's the water that must be refreshed and purified if we are going to see any improvements in our performance as measured by the four perspectives on the scorecard.

Let's look at each of the perspectives as we contextualise the BSC model and apply it to our nation.

Customer perspective: A success – the customer satisfaction survey is none other than the democratic elections, and by all accounts the voters are happy with the ANC. So there is a high level of customer satisfaction. However, there is also a high level of expectation based on President Zuma's promise to change things for the better.

Growth perspective: A disaster – think of the poor literacy and numeracy levels of post-1994 school leavers.

Operational/internal perspective: A disaster – look at the municipal collapse and lack of service delivery.

Financial perspective: A disaster – the gap between rich and poor has increased; we define economic growth in terms of money and not in terms of job creation.

So why is there such a high level of customer (voter) satisfaction? The only explanation must be that it has to do with race. Votes are based on race and not on competence. The ANC, among the liberation parties who made the shift to government, accommodated itself best to governing. The PAC has almost died. Cope is struggling. The ACDP is a religious- as opposed to a race-based party. The DA attracts mainly whites even though its party rhetoric is not based on a race card.

We are back to the score card and issues of performance. How do we measure nationhood? What welds a nation together? Is it the threat of war? How do we clean up the water in the well?

Solution

There is nothing wrong with the infrastructure of the well (the Constitution, parliamentary democracy, etc.). Replace the poisoned water with fresh water, and call this water "industrial consciousness" – an inquisitiveness about how things are made and how they work.

Consider this scenario

Go back 16 years to a black woman, Mrs Khumalo, living in a shack as a result of apartheid and forced removals. The solution to her problems is to dispose of the white racist government that destroyed her and several generations of her family's chances of a comfortable life. Mrs Khumalo eventually votes for a black government – with faith in the liberation movement to bring about change and a better life than life under apartheid.

Today, 16 years later, Mrs Khumalo's life has not improved – yet she again votes for the ANC. She wants to give the black government another chance. Even if black rule does not deliver the goods, Mrs Khumalo is sympathetic because she feels she has something in common with her leaders and believes they have her interests at heart.

The assumptions are:
- Blackness unites – it provides solidarity (Hubbard's tribal phase analysis).
- Black morality has a higher value than the white morality that caused her poverty.
- Black leaders have not yet had enough time to prove that they can do it. She acknowledges, in fact, that there has been transformation and the lives of many have improved under black rule (95% of people now have water, electricity, etc.)

Mrs Khumalo's thinking is driven by race. However, lack of basic service delivery is causing Mrs Khumalo to rethink, although she is comforted by the belief that BEE is the solution. BEE is a strategy to reconfigure the economy for the benefit of those previously disadvantaged under white rule. But the outcome has been that it has benefited only a few. Hence a change is made from BEE to B-BBEE (broad-based black economic empowerment). And still the mass trickle-down does not happen. A verification agency is set up to ensure that people who claim to be black are in fact black. It goes further, with scores for every shade in the hierarchy: black, female and disabled gets the highest reward. With due respect to the disabled, what turns an economy around is not a band of disabled people – what turns an economy around is a band of industrially competent and able-bodied workers. South Africa has defined these workers to be artisans – but we have not given these rescuers a score yet. Where do they fit in in the hierarchy of reward?

B-BBEE is not driven by economic growth imperatives. It is driven by redistributive imperatives. B-BBEE's philosophy says you must reward the person who is the most disadvantaged and then move down the ladder to the ones who were previously most advantaged and, in effect, exclude them from any rewards since the old system has rewarded them already. But the masses are being excluded from the rewards or the "redistribution of wealth".

The issue is this: After we have shared the spoils we need to get the country to function and generate its own wealth. How do we do that? Do we depend on race as a factor or should we rather depend on competence?

Mrs Khumalo's new mindset

If Mrs Khumalo accepts that it is not race that fixes the roads but an industrially competent company, then the question that she will ask is: Which company will do the best job? She may still give a black company a chance because it is culturally closer to her heart. But if that company does not perform, will she give them another chance or will she fire them for underperforming and employ (vote for) a new company to do the job?

Whether we base our decisions on the past or the future, or simply on results, the question is this: If the government continues to underperform, should we continue to vote for them? Our demands for better wages or better levels of service are intensified by our moral indignation that our comrades are now the bosses and should look after us.

Forget the dream. Greed is greed and power is power. It is not race-specific. We need industrial consciousness to detoxify the poisoned well. It's that consciousness inside the psyche of Mrs Khumalo that says: If you do not deliver the services I am paying you for – or which I will eventually pay for once I get a job – then I will get rid of you (i.e. I will not vote for you again).

Herein lies another problem – a dominant black culture of *paying for services* does not exist. Apartheid has disabled many black people in this regard, mainly because they could barely survive, given their poor wages and the repressive laws against them. So an attitude of "why should I care for something that is not mine?" has arisen. Psychological and emotional ownership has not occurred.

If you do not pay for something from your own hard-earned money, you will not fully appreciate it. This is why a welfare system is dangerous and will never lift our nation out of poverty. But if you create a job and enable a person to earn cash and have the ability to buy services or education or better food and a better home and so forth, you then have a different person on your hands. You have a citizen who is empowered enough to hold you accountable and empowered enough to demand better service. The person now has the ability to buy services elsewhere if you are unable to provide those services. This is the kind of economy South Africa has voted for. So the chief challenge is to create jobs which produce decent wages, which in turn produce citizens who can then decide who should provide their services, be they political, business or educational services. At the moment, there is a dependency syndrome and the masses are only too happy to live off the crumbs that fall off the rich man's table. But the masses can't see this because they have been poisoned by the race-conscious water in the well.

Questions

1. What is the aim of B-BBEE? Is it to reinvigorate the economy so that it becomes more productive or is it a redistributive mechanism to ensure that existing wealth is shared among previously disadvantaged people?
2. What will cause the masses of poor people to shift their thinking? Is it the lack of service delivery? What if the government delivered the basic services? Would this be sufficient to sustain our economy?
3. What is needed to grow the economy? More B-BBEE?
4. How does a nation create wealth?
5. Who should be creating jobs? Government or business?
6. How do we measure nationhood and its success or failure?

Notes
1   See Mbeki M (2009) *Architects of Poverty: Why African Capitalism Needs Changing*. Johannesburg: Picador Africa.
2   See Onyeani C (2006) *Capitalist Nigger: the Road to Success – A Spider Web Doctrine*. Johannesburg & Cape Town: Jonathan Ball Publishers. (Originally 2000, Tibuktu Publishers).
3   See Mbeki M (2009) p.88.
4   See Van Beek UJ. (2005). *Democracy under construction: Patterns from four continents*. Pretoria: Van Schaik.

5   Bond P (2000) *Elite Transition: From Apartheid to Neoliberalism in South Africa*. Pietermaritzburg, South Africa: University of Natal Press.
6   *See* Presidency (2008) Address to the Nation by the South African President - Thabo Mbeki - Resignation speech 21 September 2008 http://www.politicsweb.co.za/politicsweb/view/politicsweb/en/page71619?oid=103889&sn=Detail Another useful document to be read in conjunction with Mbeki's last speech as President of South Africa is that issued by the Presidency in 2003 called: *Towards A Ten Year Review – Synthesis Report On Implementation Of Government Programme – Discussion Document* (Policy Coordination and Advisory Services – October 2003 – Presidency) – See http://www.10years.gov.za/review/documents.htm
7   Bond P (2000) p.11.

12 | Ten do's and don'ts – the new ground rules

Who said compliance was boring!

This chapter identifies a new set of ground rules. In many respects these fundamental principles already exist in various forms in our society, either in the Constitution or the various manifestos and vision and mission statements that form part of the strategic plans of companies and government departments. The challenge is to give life and meaning to them.

The inherent danger is to create yet another code of conduct which is either not enforceable, or simply makes us feel good knowing that we have such a code.

The earlier chapters of this section of the book have each dealt with a component of the practical aspects of the solution. This chapter consolidates and summarises the discussion, as we begin to construct, reinforce and entrench an industrial consciousness for South Africa.

Create a large industrial middle class

The ideal solution to crime, unemployment and poverty is the creation of an industrialised economy with a middle income and independent large middle class.[1] This is the only class that has and will have the ability to hold government accountable, since they wield economic power which translates into real power at the ballot box. It's easy to appease poor people who are desperate – even a few crumbs will do. It's a different story dealing with a middle class. Nowhere in post-colonial Africa has such a class been created. What we have seen develop consistently and almost predictably in Africa, and now also in South Africa, is the creation of a super-rich upper class with an ever-widening gap between the rich and the poor.

The creation of a middle class – beyond the phenomenon of what has been called the black diamonds[2] – is an urgent necessity. The immediate benefit is the stabilisation of democracy as the governance framework, and a tangible and sustainable approach to addressing poverty. None of these interventions will happen overnight, but we need to find a way to signal that this is the direction in which we want to go – and then invite, excite and energise the nation to achieve this goal. The first step is the creation and adoption of an industrial consciousness as the operating principle for such a massive project – a project aimed at fundamentally reordering the socio-economic relations of South African society.

The ten big things to do

1. Make a policy decision that industrial development is the central organising principle of the South African nation – and that all other priorities are secondary. Explain to the nation that industrial development is the only solution to our poverty problem and that we all need to put our support behind this plan.
2. Establish a national convention on the theme of industrial development. Appoint a senior administrator to manage it and a chairperson from private industry to chair the sessions. Get the best industrial brains in a room; have their discussion televised live. Show a nation in search of solutions, where every citizen, organisation and union is invited to make a contribution – beyond the Nedlac process.
3. Persuade the nation that we need 4 000 entrepreneurs to create 4 000 labour-intensive businesses, which will be financed by government. Make sure that every province has a plan to industrialise; and reward innovation and entrepreneurship. Create a team of entrepreneurs; expand the funding risk profile to at least 40% of government agency funding. For example, 40% of Industrial Development Corporation (IDC) funding should be spent on greenfield projects where the IDC itself stands surety for the projects.
4. Impose a once-off BEE reparations tax or wealth tax. For example, require all BEE kings and queens to make a refundable loan to the value of 5% of their net asset value (in cash) towards an entrepreneur fund – to be repaid on the successful execution of projects related to the 4 000 factories project.
5. Emphasise mathematics and science literacy – find the talent, improve literacy and reward success. Re-energise the minds of South Africa to be inquisitive about how things are made.
6. Dramatically enhance government's administrative capacity so as to improve service delivery.
7. Visibly welcome foreign labour – acknowledge that we do not have all the skills. Reactivate the homecoming campaign.
8. Restore respect for the police service. Make an assault on a police officer a treasonable offence. At the same time, make the abuse of power by a police official an immediate and dismissible offence with no benefits.

9. Make industrial development a core subject at school and not part of an optional careers section.
10. Create an industrial army of blue-collar workers (i.e. artisans) – these are the people who make an economy grow. Make them the new heroes and heroines of a modern South Africa.

The new ten commandments

Do not encourage entitlement based on race.
Do not trade colour for competence.
Do not collude with corruption.
Do not condone poor performance.
Do not tolerate the abuse of our police officers, teachers and healthcare professionals.
Reward risk-taking and entrepreneurship.
Reward diligence and dedicated work by the service professions.
Invest in increasing mathematics and science literacy.
Welcome skilled foreigners.
Celebrate the acquisition of skills and the contributions of our people.

Code of good practice for government

- No government contracts are to be awarded to any government employee.
- No government contracts are to be awarded to a minister in office.
- There is to be a cooling-off period of five years before awarding a government contract to any person who has left office.
- No one in civil service or their immediate family members may be awarded a government contract.
- Appoint an anti-corruption tzar, legislatively empowered to act without fear, favour or prejudice.

Recommended specifics

- Farming – commercialise all farming; establish incentive programmes.
- Skills – host a skills jamboree. Call all artisans to a central place and turn them into a manufacturing industrial army of specialised squads.

Publicise this exercise as an incentive to the masses to become artisans.
- Education – double the pay of all primary school teachers. Stream learners from Grade 6 into academic or technical fields – which means opening and prioritising technical schools.
- Church and the religious community – encourage them to preach sermons about work ethic.
- Service delivery – identify the worst-performing municipality and make it a test and model case.
- State-owned enterprises – privatise state-owned enterprises (SOEs). Suggestions include instituting a lottery available to a limited number of South Africans for shares in, say, Eskom or PetroSA; make shares available for purchase (10% and shares via lottery); limit applicants, for example, to registered shack dwellers.
- Minerals – all mineral raw materials should be processed in South Africa.
- Tax incentives – if you employ more than 50 people, you get a 5% tax break.
- Unemployment grant – every unemployed person, and citizens earning less than R50 000 per annum, are to get a once-off grant.

Conclusion – "Yes we can"

There are signs across many sectors that the atmosphere is ready for a brave and bold solution to South Africa's problems. We need something dramatic to shift the country in a positive direction if South Africa is to survive as an independent and true democracy. We must activate plans to rapidly create an industrialised middle class. "South Africa first" must become our motto.

Notes
1   Mbeki M (2009) *Architects of Poverty: Why African Capitalism Needs Changing.* Johannesburg: Picador Africa, p.36.
2   "Black diamonds" is a term used to refer to upwardly mobile young black professionals whose numbers swell the ranks of what is commonly called the middle class.

Part 3.
Knife-edge transformation

13 | Three moments of consciousness

What the mind perceives, the heart can feel and the eye can visualise.

This short chapter creates a conceptual framework and overall context in which to locate three significant moments in the life of a transforming South Africa – three moments illustrative of the power and ability of the nation to change the way it thinks and believes. The nation building of the past 16 years is still very much a work in progress. The racial polarisation of pre-democratic South Africa has given way to an era of economic polarisation – a shift from race to class differentiation.

The significance of the three moments is presented as the interpretive grid through which the well-known details will again be filtered. This time, the nuggets found as a result of this second filtration process show that the South African nation has the capability to again sift and shift its psyche – this time hopefully towards an industrial consciousness.

A view from the eye of the storm

The three significant moments of national consciousness that have positively affected the nation-building programme of democratic South Africa are the TRC, the Scorpions and the Joint Initiative for Priority Skills Acquisition (Jipsa). Each of these moments will be dealt with in more detail in subsequent chapters in order to make explicit the power of consciousness and the way in which it can positively affect notions of nationhood and national identity.

I have been privileged to be integrally involved with each of these moments and have acquired a unique close-up view in my capacity as an executive manager. This may have made my view biased and myopic. It was certainly an intensely personal experience, which has caused me to reflect on my life's journey as the next chapter will show. My view of the transformation process is not unlike a view from the eye of the storm and I share it in that context. I have thus peppered the discussions that follow with illustrations drawn from my personal experiences as I participated in these moments.

Moments of positive consciousness

The three moments that provide a context for reflection on issues of national identity and patriotism of transformation are: the TRC moment, with an emphasis on its impact and contribution to taming state security; the Scorpion moment and its impact on and contribution to the modernising of criminal justice; and the Jipsa moment which signalled the realisation of a crippling skills crisis.

The character of these moments is profound in that they provide a "before and after" perspective. For example, the TRC moment enabled the articulation of a national self "before" the TRC and "after" the TRC. In the "before" period, we had a certain understanding about the character of our nation and what joins or divides us. These concepts were driven mainly by ideology and largely in the absence of commonly shared facts about reality. The TRC moment placed on the national table a set of facts previously known only to a few. For the first time the entire nation was confronted with data that profoundly affected not only how the past was to be interpreted but also how the future is to be envisioned.

Positive and profound change has occurred in South Africa in the first 16 years of democracy. It has, however, been a knife-edge transformation journey. The margin of error allowed continues, with leaders making mistakes that bear enormous consequences for the vast majority of people. The transformation process still has the potential to slice the nation into opposing halves rather than to knit disparate pieces into a patchy national fabric.

In this make-or-break period, the focus of transformation attention was essentially on the stabilisation of the country. This was done by taking control of the state security machinery and the criminal justice system which apartheid had used to legalise repression, torture and state-sponsored murder. This was essentially Nelson Mandela's task. A second focus area and activity of transformation was to stabilise the economy and activate an economic growth trajectory for a nation of over 40 million citizens as opposed to a nation of three million white citizens and 37 million black non-citizens. This was Thabo Mbeki's job. The rude realisation of the profundity of this challenge came in the form of an awareness of a lack of skills. According to the leaders of our nation and their analysis, the greatest impediment to the growth of the economy was deemed to be the shortage of skills – hence the Jipsa moment. The major challenge now facing South Africa is rising unemployment, crime and government's inability to deliver basic services. This is the job facing President Jacob Zuma.

The socio-economic outcome of the rapid years of transformation has unfortunately been spoiled by a global recession, internal management incompetence and a growing gap between rich and poor. The result is a growing sense of anger and despair on the part of the masses who have not yet fully tasted the fruits of freedom where it matters most – namely money in the bank. In more academic language we could describe the same reality as the delayed socio-economic gratification associated with freedom from apartheid.

The critical commentary and review of the transformation process must not be seen as dismissive of the miraculous efforts of the past 16 years. At the same time, we must not be lulled into a false sense of security about our own perceptions of success. This book is to be located in the context of a transformation journey that has only just begun – moving from a new nation led by an ideologically driven liberation movement, to a patriotically driven political leadership and government where South Africa's needs as a nation come first, and narrow political party gains and the self-interests of an elite few come second.

Appraisal of the recent transformation must take into account the awakening of government and society at large to apartheid's "industrial terrorism" and its resultant skills shortage on the one hand, and the post-liberation scourge of unexpected xenophobia emerging from the ranks of ordinary South Africans on the other. That the xenophobic attacks from 2007 to 2009 are linked to the skills crisis there can be no doubt, as the unemployed compete for jobs. As a result, the government is scrambling to remedy the lack of skills. The xenophobic attacks caused the government to institute a national day of forgiveness and repentance for the violence and dislocation caused by the "ethnic cleansing"-type behaviour.

Analysis will show that the three moments under review reflect a similarity across a number of areas. First, they were all brief moments. The TRC and Jipsa moments were designed to be short. The exception was the Scorpion moment where government itself aborted the specialist anti-corruption unit. Second, the moments all had a high impact value. Their visibility was national and their presence unavoidable if one lived in South Africa. For example, the TRC hearings were broadcast live on TV. The Scorpion activities were very visible in terms of the high-profile arrests and seizure of assets of suspected criminals. The Jipsa initiative emanated from the Presidency and any announcement attracted the attention of the nation. Third, each of the moments was considered to be a national imperative, driven by the Presidency itself. Fourth, each was of such national importance that it changed the way in which we viewed reality, enabling "before and after" comparisons. Fifth, the energies of each moment were unfortunately muted when incorporated into the larger bureaucratic structures of the state. The post-TRC prosecutions became the responsibility of the National Prosecuting Authority which still limps along causing a lack of adequate national closure to the gains envisaged by the TRC process. The Scorpions were disbanded and subsequently lost their edge as what was left was incorporated into the police and rebranded as the Hawks. The Jipsa moment was by design a high-impact, short-lived initiative. The incorporation of the Jipsa imperatives into the Human Resource Development South Africa (HRD-SA) strategy under the tutelage and governance of the Education Department is a matter which only time will confirm as being either wise or foolish. Each moment was profoundly transformative and part of the deliberate national building impetus of this first post-apartheid phase of reconstructing South Africa.

The primary purpose of reflecting on these three specific moments is to show that it is never too late for innovative solutions. The national consciousness of South Africa can be positively and powerfully affected and activated in order to mobilise transformative action. If we accept that industrial development is key to success, then we need an "industrial consciousness moment" to serve as a reference point as the nation shifts paradigms in its efforts to effectively address poverty, crime and unemployment. We need another TRC-type, Scorpion-type or Jipsa-type industrial moment if we are to make any significant impact.

Tired or inspired nation building?

We need a fresh dose of inspiration and leadership or South Africa is likely to remain industrially backward and crippled.

Alex Perry, writing on the eve of the election of the Zuma government, reflects the anxiety that many conservatives would have had about the incoming Zuma administration and the feelings of pessimism regarding the limits of the politics of diversity. He writes:

> During those early years, with Mandela presiding as the founding father of what Tutu dubbed "The Rainbow Nation", diversity, it was said, was no longer a source of division, but one of strength,

hope, even beauty. Mandela's embrace of the new vision hid the fact that many in the ANC rank and file were struggling to discard their old monochrome view of the world. The ANC was – and still is – confronting the same dilemma that faces all liberation movements once in power. Simply put: good revolutionaries often make bad democrats. Revolutionaries plot in secret, follow orders and serve the people by leading them. Democrats debate openly and serve the people by listening to them. Revolution is resolute, romantic and self-righteous. Democracy is flexible, often boring and riddled with doubt.

History is full of revolutionaries who failed to make the switch. Most promised people's rule but, once in power, embraced a permanent state of revolution – some, like Robert Mugabe and Hugo Chávez, conjuring up fantastical foreign enemies to fight. (To those ranks, now add the leader of the influential ANC Youth League, Julius Malema, who told the East London rally that the young would "never allow them to donate this country to Britain, to the hands of the colonisers".) To their people, this never-ending war is generally experienced as dictatorship. Too many liberation leaders leave office only when another revolutionary seizes power.[1]

While Perry reflects a conservative, reactionary and pessimistic view about revolution, he raises a point worth considering: Have we made the transition from "inspired" revolution to "boring" nation building? If Mandela's personal leadership and vision overshadowed the internal racial cracks of the ANC, we should consider how deep those cracks go. Furthermore, we should think about what it will take to inspire all citizens to get to work so that our country can liberate itself from further generations of looming economic bondage.

South Africa needs loyal patriots to help build a nation, as opposed to party loyalists and ideologues who first want to build a political party. This is the challenge and dilemma facing the Zuma presidency. There is no doubt that Jacob Zuma, the individual, graphically embodies both the revolutionary touting a machine gun and the devoted democrat; at the same time he is faced with the challenge of building a nation that is still deeply divided – this time not necessarily divided by race but increasingly divided by growing economic disparities resulting from race-based policies. Something has to change. We cannot proceed into the future with a plan for the past.

Excursus: A word on xenophobia

In the Balkan states of Eastern Europe it was called ethnic cleansing. In South Africa we use a less inflammatory expression – xenophobia – for the same barbaric practice. If we define xenophobia as a state of mind, i.e. an unreasonable fear or hatred of foreigners or strangers or of that which is foreign or strange, then ethnic cleansing is a state of action designed to give expression to that state of mind.

One of the most embarrassing and numbing moments experienced by the liberated, democratic and non-racial SA is the vicious and deadly xenophobic attacks which swept through the country in May 2008. South Africa suddenly awoke to the reality of a tide of intolerance of fellow African citizens which had been steadily growing over the years.[2] Thabo Mbeki's eloquent speeches and vision regarding African Renaissance were suddenly confronted with the harsh reality of a disjuncture between the consciousness of the political leadership and the harsh economic realities of entrepreneurial competitiveness underpinning and informing survival issues in the townships. The extent of South Africa's shock and horror is evidenced by government's rapid and publicly declared intention to host a national day of repentance and healing on 24 June 2008 – an intention that government delayed at the eleventh hour "to enable more planning and to ensure that more people participated in events of the day".[3]

One can only imagine that such an event would have gone a long way towards refocusing the consciousness of the nation towards a non-racial and inclusive society. The xenophobic sentiment continues to linger in spite of South Africa pretending to have purged itself of such tendencies. The "official" silence on matters relative to the proposed and intended day of healing serves only to deepen a sense of national anxiety on this matter.

Many critical questions remain unanswered. For purposes of our discussion here, one such question is: Were the xenophobic attacks a mere lapse in the consciousness of a liberated post-apartheid South African nation which has one of the most progressive non-racial Constitutions and bills of rights in the world? Explanations or justifications for xenophobia are not the central focus of this book. However, it appears that the default consciousness of a liberated South Africa is still tainted by race-based considerations.

Let's debunk the myth that xenophobia is linked to social class. Confining xenophobia to the poorer classes of society is probably the most fallacious mistake we can make as South Africans. Xenophobia is not easily measurable in the better-off classes since there are multiple layers of social and economic sophistication that mask the depravity of such thinking and behaviour. The poorer classes don't have the luxury of intellectualising (not that they are unable to) and neither do they have sufficient resources to buttress the onslaught of a competitive attack on their space and resources. The ugliness and viciousness of the attacks in the peri-urban and informal settlement areas is what was visually captured by the media and presented to South Africa and the world. And yet, the upper classes can be no less welcoming of foreigners, especially when such foreigners have a better set of skills.

One of the more public xenophobic cases pertaining to a professional is the case of the principal medical officer at a Cape Town clinic who was Nigerian and female. A formal investigation revealed that the clinic staff, including management (i.e. the subordinates to the principal medical officer) "… had actually mobilised the community to protest against the doctor." Nowhere in the article is the word xenophobia used. However, through further personal investigation and interviews, it was revealed that this was indeed a case of xenophobia. Furthermore, the Cape Times article was careful to simply report that "in June 2008, the doctor was threatened by patients demanding she return to Nigeria, her country of origin."[4]

Xenophobia, in my view, is essentially a battle over scarce resources, where ethnic or national origin serves as the defining criterion. It is about who possesses the skills to be more effective in making things happen, especially in the poorer areas where these become survival issues. The ugly truth is that entrepreneurial African immigrants outshine the local black people at the level of "making a plan". The immigrants have a different mindset. They come to South Africa with the intention to "make it happen". They see South Africa as a land of possibilities and assume that the country's Constitution and its people, with such an illustrious history of fighting against racial oppression, will facilitate a warm welcome. Ubuntu and a sense of African spirituality is, after all, that aspect of our national cultural index we actively market to the world as our competitive edge and the basis of our political miracle of 1994.

A crude contrast between the common South African attitude and that of the "go-getter" attitude of the foreigner suggests that a completely different consciousness governs the behaviour of the respective groups. Our local people have a more passive "let's wait for government to solve our problems" mindset. By contrast the fellow African from another country (i.e. the foreigner) is entrepreneurially driven. South Africans interpret this energy negatively and respond murderously as they perceive that the entrepreneur is "taking away" something from them rather than invigorating an economic base from which locals can also benefit.

It appears, therefore, that non-racialism in the context of scarce resources is a meaningless concept. Rather it seems to be, first, all about the control of access to the resource and secondly, about the skills required to turn limited resources in business opportunities.

We need to have certain conversations if we want to turn the economy around. Consider that we borrow skills (at a premium) from elsewhere to help us manage our economy. In some instances, business owners prefer foreign labour because it does not carry the political and entitlement baggage that comes with local labour. Owners are thus prepared to pay extra for foreign labour, not solely because there is a technical skills shortage here, but because the South African workforce has an attitude problem – they are not productive enough, they strike at the slightest difficulty. As chairman of an industry body representing 140 companies interfacing with government, I have come across these kinds of sentiments which are always expressed "off the record". It's unfortunate but true – businesspeople pay for good attitude first, and for skills second.

It is therefore not surprising that South African companies are not wholly committed to creating a South African skills capacity given the current mindset of the workers. It's easier to simply "buy in" the required labour. At least, you can be certain that, with the correct management supervision, the job will get done.

So what do we do? How are we going to progress if we are still subconsciously harbouring these latent racist attitudes which impede the growth and development of our country? My proposed solution is that we nurture an industrial consciousness that is driven by competence and industrial innovation and not racial entitlement. Transformation models exist that can guide the thinking and planning required in this regard such as, for example, the rolling out of the TRC process.

Notes

1. "Why South Africa's over the Rainbow." Letter by Alex Perry / East London. Thursday, 9 April 2009 Time Magazine.
   For more see http://www.time.com/time/world/article/0,8599,1890334,00.html?iid=sphere-inline-bottom#ixzz0bHZ3qIQz
2. Prior to 1994 immigrants from elsewhere in Africa faced discrimination and even violence in South Africa, though much of that risk stemmed from the institutionalised racism of the time rather than xenophobia. Post 1994 and democratisation, and contrary to expectations, the incidence of xenophobia increased. Between 2000 and March 2008 at least 67 people died in what were identified as xenophobic attacks. An inter-ministerial task team investigating the xenophobic attacks in which 62 people were killed, reported to President Thabo Mbeki's Cabinet that at least 21 (approx 34%) of the 62 persons killed were South Africans. (See article in Mail and Guardian (June 12, 2008) Xenophobia deaths: One-third was South African http://www.mg.co.za/article/2008-06-12-xenophobia-deaths-onethird-was-south-african) Whether or not these were victims or perpetrators remains an open question. Some South African victims have indicated that their mere familial links or shade of blackness of their skins has made them the target of the sometimes indiscriminate violence directed at black African "foreigners" or, in this instance, people who look like the foreigners (i.e. the enemy).
   In analysing xenophobic violence, it is sometimes the police itself that creates more problems than it provides solutions and safety for foreigners. Xenophobia in the police, for example, was given a public face in South Africa in 1999 when six white police officials were shown on national television racially assaulting and abusing two illegal immigrants from Mozambique commonly known as the "dog incident". (For a detailed examination of Xenophobia in the police see Themba Masuku's article, TARGETING FOREIGNERS – xenophobia among Johannesburg's police – Centre for the Study of Violence and Reconciliation – published in Crime Quarterly No 15 2006) http://www.iss.co.za/pubs/CrimeQ/No.15/Masuku.html
3. Taken from *Mail & Guardian*. http://www.mg.co.za/article/2008-06-24-xenophobia-national-day-of-mourning-postponed
4. See *Cape Times*, 10 February 2010, page 8.

14 | Life comes full circle

Life is a wild and exciting journey ... if you let it be.

> *Sometimes the ironies of life are sweet and life does come full circle.*

This chapter locates my personal career history in the context of the change and transformation journey of the country as a whole. The three moments of consciousness which provide the conceptual framework of this section of the book also have a personal significance for my life. Whether the accumulation of these experiences is a result of career design, divine ordination, pure luck or being in the right place at the right time will remain a matter of personal uncertainty and conjecture. All I know is that opportunities confronted me and I grabbed them with both hands.

In humility, I share my reflections of my personal life and career experiences, recognising that the miracle of the new South Africa has benefited and enriched my own experience. I am appreciative of the privilege of being a vital part of momentous paradigm shifts, transformation moments, as well as significant moments of national consciousness in South Africa's recent nation-building history. I reflect on these experiences, while at the same time envisaging a positive future reality for my beloved country.

My story is essentially of an ordinary guy privileged to live in and through some extraordinary times and historical moments in South Africa … and the story is not yet over, it seems.

Biographical meanderings

Full circle ... twice

Sometimes life comes full circle – more than once! One of my full-circle experiences is within the academic arena. I left the glamour and safety of the ivory tower (i.e. university) and got lost in the trenches of transformation and nation building in South Africa for 16 years, and I now find myself temporarily back in the ivory tower. This time, however, I have a better understanding and a deeper appreciation of what goes on in the world of work where the majority of people live their daily lives.

My second full-circle experience is within the engineering services arena of the private sector. I left the blue-collar workshop floor as a young tradesman and returned almost three decades later as CEO of the same company, this time wearing a white collar and with a lot less hair on my head.

With this chapter I share the perspective from which I interpret reality, namely my own career experience. In that sense this is a deeply personal perspective, patriotically subjective and, hopefully, managerially sober.

My career-life in short

I am Cape Town-born and schooled, miraculously matriculating in 1977 at the age of 17 years old. I did not achieve a university entrance level pass since most of my high school subjects were taken on the standard grade as opposed to the higher grade – a pre-requisite for university entrance.

Two months after completing high school, I started my formal working career as the first male supervisor in a clothing factory in Cape Town. This lasted for six months before I left the clothing and textile industry and joined the maritime world. By 1984 I had served two apprenticeships and was a qualified fitter and turner in the marine, general and heavy engineering sector in Cape Town. So, by the time I was 24 years old, I had sailed the seas and acquired some technical knowledge. I was set for life, I thought – a qualified tradesman and earning well.

Following my tradesman life, I subsequently completed a range of engineering, theological and social science studies locally and internationally (USA, Germany, Switzerland) graduating with a PhD from the Social Science Faculty of the University of Cape Town in 1995. I was 35 years old and had now added some academic flavour to my growing skills and knowledge base. I was a fitter and turner with a PhD. I did not think it odd at the time!

My subsequent acquisition of executive leadership and management skills and experience enables me to be an advisor and consultant on scarce and critical skills with particular reference to accelerated artisan training within the manufacturing and engineering sector.

I was recently appointed as a visiting adjunct Professor to the Graduate School of Public and Development Management at Wits University, Johannesburg, with a focus on studies in Defence and Security Management. It is from this renewed academic platform and placement that this book emerges.

My career path has in many ways been driven by the transformation imperatives facing the new South Africa. My call to join the TRC in late

1995/early 1996 presented the opportunity to serve my country in a brand new way. As a result, I became intimately involved in the practical rebuilding and healing of the soul and psyche of South Africa as it transitioned from apartheid to a free and democratic society.

My moral service to the nation did not end with the TRC call-up. I subsequently applied and was appointed as the head of South Africa's then defacto police academy for post-basic training, namely the Police Practice Department of the former Technikon of Southern Africa. The institution has since been integrated into UNISA in the context of the realignment of educational institutions in South Africa.

My stay at the police academy was short-lived. Towards the end of 1999, I resigned my well-paying academy job with all its perks to take up a non-existent position, later called the Deputy Director-General of the Scorpions, serving as Head of Investigations and Training. I was 39 years old and the first legally employed Scorpion by virtue of being the first "outsider" (i.e. person from the private sector) to be formally employed and contracted into the Scorpion unit. All the others were secondees from within the state service. I was soon joined by Frank Dutton, the legendary South African police whistle-blower and investigator who had earlier agreed to be the CEO of the Scorpions. He was based in The Hague, on secondment to the United Nations War Crimes Tribunal probing Bosnian war crimes. Two other colleagues from deep within the secret service and the intelligence agency also joined, and the four of us made up the first management team of the Scorpions.

I left the Scorpions in late 2004 to explore business opportunities which interestingly took me back to my previous engineering environment. Someone should have told me that you don't do things like this when you are in your mid-forties and with no business experience to fall back on! In 2009 I was invited to Wits University on a pro-bono basis to once again take up the academic mantle. By the time this book is published I will have turned 50 years old – probably flat broke in money terms but an absolute multi-millionaire in experiential terms!

One head and many worlds

My diverse career engagements have enabled me to inhabit many different worlds – tradesman, CEO, law enforcement tradecraft developer, human rights activist, company director, wannabe aspiring capitalist, and more recently an industrial entrepreneur and academic. I am in the process of finding my own voice given the many and varied windows of meaning through which I view life and experience reality.

The variety of windows to look through is for me both a blessing and a curse. It's a blessing to the extent that my own inner soul feels enriched and liberated from narrow and singular interpretations of reality such as the one characterising my conservative and fundamentalist Protestant Christian upbringing.[1] It's a curse to the extent that I have no career or profession truly to call my home.

I was born to parents whose love was colour-blind. My late father was a tall very dark-skinned man of slave descent and my mother a very fair-skinned short and stocky woman of Dutch descent. I have come to realise that this is classic Cape Town and coastal-oriented narrative where the mixture of the races was the norm.

All I know and remember about my parents is that they were in love. Only much later did I become aware that they, and indeed myself, were representations of socially constructed meanings, racially speaking. The apartheid label "Cape coloured" was inscribed on my birth certificate in 1960. With the help of the philosophy of black consciousness I have become comfortable in my skin and have ideologically adopted the label "black" to describe my identity. There continue to be enough people in South Africa who take pleasure in reminding me that I am not black or African. They insist that I am coloured and that I should behave like one. Generally this means that I should be docile, mind my place in society, and be thankful to the white man at whose mercy we live. How tragic.

I consider myself to be young, even though I am 50 years old. This is a scary thought since the average life expectancy of a black male in South Africa these days is about 50 due to the ravages of HIV and AIDS. So while I am beginning to think that life begins at 50, I am aware that life for many others is expected to end. I am not sure whether I am a wise old sage, a pensioner, or a pretentious man suffering from a delayed mid-life crisis, living and taking risks as if I were a 17-year-old school leaver.

My personal and career skillset within my framework of being a middle-aged man in South Africa, incorporates technical training, academic training, public service as well as private sector work experience. I have been blessed to occupy executive management positions which have at times afforded me complete freedom to be creative and explore the realm of impossibility – and to enjoy myself while doing so.

Making theoretical sense of a practical life

Each of my career moments and shifts has been accompanied by an opportunity to write and reflect on that particular moment – at that point in time. These moments of critical reflection serve, in part, as the reservoir from which I constantly draw in order to make sense of my life and career journey.

My decision to leave the industrial work space and pursue higher learning was driven by a crazy idea that I needed to prepare myself intellectually to be able to contribute to a new South Africa when it did arrive. To be honest, I did not think it would happen in my lifetime. When we said goodbye to our families in the late 1980s to pursue studies in the USA, there was a sense that we may never return since it seemed that apartheid was there to stay. But we were young and idealistic. And at another level, even though apartheid seemed so entrenched, we, like millions of others, prayed, believed and hoped for a miracle.

Then, of course, 1994 happened in South Africa.

What I sense now, 16 years later, is that South Africa needs a second 1994 moment to adequately deal with runaway crime and increasing unemployment. We need an economy that produces prosperity for the citizens of South Africa. We need an industrial workspace that embraces the transformation agenda and in a very practical way "fixes" the economy.

Finding eclectic solutions

From the ivory tower to the trenches, and back

Sixteen years ago I resigned, in protest, from my post as a junior lecturer at Wits University because the university did not deem it appropriate to second me, then, to the Truth and Reconciliation Commission that had invited me to take up a staffing position.

Sixteen years later, I have been appointed as a visiting adjunct Professor to Wits University, in part because of experiences and insight gained as a result of joining the Truth and Reconciliation Commission, and subsequent exposure and writing in the context of transformation in the defence and security arena.

The early years of political transition post-1994 were rough and unpredictable with both sides (the apartheid die-hards and the incoming visionary liberation cadres) suspiciously interacting with each other until such time that sufficient trust existed for a more relaxed transition.

The areas of focus of my professional career and activity during these early years of societal transition and nation building is the subject focus of this book, namely, crime, unemployment and the attempts to re-industrialise the base of the South African economy.

During the fourth quarter of 2009 I surfaced, like the periscope of a lost submarine, after 16 years of being in the proverbial eye of the storm. Put differently, I spent the first 16 years of South Africa's democracy and nation building programme essentially in the trenches of government, occupying executive management positions with an added five years in hard-core capitalist, entrepreneurial and a range of business pursuits. I am now in the process of re-ordering some of my thoughts, ideas and action plans, based on my experiences from the trenches of transformation.

A diffuse personal trajectory

Back to my roots. I am the third-born and only son of Robert Richards and Joan Webber. I was born in Cape Town in 1960. I attended two primary schools because the suburb where the first school was located was declared for whites only. A new school was built on the marshy farmland in the next suburb and the entire population of pupils relocated. I completed high school in 1977 (one year after the Soweto 1976 uprisings) but without a university-entrance qualification. In fact, university education was never part of my consciousness at school, neither was it part of the psyche of my parents or our social community. My parents barely finished primary school education, with my father, a deeply religious man, completing a 40-year career as a postman. He died at the age of 57. My mother was a domestic worker all her life, working for white people, notwithstanding that her own parents were white. She died at the age of 66 years while I was living and studying in Switzerland. Unfortunately, neither of my parents lived to see the new South Africa. I have three sisters, two older and one younger than me.

After an initial stint as a candidate cadet marine engineer for a private shipping company, I served on board a ship in the SA Navy as an engine room labourer. We were commonly called grease monkeys since it was our job to climb up and down a pumping and hot engine casing ensuring that all moving parts were sufficiently oiled and greased during a four-hour shift. I assumed that the grease-monkey business was just a temporary step in my journey to becoming a marine engineer. I soon realised that I was never going to be allowed to become a marine engineer – then the exclusive domain of whites and the lucky few who had excellent school results.

In the Navy I had to force my way into the engine room of the ship and after much clandestine manoeuvring, a near court marshal and dishonourable discharge for "going over the head of the white chief petty officer", I completed an apprenticeship as a marine engine-room mechanic. Now I was an educated and skilled monkey. I studied how engines work, learnt engineering drawings, worked on a range of workshop machinery and tools, traced the piping of the ship and got to witness engine repairs and overhauls.

All the young coloured men in the engine room were excused when the engineers worked on the insides of the engine. I declined the offer. My mates were not impressed with me, and neither were those who wanted to monopolise the engineering knowledge and know-how. It's amazing what one can steal with the eye.

I had already completed a technical career and had earned extremely well as a tradesman by the standards of my peers. While I earned less than the white tradesmen, I was earning more than my mother's domestic worker salary and more than my father after his 40 years of delivering letters on a bicycle. This did my father's ego no good and he refused to take money from me, his only son. Instead, my dad instructed me to hand over my wages to my mother. It was a particularly sensitive time for him since he had had his leg amputated due to chronic diabetes, was going blind and was becoming increasingly dependent both financially and emotionally.

At the time, I was a 21-year-old young man, with a beautiful girlfriend who became my wife. My testosterone levels and emerging ego blinded me to my father's plight and what it meant for him to have lost his physical capability that had put bread on our family's table for all those years.

From the Navy, I joined an engineering company in the private sector in 1981. Naval technical training was not recognised by civilian companies and so I was forced to redo my apprenticeship. This time I was registered as an apprentice fitter and turner – a trade which had only just recently opened up to people of colour via an amendment to the Manpower Act. I completed my trade and subsequently worked as a tradesman at other heavy engineering companies in Cape Town.

My varied marine and mechanical engineering workshop experience soon after my apprenticeship, and a short stint of working as a tradesman till the mid-1980s in both the heavy and light engineering sector was followed by a period of approximately ten years of pursuing higher education both inside and outside South Africa, in the USA, Germany and Switzerland. Notwithstanding that I was four subjects away from my Mechanical Engineering Diploma, I changed career focus to that of religious studies and the social sciences. It was a kind of Damascus Road experience which led me to pursue my theological studies. I subsequently completed four degrees in three countries. My PhD is from the Religious Studies Department of the Social Science Faculty of the University of Cape Town. I specialised in ancient religious texts (i.e. Old Testament). Along the way I became ordained as a protestant Christian clergyperson within the African (i.e. Bantu) Baptist denomination and served as pastor to congregations in over-populated and congested townships in Parkwood, Cape Town and Soweto, Johannesburg.

My intense pursuit of academic training was a conscious decision that turned into an obsession to "study my way to freedom". There was no predetermined or glamorous South African career pathway for a biblical scholar of colour or a "liberation theologian".

I graduated with my PhD in 1995, barely one year into the new South Africa after almost ten years of full-time academic study in three different countries. My main source of financial support was my wife who worked tirelessly as a registered nurse while I studied in South Africa. We decided not to have children for the first seven years of our marriage. My wife resigned from her full-time nursing job and accompanied me throughout my international academic pursuits, working as a domestic worker in the USA and Europe.

In the USA and Europe I sold my skills as a hospital chaplain, office receptionist, typist and a summertime handyman and gardener who knew how to handle mechanised First World garden tools. My Swiss summertime employer was particularly impressed that a black man from Africa could so adeptly manage his expensive and complicated garden machinery. My fellow students from other African countries worked as packers in a chocolate factory. I guess it helped having some tradesman skills!

I have spent the past five years (2004-2009) entrepreneurially chasing business deals and for a short stint served as CEO of one of the largest marine and general engineering companies in South Africa. Ironically, 26 years after joining the company where I completed my fitter and turner apprenticeship, I returned as its CEO and one of its shareholders. As luck would have it, the shareholders to whom I made the sales pitch, were in fact the same shareholders when I was an apprentice at that company many years before. Another full circle of sorts.

A different and earlier BEE deal saw me appointed as the managing director of an autobody repair shop. The preceding nine years or so (1995-2004) saw me living in Johannesburg as an academic and a defence and security practitioner working in the TRC, Scorpions and policing environment.

My perspective is thus one which, by diffusion of career activities, combines years of formal defence and security experience with my more recent entrepreneurial perspective. My foray into private industry has provided me with a unique first-hand perspective regarding efforts to contribute to re-industrialising South Africa and addressing the skills crisis.

My ultimate aim as a patriot is to make a positive contribution to crime reduction through building job-creation capacity and skills. My experience at the coalface makes it a lot easier for me to recognise when policy is out of step with reality, and when management is out of step with performance criteria as dictated by policy.

Cynicism and reality

Of course, it is also likely that my "trench-based" experiences and perspective may cause me to be more cynical and critical about the disjuncture between policy and practice, whether in business or government. By the same token, a view from the trenches is not intended to minimise the view from the ivory tower, where I am currently housed, since it is often the ivory tower perspective that enables the sometimes much-needed "one-step-removed" perspective (viz. that macro perspective) which in theory is supposed to be more objective, independent and sober.

My post-1994 career path has encountered three critical moments relevant to the quest of this book. These include human rights activism in the context of the TRC, building investigative and criminal justice capacity in the context of policing, and building technical capacity in terms of my industrial activity. While each of these moments will receive more detailed attention in later chapters, I now will reflect on them briefly as a means of locating my career path in the context of the evolution of transformation in South Africa.

Transforming a racist society

Joining the TRC

The much-awaited and primary finding of the Truth Commission was that the defence and security apparatus of the apartheid state were found guilty of committing acts constituting gross violations of human rights. The ANC and other liberation movements were similarly found guilty. But the scale of violations committed by the apartheid state remains without parallel. Therefore any attempt at transforming the apartheid security machinery was not going to be easy. The analogy of being confronted with an armed person comes to mind. In this regard it must be said that trying to disarm and transform a person with a loaded gun in their hand, and that person having a proud track record of having used that gun effectively, always focuses the mind of the transformation and negotiating agent. For my sins, this is the transformation storm I lived in and through for the first ten years of our democracy with a prime seat in the eye of that storm – or was it the trenches in which I took refuge!

No sooner had I been appointed as a junior lecturer at the University of the Witwatersrand, than I was hastily absorbed onto the staff of the Truth and Reconciliation Commission (TRC). My academic career plan was to enjoy the hallways of academia and bathe in the luxury of intellectual and academic abstraction especially given that I was, then (i.e. in 1995/96), one of only three black PhD academics at the university. At least so I was told and I left it at that. I had no interest in verifying my minority status. I just wanted to teach and write. The view taken by the university (via the opinion of the Dean of the Arts Faculty at the time) regarding my invitation to join the TRC, was that I was too junior to be seconded to the TRC on behalf of the university and that I should simply not take up the position.

I immediately resigned from my position at the university, hoping to show my level of disgust that a "liberal" English-speaking university would take such a position. I had no idea that this step into the unknown world of criminal justice would take me on a journey into environments I never knew existed.

Joining the TRC as a researcher / investigator, and my later appointment as Executive Secretary for the Human Rights Violations Committee as well as the Amnesty Committee, changed my academic aspirations rather fundamentally. And so commenced my decade-long journey into the bowels of the security, defence and criminal justice system of the, then, still untransformed, untamed, white-managed and white-controlled apartheid state security machine.

The TRC challenge wrenched me from the comfort of my ivory tower into the trenches of transformation where the apartheid security beast was in the throes of its last attempt at clinging to power and control. The 1994 miracle is often thought of as a bloodless coup and a miracle transition. While both these notions are accurate, we must not forget that the preceding four years of negotiations between the apartheid status quo and the liberation movements led by Nelson Mandela, much a bloodletting took place. The apartheid security forces were responsible for orchestrating a range of killings and incited civil unrest so as to give them an excuse to shoot-on-sight. In excess of 10 000 people, mainly black, were killed in clashes between the security police and "the people". The last shivers of the security beast had deadly consequences for the liberation movement who had, in good faith, suspended the armed struggle against apartheid.

Nothing had prepared me for what was about to dominate my professional career for almost a decade, except that my reading and writing skills together with my ability to repair a broken ship's engine, were fairly well honed. And perhaps my boy scout motto came in handy, namely "Be prepared". I was, after all, a proud Springbok Scout.

My TRC working days introduced me to many different security-related realities, all of which posed fundamental and critical personal challenges, especially noting that these new practical, managerial and leadership challenges took me completely out of my previous engineering and academic comfort zone. What was I doing in a high-risk security and military-dominated environment pushing a human rights agenda in the context of brutal killings and assassinations? I wished it were a movie which had an ending. But every morning I arose and went to work, to face not just another day at the office – but another day of contributing to the reconstruction of a nation badly damaged by its past.

Organised educational crime and the police

What was envisaged to be a 12-month TRC process lingered on for almost five years as the country came to terms with its brutal past. I remained with the TRC until the handing over of the final report to President Mandela, at which point I sought other employment. I had hoped to return to my previous academic post, however by now the higher education system of South Africa had rationalised and removed departments of religious studies, noting that such departments served as the ideological hotbed for the justification of apartheid. I thus had no academic home to which I could return, especially given that my academic qualifications were now meaningless in a transforming South Africa. So what was the point of investing ten years of my life to acquire a qualification which was not going to be used by the very country for which I was studying and preparing myself as a scholar and theologian? I had acquired a dead-end career qualification.

I was fortunate to be selected and appointed to Technikon SA as Executive Director – Police Practice. The position was an academic managerial position. The portfolio included responsibility for some 50 full-time academic staff, and 60 000 distance-education learners registered through my department and linked to 17 learning centres peppered around South Africa. A large portfolio indeed for a young inexperienced academic and black manager. I was never more conscious of my "blackness" than in this particular post.

The challenge posed by my new position was, among other things, entrenching a new ideological base for police education and policing in a new democracy – requiring a paradigm shift from tyrannical enforcement practices to community-based police service. At the time there were many initiatives underway to transform the police. Many of these were NGO-based or donor-funder driven. There were very few change and transformation initiatives, if any, driven from within the ideological belly of the beast. I took up office within months of the TRC report announcing the official finding that the SAP was guilty of committing gross violations of human rights.

Suddenly the intensity of human rights training grew. The "in-thing", academically speaking, from 1995 onwards, was human rights awareness and training for police and all other criminal justice practitioners..[2] The police had not yet been integrated into one organisation. There were still 11 different police forces in South Africa with 11 different standards of policing and different interpretations and understandings of human rights. The institution which I represented, namely Technikon SA, represented the opportunity at a macro-educational level to weld together as well as create a new conceptual and ideological operating base for policing in the new South Africa, in a way that the police as an organisation could never accomplish.

When I accepted the job and all the corporate trimmings and luxuries that came with it, little did I realise that I had moved from the TRC frying pan into the police fire. Up until no more than two or three years before, almost all post-basic police training in South Africa was conducted by and through this academic department, of which I was now the ultimate academic head and managerial boss.

During the early part of my short tenure, I also learnt that formal study opportunities through my department had previously been reserved exclusively for white South African police officials. Over 90% of my staff were former police officials, predominantly Afrikaans-speaking. Successful completion of a year of study through my department as a white police student came with an automatic rank and salary promotion within the police force of the South African government. If it was not official policy, then it was certainly official practice. In the midst of such an institutionally entrenched advantage for white police, the police "force" as it was then known had been renamed police "service" and was struggling to shrug off the findings of the TRC.

I soon came to learn that that my position was originally designed to protect and give educational respectability to the white domination of the police through this preferential education and practice in South Africa, via my department. You could not get a more sophisticated form of institutional and organised educational crime than this. My personal academic rating as one of very few black PhD professionals in South Africa, coupled with my generous salary and my new-found access to the corporate trimmings, were meant to blind me to the harsh ideological warfare in which I found myself embroiled. I realised that I was the token black face to help perpetuate white domination of policing in South Africa, in exchange for a very good market-related salary and perks. In fact, I was even more acceptable since I was not really black – I was coloured – a kind of cousin to being an Afrikaner. I was not African, the traditional enemy. I represented family – albeit distant relatives. My mother was after all a

Dutch woman. As an Afrikaner ideologue told me – I was a black Afrikaner. Phew! Credit must go to the appointment committee who must have seen the need for the transformation of this systemically designed educational and management advantage for white police students. The appointment committee assumed that collusion with this relatively unknown and unchecked education system would receive my support, given the corporate trimmings and power with which I was now entrusted.

Of course, one makes all sorts of assumptions when you are sitting on the outside of things. This is what I did as I engaged my interview panel at the time. However, once I had been invited in and took a closer look, I could not help but see the ill-fated race-based structural flaw governing the promotion and creation of the next generation of police leadership and management. And I was now the boss of this system, it seemed. At the very least, my role was to lend legitimacy to the system.

I very soon realised that it was going to take tremendous effort and focus to change the culture of police education and training and the ideological base of policing in South Africa. But given the platform on which I was now standing, and the positional and managerial power I enjoyed, I was aware that it was certainly possible. Liberation, after all, happens first in the mind.

Taming revolutionaries

While I occupied the Executive Director – Police Practice post, I was approached by someone claiming to represent President Mandela's office, requesting that an educational bridge be constructed to facilitate the incorporation of the former SDUs and SPUs of the East Rand of Johannesburg into the statutory forces. These former revolutionaries were to be integrated into the statutory forces via an educational bridge.[3]

The representative explained that he had approached other education and training institutions, all of whom had turned him away. They would not touch this particular student population, namely revolutionaries. I conceded, based on the fact that I was the only person of colour heading up a capacity that could be a solution to this particular challenge. It would mean a huge adjustment and shift within the Technikon, which was very Afrikaans, pro-police and anti-terrorist. I agreed without consulting upwards in my managerial chain. I just assumed that it was the right thing to do and that from a marketing point of view, this would be a huge plus for the institution – an opportunity to show the institution's on-paper pro-democracy and pro-freedom stance. Sometimes there are lessons that textbooks simply do not teach. This was one of them. I mobilised my staff and set in motion the solution to the need, which was identified as a simple academic bridging course.

The young men and women who needed to be integrated apparently had an audience with President Mandela demanding that their military sacrifices to bring about change in South Africa be honoured by their incorporation into the statutory forces. Unfortunately, many of these cadres did not have the mandatory school-leaver qualification. Both the police and military management used this as a legal and systems-based exclusionary mechanism.

The entrance requirement to join the police or the army was matric. The fact that the police service was in the process of integrating 11 police forces into one, where the vast majority of black members did not have an education, was a detail that seemed to escape the managers. But it did not escape the young revolutionaries. Most had left school at around Grade 6 or 7 to pursue guerilla and military training aimed at freeing South Africa from the shackles of apartheid. The SDU and SPU were unfortunately not on the same page, ideologically speaking. The SDUs were ANC-based and the SPUs were Inkatha Freedom Party sympathisers.

The military skills of both these terrorist groups, who were in essence at war with each other, was legendary. Even the apartheid military machine did not dare enter the East Rand areas after dark for fear of being ambushed by either SDU or SPU cadres. A complicating factor was the media spin at the time concerning black-on-black violence and war. The period I am referring to is that period between the release of Mandela and the first democratic elections.

Needless to say, my portfolio assumed the proportions of liaison between warring factions of the SDUs and SPUs as well as trying to convinced well-armed police and army managers to reconsider their exclusionary criteria and find a creative way to incorporate into the statutory forces these urban-warfare soldiers of the liberation movement. This is a topic for a different discussion, but what can be said here briefly, is that I needed to restructure my department to deliver on what I had promised vis-à-vis the SDU and SPU learning programme. I also needed to deal with the fears of my fellow academics who, as part of my negotiated deal, needed to teach these black revolutionaries in the black township with their weapons next to them – just in case.

Initially, my immediate superiors were not impressed. But the R1m payment which was transferred from Mandela's office into the bank account of the Technikon helped to smooth things over. My superiors, of course, took all the credit when it seemed that the academic programme was going to be a success and the integration into the statutory forces of formerly excluded young revolutionaries was the politically correct thing to do. I guess another one of the non-textbook lessons is that it takes a big-hearted superior to acknowledge a sometimes impulsive subordinate – instead of charging such a person with insubordination and reckless managerial behaviour.

A critical design feature of apartheid was its educational philosophy of denying black people access to educational opportunities, and thus stifling growth and artificially reinforcing white superiority and privilege. When such a design feature is coupled with and supported by live ammunition and preferential access to armories and ammunition centres, the challenge becomes more than academic.

The police and security forces were the killing machine of the former apartheid state and were in the process of being tamed. The TRC process was the first attempt to achieve this end. Of course, the TRC was not only about taming the security forces. I left my Technikon post in 1999, noting that there was still a long way to go in the context of educational as well as police reform. We were barely five years into the new South Africa. The nation was walking a tight rope.

My next assignment was to show me just how dangerous walking a tight rope was going to be. I was appointed to the position of Deputy Director-General of the Scorpions – an organisation which existed in the mind of the President and his advisors but something that still needed to be created on the ground. And this is where I fitted in, I was told.

Creating the Scorpions

In June 1999, President Thabo Mbeki ascended to the throne, voluntarily vacated by Mandela. In his first state of the nation address, designed in part to show he planned to fill Mandela's shoes, Mbeki promised the nation a high calibre anti-corruption police-type squad. In September 1999, Mbeki launched the squad commonly called the Scorpions, in Cape Town, with great fanfare but little else by way of substance. It was merely an idea, a vision, a desire. It was in October 1999 that I was drafted into the closed leadership-management circles of the Scorpions and was politely told that I needed to create this capacity which the President had launched the previous month.

It was the view of the incoming President, Thabo Mbeki, as expressed in his first state of the nation speech, that the police in its current form was not suited to dealing effectively with the upper levels of organised crime. And it was certainly not suited to dealing with corruption within its own ranks. And so was born the need for a brand new "police" unit that would be able to not only bring to bear effective law enforcement tradecraft, but also to engender a different level of confidence from both the South African public as well as the investor community both local and foreign.

The Scorpions was envisaged to be a totally separate law-enforcement entity in South Africa. Officially, the mandate of the Scorpions was to deal with organised crime and police corruption. Subliminally, however, there was a view being nurtured by the inner circle that the Scorpions would eventually become the core of a new policing order in South Africa. Some argued that the Scorpions would and should replace the police and its death squads. It was clear to me on day one that the Scorpion project was going to be a complicated and contentious one.

I thought that moving from the TRC frying pan into the police fire was about as far as one goes in terms of heat. But then came the Scorpion tight rope-walking challenge, which the Scorpions eventually lost by falling prey to the democratic processes of Parliament and the will of the people. Recent parliamentary and government decisions, which came barely ten years after its formation, have seen the Scorpions ultimately disbanded and incorporated into the management structure and control of the police, away from its former parent body, the National Prosecuting Authority.

My initial appointment in the Scorpions was as Investigating Director – Head of Investigations and Training. The government authority and home-base for my appointment was to the prosecuting authority which did not use regular civil service labels and titles for its appointees. A complicating factor is that I was not a lawyer, which immediately created an out-of-the-system challenge. In fact, none of the initial top management of the Scorpions were lawyers. So while we were appointed as Investigating Directors in the Justice Ministry, our level of appointment was the civil service ranking of Deputy Director-General (DDG). In terms of the powers of the prosecution service, however, we needed to be imbued with a range of legal and other powers which a regular DDG did not have. And then we reverted back to what would become the eventual downfall of the Scorpions – we were not lawyers – something that irked the high-ranking legal professionals who were the kingpins of the prosecution service.

As I drove home from what turned out to be my Scorpion job interview, it crossed my mind that I am either a sucker for punishment or a certified case for a mental institution. The need to create the required capacity with the Scorpions meant that my portfolio became exclusively focused on Training and Development. This meant, inter alia, being buried in the academic and learning hallways of the FBI academy at Quantico in Washington, and those of Scotland Yard's Hendon Police Training Academy just outside London. The idea was that, with the overt assistance of the FBI and Scotland Yard, I would glean from these institutions their best practices and together with a managerial leadership team, construct a law enforcement agency with an educational and training base that would be loved by the people, feared by the criminals and respected by our peers. Since my Scorpion assignment, I have found James Bond movies rather boring and poor imitations of reality. I do, however, watch mafia movies with a new set of eyes.

In 2004, having completed almost ten years of moral service to the nation and being part of the nation-building programme from a managerial-leadership perspective, I left the Scorpions as it began to zoom southwards. My stay in the Scorpion organisation was long enough for me to see the changes in leadership and in investigative priorities, which ultimately laid the foundation for the demise of one of the country's foremost law enforcement agencies. My time in the trenches of transformation was nevertheless illuminating, and has made subsequent travelling in rough and stormy seas a lot less daunting.

From tradesman to CEO

A critical gap in my experience and knowledge base was the industrial economy of South Africa, and the mystery, for me, surrounding wealth creation. And so, when I left the Scorpions I joined the private sector to pursue various business opportunities. As a result of my inquisitive nature, I got burnt in the process, realising that the world of business is not for the fainthearted. When it comes to money, many are prepared to kill, and few are guided primarily by moral and ethical sensitivities.

In 2004, I rejoined the forays of the business and industrial world, but this time with a pen in my hand, having traded my overall and toolbox for a suit in the boardroom.

Some concluding remarks

My personal journey through the first ten years of democracy in South Africa as an executive manager provided me with a unique perspective of our ongoing nation-building programme. There is nothing like one's experience from the dirty trenches to re-appreciate the view from the ivory tower. I constantly remind my comrades that prior to 1994, I spent 34 years consumed by the desire to be an engineer and to be the best I could be under very difficult circumstances. I never managed to become the engineer of the plant, but I did enjoy the satisfaction of employing engineers and being their boss.

The 1994 miracle of South Africa changed all our lives. In the context of the discussion here, the successes in the transformation of the criminal justice system must not be underestimated. The challenge of facilitating a paradigm shift from an over-militarised law-enforcement and police-led killing machine of the state, to a service-based and human rights-sensitive custodial safety and security framework for the same police was enormous. Such a transformation experiment on such a scale has not been attempted anywhere else in the world. Those of us tasked with managerial responsibility at the coal face knew just how fragile and fickle the process could be, given that we were dealing with a well-trained, well-armed and superiorly connected military and police personnel. Mistakes would have fatal consequences.

A consciousness postscript

My social science-based intellectual and academic journey has exposed me to the notion that real freedom starts in the mind. Furthermore, I learnt that the greatest weapon in the hand of any oppressor is the mind of the oppressed. As long as the oppressed are made to believe that the solutions proposed by their leaders or bosses will lead to Utopia, there will be little rigorous engagement with the policy framework or approved implementation plans. Most people are like sheep, who have an incredible trust in the leadership abilities of the shepherd. It does not mean that the sheep are stupid. They are just programmed to follow loyally. Many leaders abuse this loyalty.

My life journey has been characterised, to some extent, by blind faith, but it is also a combination of zest for the impossible, and a heightened level of inquisitiveness. All this is coupled with a consciousness I absorbed from my father who, in spite of minimal education, had the self esteem of a professor. I suspect his determination to accomplish what he set out to do must have rubbed off on me.

It was only later in life that I came to appreciate that my father was consumed by a vision to travel to the USA and study to become a missionary. I remember him boarding a plane in Cape Town in January 1971. I was ten years old. He was 45. He had only had five years of primary school education and had started work at age 14 years as a telegram boy in the post office. Yet, he had a vision. He saved up his pennies over a period of 20 years to be able to afford a Cape Town-USA return ticket. He was not accepted for study in the USA, but remained determined to visit the USA anyway.

Upon his arrival in the USA, people began to listen to him articulate his thoughts and views about the Christian message. It was not long before the missionary school to which he had applied to be a student, appointed him as a guest teacher and missionary. My father returned to South Africa after six long months in the USA where he travelled that country extensively. As a way of coping financially and reducing his costs, my father chose to house himself at a mission and welfare centre in Grand Rapids, Michigan. He shared his space and meals with hobos, alcoholics and other downtrodden types who were fed daily by the Christian mission. This was a small price to pay for free accommodation and food, he told me. I remember his absolute amazement when recalling how he saw white people so poor and begging for food – and being alcoholics. As a black South African, this must have been mind-boggling given that "poor white-ism" was a feature apartheid ideology desperately tried to eradicate.

My father returned from his trip a changed man. It was as though he had seen and experienced something he could not explain. This moment revolutionised our world and consciousness as a family. It created a different realm of possibilities for us as children. I recall a recent visit and conversation with the person who became my dad's best friend in the USA,

Phil Longstreet. When Phil and my dad befriended each other in 1971, Phil was a 35-year-old white Christian leader. Just before Phil's death in December 2008, I sat at his bedside watching the snowflakes of Michigan flutter gently to the icy ground. I listened attentively as Phil, struggling to talk, retold an event which illustrates graphically the disjuncture my dad must have felt, but never expressed to us as children.

The event was an outdoor adult baptismal service to which my dad was invited as both a guest preacher and one of the officiating ministers to baptise those who desired baptism that day. This was a very conservative evangelical Christian church grouping so there was no overt political or ideological solidarity that prompted them to invite my father to participate in the event. Being a "blood-washed child of the Lord" was sufficient. Adult baptism by immersion (i.e. when the whole body is submerged under the water) was a regular Christian ritual performed by this group of Christians who happened to have a guest from Africa, my dad. The baptismal candidates on the day were all white. Phil pointed out to me a confession my father had made to him privately after the service, that this was the first time in his life that he was at a "beach" (it was actually a huge lake) in the same water as white people.

As I listened to Phil recall this event, I became aware of how profound a moment this must have been for my father.

Certainly, America had its own fair share of integration challenges as the civil rights movement has brought to our attention. However, as Phil recalls, he and my father walked into the lake hand in hand. What was seemingly routine and minor to Phil must have been deeply moving and revolutionary for my dad, who never shared with us his reflections of this event which must have profoundly affected his own sense of self worth. The profundity of the moment was the fact that he, a black man, was baptising white people – something one could not conceptualise happening in apartheid South Africa. My father never spoke about it to his dying day. I discovered these details for the first time almost 40 years after the event and by sheer accident as I visited Phil in the USA, shortly before he himself died.

Now imagine a South African black man returning to South Africa in 1971, having been "educationally and culturally affirmed" for his talent and competence in the USA, and then returning to his homeland to be a postman again and not allowed to preach or teach to the white mission churches as he did overseas. He was 45 years old at the time – in the prime of his life.

Dad spent the remaining 12 years of his life in South Africa consumed by a passion for children's Christian ministry. He was convinced that this is where one needed to invest time and energy. His focus was on kids between eight and 14 years of age. It was customary to expect between 800 and 1 000 kids attending the afternoon children's "shows" which my dad used to put on for the kids. His repertoire included magic, exciting picture-book stories depicting black kids as the actors, and a series of lucky draws which included prizes such as blankets, tinned food and other practical items. In addition to the lively music, the kids needed to endure a bible story as told by my father, and then it was time for them to go home and tell their parents to attend the evening service.

Although my father did not experience the new South Africa, in his small way, he knew the feeling of being accepted for his competence and not his colour – even though in his own country this would not be a reality in his lifetime. Back home, my father needed to confine his ministry to the coloured townships by virtue of his race classification. I do recall the surprise of an African pastor when my dad agreed to conduct a series of children's services (then called campaigns) in the African townships. I can remember accompanying my father into this world of poverty and degradation – a world even worse than the one on our side of the railway tracks. It seemed that we could go down the racial hierarchy with the Christian gospel message, but not upwards to the whites. Only whites could preach the Christian gospel to whites.

Of course, the white missionaries could preach to blacks in the black areas. What must my dad have been feeling about this as he silently reflected on his USA experience with Phil? My father subsequently became known in the Cape Flats as Uncle Robbie, the postman child evangelist. All the while he continued to work full time as a postman since his Christian ministry work was an act of charity and goodwill. He remained a postman until he was medically boarded and eventually had to have his leg amputated due to complications resulting from his chronic diabetes. He died at the age of 57 years, suffering a heart attack while washing at the basin.

My father died while I was still a young apprentice with a passion for engines. He and I had only just started to connect, having been through some bumpy adolescent years. Unlike what my father did with his 20 years of savings, I combined my savings with that of a friend and we bought a broken car. We were convinced that having a car would attract the right girls. We felt we got a bargain since only the engine needed a major overhaul. The car was otherwise good to go – a little rust here and there – but essentially in one piece.

I removed and dismantled the engine. All the parts were strewn across the garage floor. My father, who was by now confined to bed, made the effort and hobbled on his crutches to the garage which was attached to our house. His leg had been amputated and the diabetes was beginning to affect his eyesight. He could only read with a magnifying glass.

He had begrudgingly allowed me to have two stripped motorbike engines in my bedroom, which was already a major paradigm shift for a postman who only knew bicycles. My motor car engine-stripping exercise necessitated a question from my father as he leaned closer to inspect the various engine parts. "I hope you know what you are doing."

When I had repaired and re-assembled the engine, I overheard Dad on the phone to a friend, proudly saying: "I can't believe it. The car is riding again. The boy has done the impossible."

Sometimes the impossible becomes possible through sheer hard work, effort and determination, and perhaps a dose of good fortune. I wish I could say that I had planned my career path and journey. However, all I can say is that it evolved as the new South African nation evolved, and presented me with challenges to which I have responded. I rode the wave and grabbed opportunities with both hands.

I am not sure what the next wave will bring, but I plan to enjoy the ride. This is South Africa after all – the place of miracles.

Notes

1 The contextual framework of meaning best suited for beginning to make sense of my multi-faceted experiences is what is called cybernetic epistemology where the concern is with "changing our conceptual lenses from material to pattern, rather than parts to wholes" (Keeney BP (1983) *Aesthetics of Change*, New York: Gilford Press, p.95). What cyber epistemology emphasizes is relationships, interconnectedness, patterns and a process-oriented and contextual approach to understanding life. This is in sharp contrast to what Auerswald describes as an atomistic, reductionist and anti-contextual Newtonian epistemology, which characterized my upbringing as a first generation child of Apartheid and at the same time steeped in conservative evangelical theology (Auerswald EH (1985) Thinking about thinking in family therapy. *Family Process*, 24, 1, 1-12). My very strict, rule-bound religious family upbringing with its clearly defined

boundaries concerning morals, values and principles served apartheid ideology extremely well until I discovered that in God's sight, whites were neither the custodians of morality nor people of colour but that all of humanity is created inherently equal – racially and morally. Suddenly the definitively clear lines of morality and order which characterised my upbringing became very blurred, even more so when I tried to make sense of the romance between my mom and dad – a technically illegal and immoral affair according to apartheid thinking.

2   New textbooks for police training and education needed to be compiled in the wake of the 1994 arrival of democracy and the brand new notion of equality and human rights protection for all. One of the first of such books eventually prescribed for police science students was Nel, F & Bezuidenhout J (Eds) (1995) *Policing and Human Rights*. Cape Town: Juta & Co, Ltd.

3   The formation, in 1991, of the ANC-aligned SDUs (self defence units), IFP-aligned SPU (self protection units) and PAC-aligned Task Force (TF) needs to be understood in the context of the collapse of policing capability in the black townships on the one hand and the rise of informal "community policing" structures on the other hand. The liberation movements had long since brought into question the legitimacy of the police as a custodian of justice and peace. Resultantly, the further problem was the mechanics of the semblance of a criminal justice system as practiced in the "no-go" zones of places such as the East Rand of Johannesburg and certain areas of Kwa-Zulu Natal where the Inkatha Freedom party and its "Youth Brigade" dominated – even after April 1994. It is in this context that one must understand what came to be commonly called "kangaroo courts". What was not commonly known was the level of rejection transmitted by the police with regards the integration of the SDUs and SPUs into the police.

Unfortunately, the political violence, ideological differences and tensions between the two main warring parties namely the SDUs and SPUs did not dissipate after the April 1994 elections notwithstanding the rhetoric of peace and disarmament. In spite of a democratically elected government, the advent of the TRC and the rule of South Africa through a government of national unity, the sentiment from within the ranks of the formally "illegitimate" police towards the SDU and SPU situation was more than abrasive. Rakgoadi captures well this sentiment when reporting that "Some members of the police service reacted to the integration of SDUs into the police services by saying that the SDUs must be disarmed, disbanded, demilitarised, sent to school and helped to find jobs, **but not in the police service**, (my emphasis) because the police is already infiltrated by criminals and their incorporation into the police service adds to the problem. They further posit that the police services is "trying to improve its image by streamlining and adopting a more professional demeanour". Moreover, their integration would mean that criminals could become policemen and would politicise the police force (service)." (See Rakgoadi PK (1995) *The Role of the Self-defence Units (SDUs) in a Changing Political Context*, Research report written for the Centre for the Study of Violence and Reconciliation, January 1995.)

These SDUs and SPUs were the "criminals" for whom I needed to develop an academic bridging programme that would facilitate their eventual integration into the police, a statutory force which made it abundantly clear that the SDUs and SPUs were not welcome in their ranks.

15 | Taming state security

People often only want to hear their truth.

This chapter provides an analysis of the gains of South Africa's new democracy. It is written from the perspective of the transformation of the security machinery of the state, as facilitated by the TRC process, and from my personal experiences while serving as an executive manager in the security sector during the early post-apartheid years, when the obsessive transformation focus in South Africa was on the security and military apparatus of the state.

The significance of what I have called the TRC moment is that it enabled South Africa to create a collective memory of the past – a contested past. Of significance is the fact that, at great expense to the state, a process was activated which averted a racial and civil war in South Africa.

The transformation gains made by the South African society under the leadership of the ANC-led government must not be underestimated. Part of the miracle is that the former killing machine of the apartheid state was to serve as the custodian and protector of the very people considered to be the enemy of the state. This new custodianship is how the Constitution redefines the role of state security.

However, the gains of defence and security transformation can be easily undone if no viable and sustainable solution is proposed to solve the ongoing crime and unemployment crisis in the country.

South Africa may well boast the best Constitution in the world, but this means very little in the context of the current and ever-widening gap between rich and poor, a runaway crime situation, an unemployment time bomb, and overcrowded prisons.

Context

No bloodless coup

A critical post-1994 priority facing the liberation movement and its revolutionary cadres was to take control of the state-based security apparatus. It was this very capacity that the apartheid regime so effectively and repressively used to impose its tyranny on the masses. The magnanimous gesture on the part of the liberation movement to suspend the armed struggle prior to democratic victory at the ballot box in the interest of peaceful negotiations failed to meet with similar magnanimity from the side of the apartheid state and its security apparatus. It is estimated that approximately 10 000 people were killed by the apartheid security forces during the four-year period between the release of Nelson Mandela from prison on 2 February 1990 and the official day of liberation, 27 April 1994.[1]

While the 1994 elections could be hailed as a comparatively bloodless coup and miracle, blood did flow and tempers raged as the leaders sat for four years trying to negotiate and broker a political deal for the future of South Africa. While the leaders were ostensibly negotiating peacefully, the troops on both sides were spilling blood. The township streets were haemorrhaging at the hands of the apartheid state security machine.

TRC precedents
Truth commissions or commissions of inquiry into human rights violations are a unique feature of countries in the midst of political transition from tyranny to some form of democracy. By the time of the South African TRC, there had been at least 15 such commissions across the world, including in Uganda (1974), Bolivia (1982), Argentina (1983/1984), Philippines (1986/1987), Chile (1990/1991) and El Salvador (1992).[2]

Overview of the TRC

The South African TRC was unique in that it was born as a result of an act of Parliament, and not by presidential decree or an imposition for international human rights courts or the United Nations. The TRC was set up by the government of national unity, and enjoyed a legislative mandate which clearly outlined its terms of reference. The legislation prescribed that *the commission shall promote national unity and reconciliation in a spirit of understanding which transcends the conflicts and divisions of the past*. It went on to say that this was to be done through a truth-telling process which aimed to:

- Establish as complete a picture as possible of the causes, nature and extent of the gross violations of human rights which were committed between 1 March 1960 and 10 May 1994.

- Facilitate the granting of amnesty to persons who make full disclosure of all relevant facts relating to acts committed with a political objective.

- Establish and make known the fate and whereabouts of victims, and restore the human and civil dignity of such victims by granting them an opportunity to relate their own accounts of the violations against them, and recommend reparation measures.

- Compile a report of the activities and findings of the commission, and recommend measures to prevent future violations of human rights.

The commission expanded its focus beyond the individual to include institutional hearings. The brief did not include an analysis of the impact of apartheid's racial capitalism. Rather, its focus was gross violation of human rights experienced at a personal level. However, through a series of institutional hearings, including one for the business sector, it became apparent how complicitous business had been with the apartheid state, and how many business practices had lent themselves to, and in some instances constituted, human rights violations. The institutional hearings afforded a range of organisations and institutions the opportunity to apologise publicly for their collusion with the apartheid state.

Period under review

The framing dates for the TRC mandate are significant in that they signify the turning points in the mindset and psyche of both South Africa and the international community vis-à-vis the struggle against apartheid.

Primary findings

The primary finding of the TRC was that:

> The predominant portion of gross violations of human rights was committed by the former state through its security and law-enforcement agencies.[3]

Findings were made in respect of a range of entities, including violations committed in the course of the armed struggle. While the ANC had accepted full responsibility for all actions committed by members of uMkhonto we Sizwe (MK) under its command, it remains instructive to express the TRC finding in this regard. The TRC found that:

While it was ANC policy that the loss of civilian life should be "avoided", there were instances where members of MK perpetrated gross violations of human rights in that the distinction between military and civilian targets was blurred in certain armed actions...[4]

A nation at risk: Context of the findings

The period preceding the TRC compromise could be described as poised for bloody civil war. The low-intensity urban warfare which characterised much of the armed struggle against apartheid could easily have escalated into full-blown civil war. The challenge facing the government of national unity was to quickly take control of the powerful security apparatus of the state – at the time an unknown quantity. In many ways, the TRC served to contain the anger of the masses, and to allay the fears of the former revolutionary cadres who had recently laid down their weapons, as well as the fear of the apartheid securocrats, who still controlled the state security apparatus and machinery.

The politics of administration – A manager's nightmare (Internal)

Structure

The commission comprised 17 commissioners appointed by the state president. Each had been subjected to a process of public scrutiny and cross-examination, and been found to be impartial, respected, without a significant political profile, and representative of a broad cross-section of the population.

Three specialised committees operated under the TRC, namely the Amnesty, Human Rights Violations and Reparation and Rehabilitation committees. The Amnesty committee was governed by voluntary, individual applications. The criterion for granting amnesty was full disclosure of the atrocity committed, indicating clear political motives for committing such violations. The Human Rights Violations committee provided the moral balance to the amnesty process. Victims came forward to share their stories and experiences of pain, thus allowing their suffering to be officially acknowledged. The Reparation and Rehabilitation committee was charged with assessing the extent of harm suffered, and making recommendations to the President concerning how victims (and perpetrators) could be rehabilitated.

Provision was made for appropriate staff, administration and a budget to guarantee independence from government and to ensure that the commission had the capacity to perform its functions. The commission's more than 300 personnel staffed four regional offices across the country.

Creating an organisation

The bottom-line challenge was that from a managerial point of view, an organisation needed to be created, structured and managed effectively within iron-clad timeframes.

From a managerial perspective the challenge was to quickly create a TRC organisation. As managers we were not comforted by the fact that the whole world would be watching. We therefore needed to have all the "bells and whistles" and at the same time keep our staff on track. We knew that a bumpy road lay ahead and so we needed to brace ourselves, psychologically, administratively and technically. There is a sense in which we did not need any performance contracts because our lack of performance would be so public and so embarrassing to the nation that failure was simply not an option. In short, we needed, in a mad hurry, to create systems, employ people and "hit-the-ground-running"[5]. The TRC legislation needed to be converted from policy into tangible and practical management reality that could be measured and managed.

There were no precedents for the TRC in terms of the objectives set out in its founding legislation. The closest organisational parallel to what the TRC would later become was that of the anti-apartheid NGO sector which focused on human rights issues. This was certainly not the engineering workshop I was familiar with.

Our challenges included setting up offices, finding premises, renovating, installing IT infrastructure, buying equipment, interviewing and employing staff, issuing salary slips, and putting in place internal information security measures to stop the leaking of information or the hacking of the TRC database.

A need for courage

A further challenge was to exact managerial courage as the TRC sometimes lapsed into government-bashing mode. We needed to remind ourselves that the TRC was the product of government statute –

an act of Parliament. Furthermore, we had an entire nation watching and waiting for the outcome of our work. We were not a human rights NGO accountable to some foreign donor far away. The TRC was a completely different organisational animal, where public pressure and scrutiny was a daily reality.

Experience has taught me that it is very difficult to performance-manage someone who holds a morally superior view of themselves and their cause. Very often the high morality of the cause masks the managerial incompetence, which is excused on moral grounds and not on organisational efficiency grounds. And this was the challenge in the TRC. The orientation of the majority of the commissioners and staff and the moral core of the organisation was that of a determined effort to hold apartheid accountable for its crimes against humanity. However, disciplining and guiding such staff in terms of managerial performance standards, without being accused of being either racist or unnecessarily pedantic, proved to be a major challenge. In colloquial and "political struggle lingo", comrades were united on moral grounds and consequently blind to each other's shortcomings when it came to performance issues.

Managing political egos

Trying to manage a politically driven process became a nightmare. As a manager you generally have to develop a thick skin and suspend your own emotions. This was especially true in the context of the TRC. Somebody needed to crack the whip and get the team to "get the job done" to the satisfaction of the board of shareholders – in this instance the TRC commissioners. As managers we could cry later when everyone else had gone home.

No clear bottom line

Hiring and firing is part of the management game plan. In the TRC it was necessary for me to exercise the latter option with a few staff who needed to be relieved of their posts. The golden performance standard used at the time was public embarrassment. The benefit of hindsight provides one with fancy words and categories such as risk management and risk mitigation. But we kept it simple. If the behaviour of a member of staff compromised the ultimate goal of the company, it was bye-bye time – no long stories and no time for remedial interventions.

Exilic versus non-exilic management styles

A further complicating factor bedevilling those days of uncharted management territory was the clash between exilic and non-exilic forms of political authority. Those returning from years of exile had developed different ways of expressing themselves and their authority compared with those who had endured the hardships of life under the scrutiny of the apartheid security forces. It was fascinating to see this happening behind closed doors. Ideological disagreements were profound, yet contained. The size of the egos was even more profound, yet contained. The TRC was a microcosm of our society and was thus exposed to the rough and tumble of everyday polarised racial attitudes and suspicions about each other.

The cost of secondary trauma

The personal price paid by staff was high. Some lost their hair. Others went grey. My neck went into spasms. Some staff even died.

The commissioners needed to be nurtured and protected. The staff needed assistance in managing secondary trauma resulting from the information flowing through the commission.

I remember one staff member typing up the details of a murder confession of an amnesty applicant, only to discover that this was the story of how her brother was killed by the security forces. She collapsed at work. She was debriefed and redeployed.

Information leaks

A particular challenge with which I was tasked was to stem leaks from inside the commission. A specific problem was the leaking of the contents of the amnesty applications of former apartheid ministers and high-ranking security personnel.

The leak was detected, certain staff members relieved of their positions, and additional information security measures put in place to manage the 7 000 amnesty applications and more than 27 000 victim statements eventually processed by the commission.

Dogma of implementation

If the TRC has done nothing else for me, it has deepened my respect for those tasked with managerial implementation, since this is where the rubber hits the road and where dreams become reality. I pay tribute to the unsung heroes of the commission who made the senior executives look good as we reported on and took the credit for the work done.

External challenges: The politics of stakeholder liaison

POWs – Ultra-right wingers demand inclusion in TRC process

Probably the most revealing of the TRC challenges and my scariest experience was being the emissary, liaison or, in military speak, "the nodal point" (i.e. point of contact and negotiation) between the TRC and the military threat emerging from the Afrikaner ultra-right wing.[6] The AWB believed that they had been sold out by FW de Klerk and the National Party. They were not only disgruntled, but well-armed with access to serious fire power and explosives. At the time, we had no way of knowing whether their military threat was significant – until they blew up part of the Johannesburg International Airport to make a point.

Part of my rapidly growing portfolio was to brief Archbishop Desmond Tutu on my secret negotiation meetings with the disgruntled military generals of the AWB, Boeremag and other Afrikaner splinter groups who had chosen not to join the Kempton Park negotiations and who felt excluded and betrayed. They were not happy dealing with me since they wanted to deal directly with the Archbishop. I rapidly learnt how to be a skilful gatekeeper. They wanted to broker a prisoner-of-war deal for the men who were wrongfully imprisoned as criminals, they argued. A change in their status from criminal to prisoner of war (POW) would open up the possibility of amnesty and consequently pave their way for release from prison.

At one of the secret meetings which took place at what seemed to be an ordinary Pretoria restaurant, but with a special door leading to a type of war-council room at the back, I recall how Eugene Terreblache, with great pride, made a point of introducing me, "Tutu se man" (Tutu's man), to his team of generals by identifying which one drove the armed vehicle, which one had smacked the black politician and so forth. Those were rough transitions as we entered the uncharted waters of what would become a new democratic South Africa.

I remember telling my protection team that the deal was that I meet Eugene Terreblanche and his cohorts unarmed, alone and unwired.

Thankfully, I am still alive. The TRC legislation was subsequently amended to incorporate the ultra-right wing as a gesture of reconciliation and goodwill.

Field visits: Crocodiles, skulls and bones

One of my most chilling experiences was the day that the commissioner responsible for TRC Investigations, Dumisa Ntsebeza, and I secretly entered the inner fields of what was a banana and papau plantation near the Zimbabwean border. Ntsebeza and I were being escorted by our own heavily armed TRC bodyguards in a beaten-up vehicle as part of our undercover disguise. The guards were on red alert and drove with their fingers on the trigger. It was a day of anticipated high drama. Rarely do I ensure that my family affairs are in order before I leave home. This was such a day.

The statement-gathering process of the commission led us to a black eyewitness who had been discredited by the apartheid security establishment. The witness claimed that liberation cadres who were trying to cross the Zimbabwean border into South Africa had been arrested by the South African Police and taken to a torture chamber on a certain farm, where they were subjected to hours of gruelling torture. The torture chamber was pointed out to us. The witness's account of the event further alleged that after the torture, many of the cadres had been thrown to their deaths into a crocodile-infested dam.

The crocodile incident was one of the more traumatic and difficult moments in the life of the TRC, since Archbishop Tutu could not promise to bring home the bones of the deceased – an expectation which began to dominate and determine the need for final closure on the part of the families whose loved ones had left to fight apartheid but who never came home. I can still hear Tutu saying to us: "What do I tell the mothers?"

It was different when we conducted exhumations of secret graves. It was part of my job to ensure that a family representative was in attendance at the exhumations. Transport, food and accommodation needed to be arranged and paid for. Only the closest relatives were to be invited. In African culture this could amount to quite a number of people.

Our graveside forensic verification system was very crude and elementary. Often, all that remained in the shallow unmarked graves were skulls, bones, rags and layers of lime.

I recall one mother identifying her son's skull from two missing teeth in the jaw bone. What she could not come to terms with was the small hole in the frontal lobe of the skull, presumably caused by a bullet.

It often fell on me to be the face and the heart of the commission in these moments of despair and pain. My clergy training came in handy in these moments. I would simply place my arms around the family members, lower my head and let my tears evaporate in the hot red soil around the exhumation site. I could never find the appropriate words at those moments.

A new consciousness emerges – outcomes

The TRC was, of course, a major political compromise which facilitated the movement of the negotiations from a "bullet" situation to the ballot box situation of 1994. The military machinery of the state, considered by the black masses as being guilty of gross violations, needed to be tamed, and the heads of these institutions held accountable. This was the general sentiment among the ranks of the liberation movement cadres and leadership.

Of course, the intricacies of the negotiated TRC deal were premised on individual confessions of military excesses rather than a focus on the structural issues and policymakers themselves. In short, the TRC deal focused on the foot soldier that pulled the trigger rather than the general who gave the command. This was the nature of the eventual compromise in which the foot soldiers paid the ultimate price, and the generals, by and large, walked free.

The commission ultimately contributed to what the Constitution calls "a historic bridge between the past of a deeply divided society characterised by strife, conflict, untold suffering and injustice, and a future founded on the recognition of human rights, democracy and peaceful co-existence, and development opportunities for all South Africans, irrespective of colour, race, belief or sex." This is best facilitated by a collective consciousness about the past.

After processing 7 000 amnesty applications and some 22 000 victim statements, and after having held over 140 public hearings and heard the public testimony of over 2 000 victims, the commission had clearly broke the deathly silence about the grotesque consequences; of the abuse of political power. The commission said no to amnesia and yes to remembrance; no to full-scale trials and yes to the possibility of forgiveness.

The TRC was unable to persuade all the political leaders to take responsibility for the gross human rights violations committed by their foot soldiers. It is also true that the "digging up" of the trauma of the past is potentially self-destructive. Time will tell whether the surgical incision of the TRC scalpel has been the right thing for our nation-building process. It certainly provides a powerful example of how the psyche of a nation can fundamentally be altered based on a given set of facts shared by the nation.

The TRC gave official expression to what millions of South Africans knew, namely that in the process of carrying out their mandate, the police violated the rights of the vast majority of citizens. I tend to be more direct in my own assessment and simply say that the police were found guilty of being the killing machine of the apartheid state.

But the power of the TRC, given that it was a formal parliamentary-sanctioned process, was that the state was forced to acknowledge its shortcomings and failures. The greatest irony is that the abused, namely the government of the oppressed masses (i.e. the ANC-led government), were now the ones in power and tasked with repairing the damage inflicted by their predecessors.

Did the TRC expose the truth about our past? It has been argued that while truth commissions may not necessarily expose the truth, they can and do reduce the number of lies circulated in public discourse. So today, for example, in Argentina, it is impossible to deny that the military threw half-dead bodies into the sea from helicopters. In Chile, it is no longer possible to assert that the Pinochet regime disposed of thousands of innocent people. In South Africa, we can no longer lie about the chemical and biological warfare programme which was developed to be used against the black people of this country. We can no longer deny that victims who mysteriously "disappeared" were deliberately abducted, poisoned and their bodies buried, fed to crocodiles or burnt on a pile of wood, their ashes thrown into rivers. We can no longer deny the secret graves of victims who were killed by the security forces. We can no longer lie about the blood-curdling torture inflicted on countless victims.

Conclusion

The TRC process was the first post-apartheid government-sponsored and civilian-driven nation-building programme. Of importance and for our purposes here, we are now able to see the following:

The TRC showcases the model required at a macro-societal level to shift a national psyche. No less of a similar process may be required for my industrial consciousness theory. In fact, my intention was to argue that a similar nationally orchestrated process is required to shift the nation once again.

The "democratic state" – under the Zuma administration – may well, with its recent regression to military ranks, have shifted the psyche into a different space vis-a-vis military versus civilian orientation to policing. So, while the TRC made some gains in taming the state and its security apparatus, it appears that the powerful "security apparatus of the state" has again and continues to assert its brutish power – with the subtext of reliance on security power to rescue an economically ailing nation.

Truth-telling: The South African DNA of consciousness

The TRC served many purposes, two of which are pertinent to what this book wishes to accomplish. The first is that it provided a forum for national catharsis – a purging of the soul and the mind for everyone to see and experience.

The second accomplishment of the TRC for purposes of our discussion here is that the TRC process created a foundation upon which a new national consciousness could be built.

Thus the TRC was the first moment for the new South African nation to "find itself" by looking into its past and sharing a view about what had taken place in that past. The challenge we now face is to find a common identity by looking into our crystal-balled future and to re-energise ourselves as a nation to achieve our national goals – of which poverty-reduction must be the number-one priority.

Notes

1. Some place the figure at around 14 000 (*See* Max Coleman (1998) *A Crime Against Humanity: Analysing the Repression of the Apartheid State* (Maudsley Monographs) – Human Rights Committee. See also Ellis S (1998) The historical significance of South Africa's third force, Journal of Southern African Studies, Volume 24, Issue 2 June 1998 , pages 261 – 299. Blade Nzimande soberly reminds us that this period was indeed a time of war. He reflects on the early days of the transitional period honouring the heros of what came to be experienced as one of South Africa's bloodiest wars. (See Nzimande B (2010) Nzimande on South Africa's seven day war http://www.politicsweb.co.za/politicsweb/view/politicsweb/en/page71654?oid=168342&sn=Detail
2. *See* P Hayner (1994) Fifteen Truth Commissions – 1974 to 1994: A comparative Study in *Human Rights Quarterly*, 16:4.
3. Truth and Reconciliation Commission of South Africa Report, Vol 5, (October 1998, CTP Book Printers, Cape Town). page 212.
4. Ibid, p.240.
5. Archbishop Tutu makes the same point as he reflects on the setting up phase of the commission (See Tutu D (1999) *No Future Without Forgiveness*. South Africa: Random House, p67.). No further detail is provided since the focus of his book and his role in the TRC was not administrative. His deputy, Dr Alex Boraine, was more the administrative organizer (See Boraine A (2000) *A Country Unmasked: Inside South Africa's Truth and Reconciliation Commission*. Oxford, England: Oxford University Press.). Very little has been written about the TRC from an administrative and management perspective – those who needed to switch the lights on and off everyday. Another useful but limited attempt to describe the set up phases of the commission is Graybill LS (2002) *Truth and Reconciliation in South Africa: Miracle or Model?* London: Lynne Rienner Publishers – especially chapter 1 (pp.1-10). The focus here is predictably on the overall political process rather than the nuts and bolts of administration and management. I echo Boraine's view namely that there is certainly a need for these kinds of perspectives to also emerge as part of the TRC story and not only those with ideologically divergent perspectives.
6. Professor Piet Meiring, an Afrikaner academic and clergyperson was appointed to the TRC as an additional member. His presence and facilitation skills helped during my negotiations with the disgruntled far rightwing leadership. While Prof Meiring may possibly have been viewed by our rightwing audience as a "traitor" he was perceived to be a friend of the Afrikaners sitting on the inside – someone with access, although Meiring would constantly defer and direct the discussions to me advising the audience in Afrikaans to "Speak to Dr Richards now. He's the Executive Secretary and will deal with the detail of your requests. He will make sure it gets to the right people." This may explain in part the permission granted for Meiring to take a photograph of the encounter with the likes of the late Eugene Terreblache and the late Robert Van Tonder – who claimed to be the real right wing leaders and who were wanting to "do a deal behind closed doors" with the Commission on behalf of their prisoners of war who were languishing in "multi-racial prisons", a sore point for the right wingers (See Meiring P (1999) *Chronicle of the Truth Commission: A journey through the past and present – into the future of South Africa*. Johannesburg: Carpe Diem Books, p.317). The right-wingers, when they eventually did make a submission and publicly testify (i.e. "confess") to the Amnesty Committee, made specific mention of the various meetings which Prof Meiring and I facilitated on their behalf. They were kind in their recollection of the various meetings (See transcript of Truth And Reconciliation Commission Amnesty Hearing Date: 12 June 1998 (Day 5), Held At: Johannesburg – Applicant Names: Marthinus Loedewikes Van Der Schyff; Andries Stephanus Kriel; Abraham Liebrecht Myburgh; Abraham Mothuphi see http://www.justice.gov.za/trc/amntrans/1998/98060812_jhb_ridora3.htm

16 | Bringing down the elephant

Equality before the law in a context of gross economic inequality remains revolutionary.

The purpose of ventilating the Scorpion story in this chapter is that it provides a body of evidence in support of the view that it is possible to fundamentally and positively affect the psyche of the nation of South Africa in the midst of its enormous challenges of runaway crime and unemployment.

South Africa's version of the FBI was a unit popularly called the Scorpions. This unit had a short lifespan of just about ten years. In fact, the Scorpions were only really operationally effective for the first four to five years of its existence. The balance of the time was taken up trying to defend its existence – a battle it lost since government decided to close down the Scorpions barely ten years after its inception.

The Scorpions were launched by President Mbeki in September 1999 and officially disbanded by presidential proclamation in February 2009. However, the impact of the Scorpions on the psyche of the South African public cannot be underestimated.[1]

Like the TRC process, the short-lived operational and subsequent legal lifespan of the Scorpions is the clearest illustration of fundamental change within the criminal justice system of a democratic South Africa. Its location within the prosecution service meant that its energy rubbed off and served as the primary catalyst for the transformation of the prosecution service as a whole. Thus, while in the office of the NDPP (National Director of Public Prosecutions), the DSO (Directorate of Special Operations) was not only a super-functioning department, it also embodied and ignited a transformation process which had implications far beyond its narrow investigative mandate.

The location of the DSO within the office of the NDPP may originally have been one of political convenience. Its subsequent placement in the police under a different name was one of legislative choice. The strategic significance undergirding the creation of the Scorpions seems to have been lost in the whirlpool of political leadership power struggles. Were the Scorpions a victim of their own success?

The Scorpions provided the nation with a visible model of successful crime-fighting – a model which provided all citizens with a sense of connection and national pride. In short, the Scorpions made the "have-not's" in society feel that there was at least one group who could be entrusted to confront the "untouchables" – be they overt crime bosses or covertly corrupt politicians.

A new era dawns

The vision and hope expressed in South Africa's post-apartheid Constitution is that its people will live in conditions of freedom and security, which will enable them to pursue the quality of life they desire. Central to achieving this vision was the criminal justice system which during apartheid, served to legitimise the racial and consequential economic oppression of the vast majority of people of South Africa.

It is in this context that the Scorpions were created. In the wake of the findings of the TRC, South Africa desperately needed to engender in both its citizens and potential foreign investors a sense of confidence in the criminal justice system, and rebrand South Africa as a safe destination for investment.

Equality before the law as heresy

The arrival of freedom and democracy in South Africa brought with it, among other things, the need for a transition from an old antiquated criminal justice system to a modern system.

Before the demise of apartheid, black life outside the confines of designated living areas was essentially criminalised, as was any resistance to the apartheid state. The inversion of what we today consider to be justice and fairness, legality and equality, was for centuries considered the norm in South Africa. Thus, the criminal justice system served exclusively to protect colonial and white minority rule and their economic interests in South Africa. The decriminalisation of black life as a whole is thus a recent phenomenon in terms of the law in South Africa and the notion of equality before the law.

It is in this context that we need to locate and interpret some of the root causes of crime. I am not suggesting that if black life had not been criminalised we would not have such high levels of crime. Neither am I suggesting that the legal protection for white privilege and status in South Africa was acceptable. What I am alluding to is the absence of a shared national psyche – a shared historical legacy where an entire nation knows what it means to live within the confines of the legal prescripts of equality before the law, regardless of colour or creed.

One must not underestimate the deep levels of mistrust of the criminal justice system held by the majority of the black population – a system which excluded and brutalised black life. Similarly, one should never underestimate the legal and legislative lengths to which the rich and powerful will go in order to protect their interests, especially their economic interests.

Thus, one of the critical areas of government requiring radical transformation was the criminal justice system, with particular reference to the police and the prosecution service. These two capacities were two sides of the same coin used by the apartheid state to enforce its racist policies.

Understandably, then, the transformation of the police and the prosecution service would need to be institutional in character, and depended more on substantive reorientation of the law than the personality of the leadership.[2]

It is in this context that the rapid creation of the Scorpions six years into the new South African democracy is located.

South Africa as a haven for criminality

The post-1994 media image of South Africa, both locally and internationally, was that of a place where levels of serious violent crime, as well as crimes committed by more organised criminal networks, were rapidly on the increase. Like many other emerging democracies, South Africa grapples with the very serious threat posed by organised crime to the safety and security of its people, as well as to the integrity of its economic and democratic institutions.

Barely 16 years ago, South Africa transitioned from a closed and isolated apartheid society to being a member of the free world. Suddenly the infant called the new South Africa had to compete with established elders in the game of global economic competitiveness. In terms of criminal justice issues and the challenge posed by organised crime, South Africa quickly discovered that the world was indeed a global village. Its antiquated justice systems needed to adapt to the modern world, which by and large recognised that the stable financial institutions of a transitioning South Africa made it vulnerable as both a base for organised crime and a conduit of the proceeds of organised crime.

South Africa thus had to modernise its criminal justice system in order to respond with dynamism and relevance to external threats. The creation of the Scorpions was in part a response to this challenge.

Material conditions facing criminal justice

A pre–1994 insular existence

A constant and justifiable refrain in the context of the review of the first 16 years of democracy is that we have come a long way in a short space of time.

The first feature of earlier times was that the criminal justice system and its enforcers of law enjoyed no legitimacy as far as the majority of South Africans were concerned. In short there was no public support for law enforcement.

The second feature of the old system was that there was a serious lack of investigative capacity within the ranks of law enforcement officials, and the police in particular. In a context where the performance indicator was the level of brute force used, there was no need to develop investigative skill or use any definable investigative methodology to prove one's case. Therefore no real investigative training took place prior to 1994. The focus of policing and indeed the broader criminal justice system was the elimination of the enemies of the white minority state, and not the protection of the civil liberties and human rights of the citizens of the country.

Of course, the greatest irony of all is that the erstwhile enemies of the state are now in fact the state. And the former enforcers of apartheid are now called upon to enforce democracy – an unfamiliar and unpleasant task for some. Yes, the balance of political power has shifted. The challenge was and remains to ensure that the practice of criminal justice reflects a similar shift.

A third feature of the pre-1994 criminal justice system was that law enforcement officials did not respect the rights of people. Suspects were convicted on the basis of confessions extracted by force. It would therefore not be inaccurate to describe the pre-1994 criminal justice system of South Africa as a confession-based system. The current challenge for both police official and prosecutor is to get a conviction based on objective evidence – a strange phenomenon in the pre-1994 era.

The fourth feature of the pre-1994 criminal justice system is that crime was predictable and stereotyped. For many years South Africa was geographically isolated due to its pariah status. A result of the isolation was that certain crime phenomena were unknown to South Africa in the pre-1994 era – for example the Nigerian phenomenon.

Another result of the isolation was that, up until 1994, South Africa had not been used as a serious transit point for the drug trafficking trade.

Challenges posed by transition

With the advent of democratic change, the adoption of a Constitution and a Bill of Rights, the criminal justice system faced a new set of challenges. Five major changes are worth mentioning.

The first and probably most dramatic was that the new Constitution outlawed torture. All evidence obtained in contravention of the rights of the people was inadmissible. All law enforcement officials were forced to operate under the provisions of the Bill of Rights. Ironically, the then dominant law enforcers saw the Constitution and the Bill of Rights as the enemy, and as favouring the rights of the criminal.

The second change facing the criminal justice system was that within a relatively short time, the criminal landscape of South Africa was populated with crime groups formerly unknown in South Africa. South Africa's unique location, relatively sophisticated infrastructure and many, and fairly porous, borders, turned the country into the playground of international criminal organisations fleeing intensified law enforcement activity in their countries of origin. South Africa had increasingly become a target for international drug syndicates, both as a market, and a conduit for onward distribution. At home, right before our eyes, we saw rudimentary criminals develop overnight into sophisticated criminal organisations, engaged in sophisticated and profitable car-hijacking rings, cash-in-transit heists, gun-running, protection rackets, and professional hit-men operating in the local taxi-industry.

The second challenge, therefore, was to accept that relatively strong infrastructure (both financial and physical) is susceptible to crime syndicates who will manipulate and maximise such an infrastructure for criminal activity. The challenge is therefore to quickly put in place systems and structures to ensure that the infrastructure is not manipulated by unscrupulous crime bosses.

A third challenge facing the new criminal justice system was the appearance of vigilante groups. The inability on the part of law enforcement to deal with the upsurge in criminal activity provided fertile ground for vigilante groups to fill the gap. In Cape Town we had the problems of groups involved in high-profile murders of gang leaders and drug dealers, ostensibly to rid the community of the scourge of crime. We experienced an upsurge in drive-by shootings, bomb attacks and other organised criminal activity. Bombings of American franchises posed new challenges to law enforcement in South Africa. Such incidents of urban terror were the cause of considerable local and international concern.

The conventional approach to law enforcement was ineffective in dealing with the challenges just identified. What we were up against were sophisticated groups of criminals who plan, organise and assess the risks involved in what they are doing and adapt accordingly. At best, as law enforcement, we were able to target the foot soldiers. The leaders of these organisations remain notoriously immune to prosecution.

The fourth challenge faced by a new criminal justice system was the issue of trust. The new black political leadership of the country needed to find a way to trust the "old guard" – those enforcers whose previous targets were the very political masters whom they were now called upon to serve. In a situation of very little trust, the challenge for law enforcement was to "find each" – and to do so in a hurry.

The fifth challenge had to do with the nature of the system itself. The inherited criminal justice system, designed for the prosecution of the majority and the protection of a small white minority, was characterised by antiquated management systems based on tradition rather than creativity, on tenure rather than excellence. The "old guard" were guaranteed their jobs, regardless of their performance. In this regard the performance-driven culture of the Scorpions facilitated the implementation of a performance-management system which later became a standard feature of the entire prosecution service as well as a benchmark for the senior management system (SMS) of the public service.

Elements of a new vision

Given such material conditions and circumstances, how then do you create a criminal justice vision for the future – and not only create the vision but deliver such a vision?

One of the elements of the vision needed to include transformation. The need to radically transform the criminal justice system was imperative.

For the National Prosecuting Authority, transformation meant that the organisation needed to be representative of the majority of the people in terms of race and gender. Furthermore, the criminal justice system needed to be people-oriented and not a system serving itself.

As time moved on, it became increasingly difficult to separate the successes of the Scorpions from those of the prosecuting authority, since the NDPP was the political and custodial head of both entities.

As top management, we had many heated debates and management-turf battles regarding the core methodological orientation of the organisation. These choices would not only determine the texture of the management culture but would fundamentally affect the orientation of the training required for young recruits and the competencies that needed to be nurtured.

One view was that the Scorpions should be intelligence-led, which would suggest that the intelligence agencies should be the ultimate home of the Scorpions. The argument was supported by the fact that no successful investigation or prosecution can take place without good intelligence, defined mainly as undercover operations.

The opposing school of thought argued that our aim should be to prosecute and not merely disrupt criminal activity. It was held, therefore, that the operations of the Scorpions should be prosecution-led.

Since we were housed in the office of the prosecution service and since possession is nine-tenths of the law, the management of the Scorpions shifted in style and focus. The prosecutors won the day. Resultantly, the umpteenth draft of the proposed DSO legislation was amended, entrenching in law what had become more and more the practice, namely that the head of the Scorpions would be a prosecutor, indeed a D-NDPP – Deputy-National Director of Public Prosecutions.

The original management team of the DSO – the team that gave birth to the Scorpions – was thus forcefully shifted to make way for a bullish prosecution service who felt that they had won the battle for the soul of the Scorpions by entrenching in law their control of the organisation.

The original hope and aim of inspiring the creation of an independently minded forensic investigative capacity gave way to an apartheid-era mindset which treated investigators as second-class professionals when compared to the status accorded to lawyers. Dark clouds were beginning to gather on the horizon.

In the final analysis, the Scorpion organisation became a prosecutor-managed (as opposed to an investigator-managed) organisation, thus expanding and entrenching prosecutorial methodology into managerial control. The Scorpion investigators found out what it was like to be treated by prosecutors who had traditionally only dealt with uneducated and unskilled police officers.

Notwithstanding the emerging organisational shifts and competing organisational cultures, the core group of Scorpion senior executives and the first generation of young recruits provided the energy for the broader transformation within the National Prosecution Service.

After many hours and consultative sessions, the Scorpions and their institutional host and new managerial bosses, namely the prosecution service, crafted a vision as *Justice in our society so that people can live in peace and security*. The direct application and mantra for the Scorpions went further and said that *We want to be loved by the people, feared by the criminal and respected by our peers*.

The second component of a new criminal justice vision was inclusivity. The design of the post-1994 criminal justice system was to ensure that it reflected the aspirations of the 40 million black majority population and not the exclusive needs of the three million white minority. The old system was not only ineffectual for the needs of the vast majority but also wasteful in terms of resources. Furthermore, a brand-new management system was needed – one that recognised performance rather than tenure.

The third deliverable in terms of vision was to *create legislation* and design structures to deal effectively with organised crime and its effects in South Africa. In a relatively short time a number of legal instruments were made available to investigators and prosecutors. These included the National Prosecuting Authority Act, the Prevention of Organised Crime Act, the creation of a Financial Intelligence Centre, and the ongoing transformation of the financial and economic architecture of the public and private sector.

From vision to strategy

To translate vision into reality two things needed to happen, namely, a focus on the money, and the creation of a world-class investigative capacity.[3] The translation of vision into reality requires a different managerial approach, especially when creating an organisation "on-the-trot".

Go for the money

We realised very early that imprisonment alone was not a sufficient deterrent to criminals. The prisons themselves simply become another operating base for sophisticated and powerful crime bosses. Our analysis showed us that organised crime is fuelled by three things: market demand, high returns and low risk.

Our challenge was to increase the risk to organised-crime bosses, limit the profit margins and if possible, eliminate the market demand. We therefore moved in unashamedly to reclaim our turf. The penalties imposed by the Prevention of Organised Crime Act are stiff and the terms of imprisonment long. The new legal instrument (i.e. POCA) also named other offences such as racketeering. Membership of a proven criminal enterprise thus became punishable under law. We found out that there is nothing that hurts modern crime bosses more than to take away their assets and freeze their money, wherever it is in the world.[4]

With the benefit of the experiences of our international partners like the FBI and Scotland Yard, we in South Africa realised very early that the most dangerous of criminals are those able to destabilise an economy through their manipulation of the money markets for purpose of laundering the proceeds of crime. Thus, the new mafia boss is not necessarily the traditional Al Capone, but more likely a corporate executive able to hide money gained by dubious means.[5]

Operating context

For the first 18 months of its existence the Scorpions operated in a context of legal uncertainty and on the basis of borrowed powers in terms of the agencies represented by those members seconded to the Scorpions.

Miraculously, within the first three years and amidst strong opposition from other competing agencies, the Scorpions managed to make some inroads into crime phenomena which plagued South Africa. A combination of prosecution-led investigative techniques, following the money, some skilful undercover work and high-visibility arrests of suspects radically altered not only the levels of organised crime, but also the perceptions and consciousness of the vast majority of South Africans with regard to the effectiveness of the new brand of law enforcement.

Integration with existing capacity

It took great effort, but within a short period the capacity building and training-and-development programme of the Scorpions was able to produce an emerging investigator resource. This gave credence to the view that the former investigating directorates, namely IDSEO and IDOC, be disbanded, and amalgamated with what was a thriving independent Scorpion investigative capacity. Traditional law enforcement did not expect a generation of young, mainly black university graduates to outperform themselves or the expectations of the President of South Africa. The fact that the President himself personally visited the trainees at their training camps outside the country, and posed with them for photo opportunities, boosted these young graduates' self esteem and sense of national pride. As management we went to great lengths to nurture the mystique surrounding the operations of the Scorpions, leaving South Africa with the impression that there was a Scorpion around every dark corner.

Legal framework and mandate

Any rehearsing of the merits of the mandate of the Scorpions is, of course, purely academic, given its disbandment and subsequently being superseded by the Hawks.[6] It is worth noting that in spite of a rather broad legislative mandate, the Scorpion management did continually prioritise their efforts and capacity. For example, during the early days, the prioritisation and focus in respect of the category of offences was a 60% focus on offences (or unlawful conduct) committed in an organised fashion, 30% on corruption; and 10% constituting a broad category of offences including referrals by the National Director and other statutory bodies and a selection of specified offences.

After 18 months of ultra-careful investigative work, noting that the constitutional basis and mandate of the Scorpion unit was not yet finalised, it was a miracle that the unit managed to be so successful. If success was not attained by way of securing a prosecution, at least the unit was successful in being able to provide South Africa with a different consciousness about what can be accomplished if there is sufficient political and managerial will to make it happen.[7]

Subsequent developments in the organisation of the Scorpions need not detain us here. Suffice it to say that the organisation eventually became bogged down in bureaucratic administration, while at the same time becoming vulnerable to powerful political forces. The flare of the first generation of starry-eyed university graduates who subjected themselves to gruelling bootcamps and survival training both locally and internationally, was fast disappearing. The private sector unashamedly began to poach these surprise products of state-sponsored training and affirmation – the world-class South African forensic investigator which apartheid could not produce, and which our new democracy was unable to retain.

A new consciousness

The legacy of the Scorpions is still to be properly assessed and debated. Strangely, former management personnel remain tight-lipped, and current political sensitivities are too high to soberly appreciate the innovation and success, against the odds, achieved by an enthusiastic squad of young, mainly black South African university graduates determined to "do their country proud". Where did their enthusiasm come from? There are three observations and matters that deserve mention as we try to make sense of this emerging new consciousness not only among the recruits but also within society at large.

Performing to international standards
The first observation is that the Scorpion organisation produced high-calibre and well-trained forensic investigators. In terms of the international training undergone by the first generation of recruits, the Scorpions were the only international unit allowed to complete the full FBI course, formerly exclusively reserved for the FBI's US citizens. The customised Scotland Yard training programme was no less intensive given its punctilious attention to the skill of accurate statement-taking.

Debunking "technicality" myths
A second observation is that it took only a small crew of competent and

well-trained investigators to change public perception about crime and its benefits. Scorpion investigators proved that it was not only criminals who reaped benefits from our democracy.

The careful forensic work of the young Scorpion investigators ensured that the cases presented in court were thoroughly investigated and well prepared, thereby reinforcing the correctness of our Constitution and its Bill of Rights which provides protection for all citizens, including criminals.

Notwithstanding the challenges from legal counsel representing criminals, the reality is that, since the inception of the Bill of Rights, our courts have developed a complex body of constitutional criminal jurisprudence that is a virtual mine-field for the average prosecutor, never mind the average investigator. Just a cursory glance at the grounds upon which cases are thrown out of court on a daily basis bears testimony to this fact.

This is a phenomenon far from unique to South Africa. Other constitutional democracies experience the same problems. Many times, initially simple concepts of fairness and justice have been woven into an intricate constitutional matrix laced with legal land mines. Law-enforcement professionals need to constantly apply the law to new situations. The young Scorpion investigators showed a tremendous amount of adeptness, thus entrenching the gains of democracy and human rights rather undermining it through less-than-superior investigative work.

Legal counsel for criminals, in general, and organised crime bosses, in particular, have exploited the need of the criminal justice system to show fairness and just cause, as opposed to rumour and innuendo or dubious confessions from those who once-upon-a-time worked for the crime syndicate. Invariably, whenever criminals are faced with a formidable case, they focus the court's attention away from the determination of their innocence or guilt and turn the spotlight instead on the manner and propriety of the investigation. Every decision taken in the course of the investigation is attacked, from the application for a search warrant to every aspect of how the warrant was effected. Complex investigations into an organised crime syndicate become easily undone as a result of some irregularity in, for example, the appointment of the investigating officer that effected the arrest. Nothing erodes confidence in the criminal justice system more than when members of the public see someone get off on a technicality.

Interception and monitoring

The third observation regarding the legacy of the Scorpions is that complex methodology was no longer considered a hurdle. It is a fact that in complex organised-crime investigations, the investigative methodologies commonly used are even more vulnerable to attack. Applications for the interception and monitoring of telecommunications, or wire-taps, and the infiltration of informants into the criminal organisation are very effective against organised-crime figures, but are also notoriously vulnerable to attack in court.

Sadly, in South Africa it is not just the fact that criminal law has become increasingly complex. We have the added problems of the low levels of education and skill of police officers, low salaries and low morale that have also contributed to poorly investigated cases, which in turn have become fair game during the trial. It is often at the investigation stage that mistakes are made, which ultimately result in the exclusion of evidence with the eventual acquittal of the accused. It is for this very reason that the primary focus of the Scorpion unit was its training and development portfolio.

Conclusion

The period immediately following the 1994 democratic elections posed some extraordinary challenges for the new black-majority government as it took office. A fundamental challenge we faced then and continue to face is to build the public trust in the rule of law – to facilitate the paradigm shift from a confession-based approach to an evidence-based approach to investigation and prosecution.

I have outlined how we, the top management team of the Scorpions, applied modern business principles to the operations of the Scorpions by attracting people with the right blend of skill and commitment in an increasingly complex investigative and legal environment.

Six years into our new democracy, Parliament passed amendments to the National Prosecuting Authority Act, 61 of 2000 which, according to its preamble, were aimed at making provision for the establishment of an Investigating Directorate (i.e. the Scorpions) with limited investigative capacity, to prioritise and to investigate particularly serious criminal or unlawful conduct, and with the object of prosecuting such offences or unlawful conduct in the most efficient and effective manner. Barely ten years thereafter, the Scorpions were disbanded and rebranded as the Hawks.

In our current attempts to address the high levels of crime and violence in our society, the Scorpions experiment provides useful lessons regarding how to fundamentally and positively alter the consciousness of a nation – from haters and despisers of the police and a distrust in law enforcement towards a unit that desired to be loved by the people, feared by the criminals and respected by its peers.

The lifespan of the Scorpions may have been short. However, the lessons regarding consciousness-building and development have barely begun. The fact of the matter is that a nation's psyche truly can be shifted. As I often said to my trainees: All it takes is a sting in the right place from a Scorpion to bring down an elephant.

Notes

1 Jean Redpath's 2004 monograph analysing the Scorpions is one of only a few texts available on the inner workings of the Scorpions. The Khampepe Commission of Enquiry (report submitted to the Presidency in February 2006) is another such document. Redpath makes the observation that outside of the police, the Scorpions were probably the most recognised law enforcement body in South Africa. She goes on to say that "The impact of the Scorpions on the South Africa public's psyche after four years of operation cannot be underestimated" (*The Scorpions – Analysing the Directorate of Special Operations* (ISS Monograph Series No.96, p.9). This was in spite of the fact that, at the time, very little was known about the inner workings of the organisation.

2 The April 2010 transformation and restructuring programme of the Prosecuting Authority under the leadership of Menzi Simelane, appointed as NDPP by President Zuma, has been controversial to the extent that no less than the President himself has needed to intervene and put on hold Simelani's intended restructuring rollout plan which would have seen many specialised units disbanded (See Zuma freezes Simelani's NPA strategy (May 14, 2010) http://www.newstime.co.za/rs_headlines.asp?recid=5384. Simelane's appointment as NDPP comes a decade after that of the first NDPP in the democratic era, Bulelani Ngcuka, who similarly embarked on a major restructuring of the Prosecuting Authority. The Ngcuka era saw a fundamental restructuring of the prosecuting authority utilising a budget of hundreds of millions of South African taxpayers' money to create a more efficient and effective criminal justice system as it related to prosecutions. As part of this process we saw, for example, the creation of specialised investigative and prosecutorial units such as IDSEO, IDOC, not least the Scorpions, AFU (Asset Forfeiture Unit), Sexual Offenses Unit to name a few. The Simelani era of restructuring of the Prosecuting Authority, on the surface, appears to be an undoing of the systems, procedures and structures put in place during the Ngcuka era and further developed by Vusi Pikoli (the successor to Ngcuka) who vacated his post after reaching a settlement with government and in the context of his quest to arrest and charge the then National Commissioner of Police, Jackie Selebi, for corruption and a range of crimes using POCA legislation.

3 The Scorpion organisation did not suddenly appear in an operational investigative vacuum. It was preceded by what could be described as a number of uncoordinated precedents. Transformation within the criminal justice sector was gathering momentum in the wake of the

1994 democratic elections and the revelations and subsequent findings of the TRC. Ongoing restructuring within the police service meant that a number of specialist police units were closed down including the infamous police "death squads" and Vlakplaas operations linked to Eugene de Kock, dubbed South Africa's prime evil. Some of the specialist police skills were absorbed by newly established commissions and investigating directorates including the Special Investigating Unit (SIU) initially headed up by Judge Willem Heath and a forerunner to the Asset Forfeiture Unit now headed by Willie Hofmeyer and located in the office of the NDPP. The SIU was an anti-corruption unit originally set up to investigate the theft of state assets in the Eastern Cape, in particular. During the early days of a transforming Prosecution Service, two investigating directorates were created and located in the office of the NDPP namely IDSEO and IDOC – both promulgated in 1998. IDSEO focused on commercial crimes and IDOC on organised crime and terrorism. Both the IDSEO and IDOC units utilised investigative personnel who were seconded from the South African Police Service. These personnel were hardly ever properly or formally trained yet had a depth of experience. There was no deliberate drive within the apartheid criminal justice system to develop this kind of specialist forensic capacity given the "confessional" approach to criminal justice in the pre-1994 era. The Scorpion intervention and innovation was the deliberate training and insertion into the criminal justice system a range of properly trained investigators and analysts. In terms of methodology the aim was to combine three intersecting areas of operational skill – prosecution, crime data collection and investigation (in Scorpion circles commonly called the "troika" approach). Hence it was decided to recruit young starry-eyed university graduates, with no political baggage but with qualifications in specialist areas such as Information Technology, Finance and Commerce, Law, and Natural Science and create a cross-pollination of the various disciplines in order to give rise to a vibrant multi-disciplinary "troika" approach to dealing with serious economic crime and organised crime. Candidates of such a calibre would by definition attract a salary superior to the average apartheid-created police officer.

4   The Prevention of Organised Crime Act 121 of 1998 (POCA) provides that property obtained by means of criminal activities may be forfeited to the South African State.

5   The widely reported 2 July 2010 Johannesburg High Court verdict of "guilty of corruption but not defeating the ends of justice" was a devastating blow for Jackie Selebi, appointed as South Africa's first black National Commissioner of Police in 2000. Selebi has been on trial for the past four years and at a cost of excess of R14m to the South African taxpayer. The prosecution case was driven, methodologically, by the mantra "go for the money" and exposed how Selebi had taken bribe money emanating from organised crime syndication. (See http://www.sowetan.co.za/News/Article.aspx?id=1157419)

6   Government decided to disband the Scorpions notwithstanding the findings and recommendations of the Khampepe Commission of Enquiry regarding its mandate and location of the DSO. The findings, in the main, were that the DSO was not unconstitutional and the its location in the NDPP was jurisprudentially sound particularly in the context of the Troika methodology. Judge Khampepe contextualised the formation of the Scorpions saying that "something drastic had to be done to curtail impermissible levels of organised crime and the strain on law enforcement compounded by certain corrupt elements within the police force. For that reason, there was a need to create a multidisciplinary unit such as the DSO incorporating the *troika* principle. There was also consensus that the unit should be placed outside the SAPS". (For a full transcript of the *Khampepe report see the Khampepe Commission of Inquiry into the Mandate and Location of the Directorate of Special Operations ("The DSO")* http://www.thepresidency.gov.za/main.asp?include=docs/reports/khampepe/index.html

Amidst the politicking around the closure of the Scorpion unit and the migration of its capacity to the police managed unit called the Hawks, Johannesburg-based businessman Hugh Glenister unsuccessfully sought from the Pretoria High Court an urgent interdict against the government's plan to pass legislation that was intended to disestablish the Directorate of Special Operations (DSO) – otherwise known as the Scorpions. (*See* Urgent interdict launched to prevent disbanding of Scorpions http://www.legalbrief.co.za/article.

php?story=20080318123924855)

7   Notwithstanding the 2010 guilty verdict, Selebi, ten years before, in his augural speech as National Commissioner of Police said that "police is not just about arresting suspects and recovering stolen property ...[but also] to ensure a stable democracy which is conducive to sound governance, create an environment that is conducive to economic growth and ensure acceptable basic service delivery for all the people of South Africa." (See www.saps.gov.za) It is further noteworthy to recall Jackie Selebi's speech to my recruits at the first Scorpion Graduation Ceremony (soon after Selebi's appointment as National Commissioner of Police) held at the "secret" police training camp somewhere north of Pretoria where the Scorpions underwent their bootcamp training. Selebi made the emphatic point that the police will sort out its own corruption issues internally and did not need the Scorpions to help with this particular task. A lot has happened since these speeches were made ten years ago.

17 | Industrial terrorism and the Jipsa moment

We are neither producing nor retaining enough skilled patriots to manage our own economy.

This chapter identifies, describes and analyses a third, short-lived, moment of positive consciousness in South Africa called the Jipsa moment.

The Joint Initiative on Priority Skills Acquisition (Jipsa) moment is not unlike the TRC or Scorpion moments discussed in previous chapters – all short yet profoundly significant moments in the transformation trajectory that facilitated a shift in the way South Africans think about their nationhood and matters relative to national identity. The central argument in this book is that South Africa needs another moment of consciousness if it is to make a substantial and sustainable shift from poverty to prosperity; from unemployment to a labour-absorbing pro-employment economy; and from crime to a more peaceful existence in South Africa. The Jipsa moment, more than any other, helps us to contextualise the ultimate solution, namely a shift towards industrial consciousness as the key determinant of our collective and prosperous future.

Scarcity and incapacity: When did it start?

The apartheid state actively sabotaged the economy by lighting the fuse of a skills-deficiency bomb, which the incoming black majority government failed to defuse when it took over the reign of power in 1994. This is nowhere more graphically illustrated and evident in the area of artisan training. In 1985, for example, South Africa enrolled 26 500 apprentices (mainly white), of which only 13 500 passed their trade test. By 2006, just over two decades later, South Africa only managed to enrol 9 041 apprentices, with only 3 222 passing their trade test that year. During this 20-year period of declining apprentice and artisan numbers and the consequential deskilling of the industrial base of the economy, South Africa's political control changed hands peacefully – from apartheid to democracy.

Some 12 years after the introduction of multi-party democracy into South Africa which occurred in 1994, the apartheid skills bomb exploded and in its wake has left enormous collateral damage to the economy and the psyche of a black majority population which had prepared themselves for decades to reap the benefit of liberation and freedom from apartheid. The explosion and subsequent damage referred to here is the realisation and official acknowledgement of a chronic skills shortage, particularly within the industrial sector.

It is often argued that the skills crisis is a global phenomenon and therefore South Africa should not be too paranoid about its lack of skills. The effect of such an argument is to diminish the dire impact of the skills crisis on South Africa – a country that has never had a sufficiently strong or racially diverse industrial skills base and therefore no skills safety net to fall back on to. It is sobering to recall that it was only as recently as 1981 that people of colour were allowed to be indentured as apprentices with the opportunity of becoming artisans. In addition, the artisans which are being produced by South Africa are being snapped up by First World countries who are able to pay a better hourly rate. So the challenge facing South Africa is two-fold: rapid training combined with a retention strategy.

The anatomy of a rude awakening

A defining moment

The Jipsa moment of awakening took place during the period 2005/06 when the political leaders were plotting an economic growth plan for the country. President Thabo Mbeki at the Cabinet Lekgotla (strategic planning session) of July 2005 appointed his Deputy, Phumzile Mlambo-Ngcuka to assemble a task team to identify constraints in the economy and to propose interventions to increase the capacity for growth to a sustainable 6% per year in the long term, and address challenges emerging within the second economy. The mandate was clearly to "think out of the box".

By February 2006, Deputy President Mlambo-Ngcuka and her team, supported by a small group of specialists from various government departments and co-ordinated by the Presidency, had created a framework document which set the overarching objectives for the Accelerated and Shared Growth Initiative for South Africa (AsgiSA). These objectives were clear and concise:

- To reduce the unemployment rate from 30% to 15% by 2014.
- To reduce poverty from one-third to one-sixth of the population by 2014.
- To increase the annual GDP growth rate from 3% to 4,5% per year for the period 2005 to 2009 and to 6% for the period 2010 to 2014. This target should create a sustainable annual growth rate of 6%.

An almost immediate realisation from the Deputy President's team showed that the single most constraining factor to economic growth was the shortage of skills. Hurriedly, a skills strategy called Jipsa was designed and launched on 26 March 2006, barely a month after the announcement of the economic growth plan which was called AsgiSA.

Thus, literally within weeks, the Jipsa initiative became government's high-level intervention (and hoped-for solution) to the skills crisis.

Jipsa cannot be understood in isolation from its mothership called AsgiSA, and its impact cannot be assessed without appreciating that its impetus came from the most powerful office in the land, the Presidency itself. The current and ongoing skills and training crisis in South Africa no doubt has its roots in the apartheid era, with particular reference to apartheid's education policy of inferior education for people not classified as white. Yet, while apartheid education policy, in general, had its roots in the 1950s, it was in the mid-1980s, in collaboration with private and white-owned business, that the apartheid regime decided against stopping the rapid decline in the training of artisans and other engineering professionals required by the last days of apartheid and indeed the first democratic economy of South Africa.

Why did it take more than a decade for the new and first black-majority government of South Africa to wake up to the scarce skills reality? Was it a lack of industrial consciousness on the part of the incoming revolutionaries?

Terrorism and the surprise factor

In 2005/06 the new South Africa's economic aspirations as articulated by the ANC-led government came under severe terrorist attack. The near-fatal blow was the realisation by the Mbeki cabinet that the major constraint to achieving economic growth was the critical skills shortage facing South Africa. The AsgiSA/Jipsa analysis was more specific in that it identified a range of artisan and engineering professional skills as being absolutely critical and necessary if the economy was to recover and grow. The required yet absent skills were thus dubbed scarce and critical skills, thereby creating a whole new discourse within the industrial mind-space of South Africa.

In many respects, the discourse is still dominated by a "scarcity" (as opposed to an "abundance") conceptual framework. In other words, the solutions paradigm is primarily driven by a solution to the scarcity and shortage needs. However, what soon became evident but had not yet dominated the discourse to the same degree was the issue of capability. The debate and emotions concerning the skills shortage factor soon gave way to the added dimension of capability. Suddenly the conceptual and real challenge shifted from facing an unemployment problem to an unemployability problem. It appeared as if training and education systems of the country were producing people that were of no use to the economy other than that of unskilled labour. Perhaps a useful window into this matter is South Africa's poor performance in the areas of maths and science outputs from our school benches. The basic language of industry is maths and science, and yet our systems were producing learners with gross deficiencies in terms of this language capability.

An undetected and growing cancer

By 1994, at the time of the democratic takeover of South Africa, there was already a 50% drop in the artisan output, with only 7 000 artisans passing their trade test in 1994. Under the leadership of an ANC-led government, the numbers continued to decline so that in 2004, only 2 548 artisans successfully completed their trade tests.[1] This means that between the mid-1980s and mid-2000s there was a more than 80% reduction in the number of artisans produced in South Africa.

Should the alarm bells not have rung in 1994 when the artisan output had dwindled to 50% of the then artisan output figures? If the information was then not available, should the question about artisan output not have been asked, at least? Stated differently, what do you do when 12 years later you realise you do not have the fuel required to re-industrialise the base of the economy, namely the required industrial skills set?

In terms of the above reframing of the artisan numbers, the political victory of 1994 suddenly seems to have a rather hollow ring to it, given that it was only a matter of time before the ticking skills bomb would explode and the economy would run out of the skills required to keep it alive.

We are left asking whether the skills crisis is the result of free market fiscal discipline and sensitivity, or instead, hard core ideological warfare where, as far as apartheid beneficiaries were concerned, it was simply a matter of time before the black government would find itself in an embarrassing and vulnerable situation with regard to a lack of skills. The net result would be that the black government would come crawling back to the former white ruling class for assistance – a class that currently holds the country hostage through superior skills. All this, of course, though speculative, fundamentally undermines the intent of BEE, since the dependency of the economy on white skill is blatantly obvious, but not something the ruling party will readily admit.

A new language is created

The net outcome of the AsgiSA and Jipsa activities was the adoption of a wide yet unspoken mantra for economic revival in South Africa; 50 000 trained and productive artisans, and an additional 4 000 engineers by 2010, if we are to achieve a 6% growth rate and begin to substantially reduce unemployment to 15% by 2014. The new mantra (i.e. new target) as per the Industrial Policy Plan (IPAP2) released in February 2010 may well be its signalling of the creation of 2,2 million jobs by 2020. To the 2,2 million jobs target one must add the visionary proposal by big business called Vision 2040 – which constitutes a target of doubling the economy over a period of 30 years.[2]

What we can say at this early stage is that by all accounts, the South African ship has been steadied and is still afloat even if many find it difficult to accommodate the political leadership change in the country. The challenge is to find a way to steady the ship even more to be able to withstand severe storms which are threatening on the horizon. Perhaps another Jipsa is needed?

The big debates and questions

Four debates

The first big debate relates to infrastructure development. It remains debatable as to whether the re-industrialisation of the South African economy via the mass-scale public works programme is the proper solution. Government has made a decision to invest billions of rands in infrastructure development – a programme which fundamentally presupposes the need for the training of at least 50 000 artisans by 2010.

The second debate relates to how the first 16 years of democracy in South Africa have been characterised by unprecedented economic growth and accompanying fiscal stability – but 16 years of largely jobless growth and the concomitant failure to systematically address the rampant poverty in our land.

The third debate relates to the systematic decline of the industrial base of the South African economy. It has already been noted that the 1980s saw a steady and, in my opinion, deliberately orchestrated decline in the industrial capabilities of our economy. The realisation in the mid 2000s of a more than 80% reduction in the industrial capacity of the required workforce is beyond a crisis.

The fourth area of debate relates to whether the epicentre of a growth and development strategy for an emerging economy such as South Africa should in fact be skills acquisition and development.

These are the debates. However, it seems that the horse has already bolted from the stable. The time for debate is rather limited. It is time for action and delivery. So if the script has been written (i.e. AsgiSA, Jipsa, and now IPAP 2), the war fields defined (i.e. industrial training with special reference to artisan training), the size of the army established (i.e. 50 000 artisans and counting) – and the new generals appointed (i.e. the Zuma government), why are we not marching to war?

The Jipsa emergency response

What was Jipsa and how did it work

Jipsa[3] was initially envisaged to have a lifespan of 18 months, which was extended for a second 18-month period to the end of March 2009. The Zuma administration has envisaged the incorporation of the content and impetus of Jipsa into a wider human resource development (HRD) strategy to be funded and managed by the Education Department.[4]

To appreciate the emergence of Jipsa, the apologists for Jipsa point out that one must bear in mind that in the years since the democratic elections of 1994, significant efforts have been made to restructure institutional support for skills development, including the introduction of the sector education and training authorities (Setas) and an increased focus on technical training. However, the lack of interface between the users and suppliers of human capital meant that these institutions were not effective in developing the skills required by the economy.

In March 2006, Jipsa was established to be that much-needed interface to accelerate the provision of priority skills acquisition.[5] The key to achieving the artisan throughput targets depended on gaining agreement on four matters:

1. The identity of 15 priority trades considered critical for industrial growth, as well as the requirements for each. These priority trades included automotive electricians, boilermakers, carpenters and joiners, diesel mechanics, earth-moving equipment mechanics, light and heavy electricians, fitters, fitters and turners, instrument mechanics, millwrights, motor mechanics, sheet metal trades workers, shutter hands and steel fixers, toolmakers and patternmakers, and welders.
2. The different pathways to attaining artisan status across the different trades (as outlined above).
3. The provision of financial support to employer-led initiatives through the fiscus, the National Skills Fund and Setas in addition to private-sector contributions.
4. Closer co-operation and co-ordination between the departments of Education and of Labour, and between government, business and labour.

The mandate period of Jipsa was too short to expect earth-shattering accomplishments. What Jipsa could do, at best, was signal the direction in which training and skills acquisition should happen.

Jipsa lessons

Where there is a political will, there is an economic way

The Jipsa moment holds many positive lessons for South Africa. The most positive is that a crisis that was detected and acknowledged by government, received urgent attention, and remedies were activated. Unfortunately, the detailed performance monitoring which was expected as the follow-through on the activated remedies leaves much to be desired.

With hindsight we may agree that the Jipsa intervention was too short, much like the brevity of the Scorpion and TRC moments. It will remain an open question as to whether the Jipsa moment actually facilitated a mindshift in South Africa. I would like to believe that at the very least, Jipsa laid the foundation for the development of such a paradigm of consciousness – something that now needs to be taken further.

Three major risks

There are at least three risk factors that must briefly be mentioned as we unpack the significance of the Jipsa moment.

Firstly, we need to ask if South Africa stands a chance of winning the race against time, given that it is currently at risk of losing its much-needed artisanal class through natural attrition and an aging workforce. The average South African artisan is between 55 and 60 years old, and mainly white.

Secondly, it is evident that both the state and private industry have a high level of reluctance to train apprentices. A point that I will labour here is that an artisan-base provides the fundamental skillset required to grow an industrialised economy. If South Africans are not employed, it is likely that industrialising countries such as China, Malaysia, Korea and India, as well as some traditional First World countries such as Germany, will be more than willing to export their labour to South Africa.

Thirdly, and probably most importantly, there seems to be a reluctance on the part of the youth of South Africa to want to become artisans. The South African psyche seems to be dominated by a prejudice against artisanal training, and in favour of university-based "engineering" education and training.

The remedy required to mitigate the risk

The three risk factors identified obstruct the imperative of getting tens of thousands of young people into apprenticeship programmes, notwithstanding the desire expressed by government to see 350 000 industrial apprenticeships and scarce skills learnerships set in place in the short term.[6] So what needs to be done to change this situation?

The primary condition required is that of an economy which offers real job opportunities supported by a state and business base willing to train and develop people over and above its own needs. The larger economic theory issue is whether the economy should be demand-driven or supply-driven. Another influencing factor is whether or not the economy should be driven by the imperatives of developmental state orthodoxy or left to the forces of the free market. These theoretical and ideological issues notwithstanding, it appears that the skills script has already been written. The targets set out by AsgiSA and Jipsa have not been met. Why have we not been able to mobilise the millions of available youth and channel them into the artisan training conduit?

In my view, the missing piece of the puzzle, and indeed the central theme of this book, is the need for a new mindset to govern the psyche of the entire population of South Africa, and not just those seeking employment in the industrial sector. It is this new mindset that will create the positive energy needed to propel the millions to find and indeed create the necessary job opportunities. Therefore, the answer to why we don't have millions of youth being industrially trained is not so much about the financial cost, but rather about the emotional and psychological orientation of our society as a whole. We need to change our mindset if we are going to make any significant dent in the skills crisis which daily gnaws away at the fabric of our fragile economy.

A further exacerbating factor and uniquely South African phenomenon is that we have thousands of industrial-skills oriented graduates flowing from our FET colleges who are seemingly unable to secure a job. It is not uncommon to find engineering graduates who have not worked since graduating ten years ago. Either there are no jobs in the economy, or the graduates are inappropriately skilled for the South African job market. Somewhere we are skipping a beat and wasting resources.

I wish to add a further dimension to this discussion, namely the issue of attitude and consciousness. A large proportion of currently unemployed graduates probably ended up at FET colleges because they could not find work in the market place, and attended the FET college in the meantime. This is unlike the approach of yesteryear when vocational training was linked to an existing job placement and you attended a block release course for a short period and returned to your work station. In this way the system ensured that the theory and practical aspects of your training were in synch. However, with the advent of the FET philosophy, the approach to vocational training was delinked from the needs and capacity of the economy. So school-leavers entered the FET college, many with the benefit of government bursaries, and the college itself heavily state-subsidised. Students thus completed their studies, for which they were probably never properly profiled either in terms of aptitude or attitude. The result is that we have ended up with tens of thousands of vocationally certified graduates whose conception of the world of work and work ethic are significantly out of tune with the demands of the workplace.

The provisions of South African labour legislation are generally pro-worker and pro-incompetence. It is almost impossible to fire an incompetent worker. An employer, being aware of the skills and attitudinal mismatch given our FET scenario, is far less likely to risk employing a South African graduate with suspect qualifications and an entitlement attitude, than he/she would be regarding the employment of foreign labour – who tend to have a very different attitude towards work. Speculatively, this may be one of the explanations why a contractor who was issued a South African government contract chose to import foreign unskilled Chinese labour rather than utilise the millions of available unskilled labourers on-tap in South Africa.[7]

The reality facing South Africa is that we, the citizens of a sovereign and independent state and proud members of an emerging democracy, will soon not be able to manage our own economy – if this is not already the case. As a result, we will be taken into economic slavery and remain in bondage in our own land for generations to come.

Dynamic private-public interface
So how do we work our way out of this deepening skills disaster? The first step, and most difficult in my view, is through the creation and adoption of an industrial consciousness as the new basis for national identity and patriotism in a new South Africa.

What the Jipsa moment displayed most brilliantly was the ability of government, in partnership with private industry, to shift fundamentally the mindset of the nation, change the discourse, and re-orientate the focus and expectations of the economy.

The challenge and solution, in my view, is to create another Jipsa-type moment – a new moment that will shift the psyche of the nation as it attempts to address a worsening unemployment and crime problem. But this time the shift in the psyche must be more deliberate, focused and sustainable if South Africa is to move from poverty to prosperity – through an economic growth strategy which is premised on a massive labour-absorbing economy. The proposed content of such a shift – and indeed the first step towards a solution to creating a pro-employment economy – is what I call industrial consciousness.

Further analytical considerations

Two steps forward, one step back
The unemployment pie of South Africa reflects that at least 60% of the unemployed (i.e. four million) is made up of youth between the ages of 18 and 25 years. So we have a youth-saturated and youth-driven unemployment problem as opposed to a mass of previously skilled and mature unemployed but employable citizens.[8]

Industrial myopia of the ruling class

With the benefit of hindsight, I suspect that it is not incorrect to assume that a necessary first strategic step for the South African black liberation movement in 1994 was to take over the security apparatus which was used by the apartheid state to brutally repress black people in the name of Afrikaner nationalism.

A logical and justifiable second strategic step for the incoming ANC-led liberation movement, it could be argued, would be to productively manage the rapidly deindustrialising economy of South Africa. In terms of timeline, one could argue that this decision was made 12 years too late.

In the wake of Mandela's reconciliation and healing presidency, I suggest it was Thabo Mbeki's job as Mandela's successor to fix the systems in the country and get the nation to work. In terms of the economy, the Mbeki strategy was a three-step process, namely to strengthen and consolidate the first economy, then meet challenges of the second economy, and finally to provide and refine the social security net.[9] The steady decline in the production of artisans either went unnoticed by the ANC-led government or was not considered an important issue as part of the takeover of the country in 1994.

The fact is that we now sit with a massive skills and education problem that is not going to go away quietly or easily. We need bold and innovative solutions which go beyond throwing more money at the problem, if we are going to win the skills war and consequently our war on crime and poverty. We need a generation of youth that are possessed with a dogged will and determination, supported by the highest authority in the land, if we are to rescue our economy and make it grow for the benefit of all.

Systems design problem

What makes university education the ultimate and desired goal of the learning pathway? Why is there only a limited aspiration on the part of young learners to go to technical school? My view is that this is a perception driven by the prejudices of the ruling party. We seem to have created a monster of tertiary-qualified young people who have skills but for whom there appears to be no demand. How do you tell a graduate that he/she does not have the right aptitude or attitude when they have a qualification to prove otherwise?

There is no doubt a systems design problem if our universities end up being choked up with students and our technical schools and technikons are empty. Traditionally sought-after and high-paying non-industrial professions such as medical doctors and lawyers do not grow an economy. It is the artisans who are absolutely critical to the growth of an economy such as South Africa.

The first generation of democracy babies have as their role models for success the BEE moguls. This generation have had no overt "indoctrination" which says that you need to work hard in a blue collar to achieve enough to shift your lifestyle options and chances of upgrading from a shack to a decent house. There is an aspirational mismatch between what government perceives to be the need to create an army of artisans to rescue the economy, and the role models flaunted by government and to which youngsters aspire. Put differently, very few school-leavers aspire to be tradesmen. They would rather become IT specialists, doctors or lawyers, regardless of their performance results at school. There is, of course, nothing wrong with such aspirations. But why is there not the same aspiration towards the blue-collar world? It is because industrial consciousness is not being promoted either at school level or at the level of social awareness.

So how are we going to get young people energised to become what the country needs as opposed to what the country is projecting as an aspirational element? The answer is simple; we need to change the messages we send to our young people – change the value that is being placed on artisans and manual labour.

Artisans are no doubt a key catalyst and requirement for the revitalisation of our economy; the ultimate liberation soldier if you will. So, what shall we call our army of soldiers and who will lead them into battle?

The AATP Case Study – a new training model

The most successful and innovative artisan training and development programme currently underway in South Africa is the Accelerated Artisan Training Programme (AATP) being piloted by the Manufacturing Engineering and Related Services Sector Education Training Authority (Merseta). Its roots lie deep in the metal industry. The challenge presented by Jipsa was to accelerate artisan training, and the Merseta, under the leadership of Dr Raymond Patel, rose to this challenge.[10] Not much has been written about this innovative experiment which is still in its pilot phase. However, two preliminary comments are pertinent to the current discussion given that the programme has just undergone a comprehensive external review.

Firstly, in terms of methodology, it was deemed important to ensure that there was a fundamental link between relevant workplace experience and the theory learnt at college. The programme was well-incentivised for the employer and the learner alike. The AATP programme required written and contractual support from no less than the CEO of a company in terms of guaranteeing placement and the application of theory to practice, which was linked to incentive payments.

This raises the second issue which is the cost of training. To date, the programme has reflected a direct claimable cost (by the employer) of up to approximately R145 000 to train a single apprentice. A further calculation shows that it costs the taxpayer approximately R1 million to train and develop seven artisans. The Jipsa target of 50 000 artisans will therefore cost in the region of R7 billion. Some analysts suggest that the real need is closer to 120 000 artisans required for the economy.

The design assumption of the AATP programme is premised on the view that it is possible to train a junior artisan in 18 months to two years and extend work experience into the next two years for further development rather than design a training programme for four years. Furthermore, the AATP programme was designed as a "training above equilibrium" approach. Companies were incentivised to train artisans over and above the needs of that particular company, hence the handsome financial incentive.

The aim of the pilot Merseta-driven AATP programme was to train 5 620 apprentices over a three-year period starting in 2007, aligned with the Jipsa imperatives. However, notwithstanding the significant monetary incentive for employer and trainee alike, as well as the infrastructural support provided by Merseta, the largest Seta in South Africa, the programme has managed to enrol only 2 194 apprentices (just under 50% of its target).

It is hoped that the AATP initiative will become an entrenched model not only to accelerate artisan training in South Africa, but also to conduct mainstream apprenticeship training. South Africa remains a long way from attaining the creation of the artisan numbers required by the economy but these are early days and the AATP represents a significant post-Jipsa attempt to roll back the deepening skills crisis engulfing the country.

A way forward – four immediate quick wins

In the short term, there are at least four easy and quick wins that can be achieved, if only to boost our morale after a depressing discussion about the scarce skills crisis.

First – somebody must tell the engineers and the artisans in particular that they are important.

Second – educators need to be reminded that they are the custodians of the standards by which we will stand or fall. The word to educators must be clear and simple: do not compromise on standards. Most educators in SA are white and very rarely will white educators challenge black laziness, stupidity or entitlement. Our educators must not do us a disservice by accommodating poor standards and shoddy work. We need to be proud of our high standards and produce a nation of likeminded, proud and properly qualified people.

Third – we need to embrace the remaining international goodwill to assist us with skills development but without selling our souls and birthright in the process. We have what it takes right here in South Africa, and therefore we should not be dismissive of our own abilities in exchange for those which come from "overseas". We are a smart people and with the right orientation and coaching, we can become world leaders in any field we so desire.

Fourth – we need to stop rewarding incompetence, be it in the public or the private sector – political or otherwise. Let's catch someone doing something right rather than emulate the traffic-control philosophy of placing hidden speed cameras whose sole purpose is to capture you doing something wrong. Perhaps we need to become more preventative in our thinking.

Conclusion

This chapter has made a case for interpreting the Jipsa initiative as a significant moment of consciousness in the transformation journey of South Africa. I have pointed out that the AATP model of artisan training represents an innovative post-Jipsa solution to the growing deficit vis-a-vis artisan training.

The challenge we face as a nation is to harness the potential and power of a Jipsa intervention and to move the country more rapidly along the path towards prosperity and away from poverty. Will we win the race against time and problematic attitudes? Or will South Africa need to concede defeat and hand over its economy to a more skilled country and coloniser?

The real threats facing South Africa are our impending inability to manage our own growth, our inability to manage our own economy, and our inability to manage our own economic future and destiny.

This chapter has also challenged the skills development orthodoxy governing the heart and minds of ordinary skills-hungry and skills-starved South Africans; an orthodoxy which by default focuses on and affirms the contribution of the white-collar professional and entrenches the prejudices we hold towards blue-collar workers.

I suggest that the glorification of the blue-collar worker may be the breath of fresh air required to infuse a new level of enthusiasm and commitment into our economy as we collectively try to reposition and reconstruct our country from the ashes of 300 years of colonial legacy, and 16 years of post-apartheid attempts to fix the ship before it sinks.

Notes

1 See Mukora J (2008) *Artisans/Trades*. Scarce and critical skills research project commissioned by Department of Labour, South Africa (March 2008) page 28, quoting from the Indlela trade test register. See also Akoojee S & Brown H (2009) Accelerated Artisan Training at the Manufacturing Coalface: responding to the Skills Challenge in South Africa (unpublished paper) Presented to the AATP Steering Committee of the Merseta, Johannesburg, August 2009.

2 See Chapter 4 above where this matter is also discussed. It is worth repeating here, Vision 2040 – a vision of South African big business to double the size of the economy over a period of 30 years alongside objectives for reducing poverty and inequality. For more detail see article by Cramer T (2010) Big business wants doubling of SA economy by 2040 to be new national goal. Article in Engineering News 23 February 2010 http://www.engineeringnews.co.za/article/big-business-wants-doubling-of-sa-economy-by-2040-to-be-new-national-goal-2010-02-23

3 See a presentation made by Gwede Mantashe (2006) JIPSA - An intervention in the skills revolution (2006) –http://www.idc.co.za/Conference%20Papers/2006/Africa%20Development%20Finance%20Week/MarieKirsten.pdf

4 Jipsa is to be integrated by March 2010 into the Education Department and will be funded from the education budget. The National Treasury would make no additional allocations to the Human Resource Development for South Africa (HRD-SA) strategy, which was on schedule to be implemented on April 1, this year. The HRD-SA strategy from 2009 to 2014 is being implemented to ensure the coordination and integration of the provision of scarce and critical skills in the country and was being managed by the Department of Education (DoE). Government's Joint Initiative for Priority Skills Acquisition (Jipsa) would eventually also be incorporated into the HRD-SA. With the release of the 2009 Budget, the National Treasury said that it would not

offer additional support for the strategy this year, noting that the DoE would have to fund any additional expenses under its own operational budget. The DoE would continue undertaking stakeholder consultation with regard to the strategy until the 2009/10 financial year, while Jipsa would only be incorporated under the HRD-SA in March 2010. http://www.engineeringnews.co.za/article/jipsareplacement-programme-to-be-funded-through-education-department-2009-02-11

5   Presidency (2008) *Jipsa – Report on activities in 2007*. Issued by the office of the Deputy President of South Africa (April 2008), page 8.
6   *See* Merseta (2009) *External Review of the Accelerated Artisan Development Project (AATP) – Draft Report* (unpublished report) – tabled at the January 2010 sitting of the Steering Committee of the Manufacturing, Engineering and Related Services Skills and Training Authority of South Africa chaired by Dr Raymond Patel, page 37.
7   *See* Eskom contractor accused of importing Chinese workers, March 19, 2010 http://www.busrep.co.za/index.php?fSetId=662&fSectionId=552&fArticleId=5397466
8   Julius Malema, the controversial president of the ANC Youth League claims that 75% of the unemployed in the country are young people (quoted in Mail and Guardian, March 26 to 31, 2010, page 3). On the other hand, Professor Peliwe Lolwana, a Wits university educationist, in an unpublished paper presented at a recent roundtable of Wits University academics and training specialists, identifies explicitly that an interesting problem has been growing over the years in South Africa namely that a staggering number of young people are jobless and often possess low and poor qualifications for employment and further study. The problems caused by lack of adequate levels of education and often consequently the inability to access the labour market, are experience by all age groups in a society. Lolwana goes on to say that young people present a particular case, since early labour market experiences are a predictor of longer-term labour market involvement as well as employment stability. In South Africa, many studies have surfaced recently that put the spotlight on the youth crisis. These studies are diverse, but all come to the same facts that allow us to conclude that the youth in the country deserves attention:
    - 41% of young people (18-24 year olds) are not in education, not in employment and not in training;
    - 65% of young people (15-24 year olds) are not in employment;
    - 12% participation rates of Africans and 13% participation rates of coloureds in university education;
    - There is less than a 50% chance that a black school leaver, with matric, will be employed by the age 24.

    Lolwana points out that her proposed project seeks to understand the nature and extent of this problem in the first place. In the second place it seeks to study the role of each of some of the key elements associated with this problem. Thirdly, this project seeks to provide some theoretical as well as empirical answers to the key questions. It will also provide a platform for examining the relationship between the elements and also explore how integrated solutions could perhaps be the answer to the problem at hand. (See Lolwana P (2010) Post-school Education and Research in Labour Market Skills (PEARLS) – Concept Document – (Wits Department of Education, unpublished paper)
9   *See* Kirsten M (2006) *South Africa's Second Economy* – DBSA http://www.idc.co.za/Conference%20Papers/2006/Africa%20Development%20Finance%20Week/MarieKirsten.pdf
10 I was appointed to the AATP Steering Committee in 2007 by Dr Patel (CEO of Merseta), and am privileged to continue serving as a founding member in my capacity as industry expert and advisor on artisan training.

Part 4.
The way forward

18 | Conclusion: True liberation starts in the mind

The impossible can be done immediately. Miracles may take a bit longer.

This book has proposed a solution to two of South Africa's seemingly insurmountable problems, namely growing unemployment and rising levels of crime, especially violent crime. These twin challenges are the tentacles of a more deeply rooted problem called poverty. History has shown that a nation moves towards prosperity and self-reliance through industrial development. My proposed solution is a radical mindshift at both a personal and a societal level. My call is for the creation and adoption of a new national consciousness – a new national identity cast in industrial awareness as opposed to politically charged racial terms.

Such a consciousness can be defined as an obsessive curiosity about how things are made. The inherent logic of the proposed solution is simple: *If you awaken the spirit of curiosity, you may at the same time also create a thirst for wanting to make the object or be part of the process that makes the object about which you are curious. If someone else could make it, then surely I can also make similar things or improve on what has been made.* Hopefully this curiosity will have a snowball effect, leading to the creation of a nation that encourages such curiosity, resulting in the creation of industry.

The first section of the book made a case for industrial consciousness to serve as the basis for re-energising the industrial base of the economy as opposed to the current politically charged race-based consciousness. If the first section was abstract and philosophical, the second section of the book was overtly concrete, practical and management-oriented. A proposed rescue plan was laid out identifying and discussing six elements of a rescue plan and inviting the reader to participate in crafting a solution to South Africa's most challenging problems. The third section was more reflective in nature and provided a basis for the hope that a positive future for South Africa is possible. Three moments of positive consciousness were identified as having taken place during the first 16 years of nation building in the new and democratic South Africa. These were identified as the Truth and Reconciliation Commission (TRC), the Scorpions and the Joint Initiative for Priority Skills Acquisition (Jipsa) moments.

On the basis of the analysis and commentary in the first three sections, a fourth and final section concludes this book by expressing faith in a brighter future for South Africa. However, such a future will require tough love, hard decisions, and courageous and patriotic citizens who want to see a better future for our beloved country.

There is no doubt that in 1994, South Africa officially shifted from state-sponsored terrorism to a democratic state. But has this new multi-party democracy further entrenched government-sponsored educational and economic dysfunctionality? Whether this is the result of an apartheid legacy or the incompetence of the current ruling party is irrelevant. The reality is that in the areas that matter most, namely education and the ability of the masses to meaningfully engage with and benefit from the economy, we have failed dismally.

If all South Africans don't join hands to fight the scourge of crime and unemployment, and ultimately poverty, we might as well concede defeat and allow a modern-day colonial empire to take over our country and dictate the quality of our existence in the land of our birth.

I have proposed that the unifying force required to defeat the scourge of crime and unemployment is not a racial obsession, but rather the explicit creation of a new national psyche that is driven by industrial consciousness. The racial polarisation must be overcome if we are to move forward as a united nation. Industrial consciousness as described in the chapters of this book holds such a promise.

I have also argued that, in order for industrial development to get traction in our society, we need to redefine our national identity in terms of the progress we make vis-à-vis industrial development. This is the new performance standard which should be used to measure our nation-building programme. It is not good enough for an individual to be positively disposed to industrial development; as a nation, we need to reprogramme our minds with new software, called industrial consciousness, so that we can maximise our collective potential.

The glue needed to bind a nation bludgeoned by crippling poverty and violent crime must be its desire to rapidly industrialise, since this is the key solution to getting rid of poverty in our society. The creation and adoption of a new psyche will serve as the new fulcrum for a prosperous South Africa.

From idea to action

I hope that the contents of this book will assist us to shift into a better state of well-being, where crime and unemployment are no longer the distinguishing features of our nation. I believe that the solution to crime and unemployment lies in the hearts and minds of every South African –

an area of focus that has been ignored by most of the strategy and policy proposals of the past 16 years of transformation.

But is a positive future really possible? We need to remind ourselves that to achieve the proposed solution, namely industrial consciousness, will require an enormous effort – and it won't come cheap either. Despite the enormity of our problems and the fact that we will have strong disagreements on certain matters, I believe that a re-energised future is possible. Just because we disagree on certain matters does not mean that our country cannot succeed. Healthy dissent is the fuel required for a thriving democracy; however once a final position has been reached, it is then incumbent on us all to pull in the same direction. In other words, we must allow the power of the ballot, and not the bullet, to ultimately decide which option and ultimately policy we should follow. Once that decision has been made, we, as loyal patriots, need to put our shoulder to the wheel and positively contribute to that future.

We must draw inspiration from the fact that South Africa has a track record of fundamentally altering the state of consciousness of its people. We are a miracle nation after all. So why can't we create millions of jobs, reduce crime and decisively fix our poverty problem? I believe we can. The problem is that we have been using the wrong formula.

There is no reason to doubt that South Africa's future can be bright and prosperous. The challenge facing us is to make smart, yet tough choices. I believe that as a nation standing together, supported by sympathetic international friends and committed patriots, we can turn the country away from death's door. Poverty is the real enemy and we need to keep the enemy in focus at all times. The enemy is not the competence of those loyal patriots who want to re-energise the nation with positive and collective action for the benefit of all. The enemy is poverty and those who prop it up with gross incompetence, neglect and careless administration.

What kind of mindset is required?

The intention of this book was to present a case for the first and most critical step in fighting crime and creating jobs, namely a change of mental paradigm. I extended the argument one step further by proposing that this new mental paradigm, which I have described as industrial consciousness, serves as the basis of a new national identity for the nation as a whole. The mindset change goes beyond a shift in one's personal and private thinking and belief system, and extends to changing the belief system of the nation in its entirety. In this way we can develop a new social cohesion as a nation – for it is only when we stand together that we will effectively eradicate poverty, crime and unemployment. But is such a change in mindset possible?

Any discussion about national identity must address the issue of nation building and that elusive thing called patriotism. In South Africa, the topic of race always simmers just beneath the surface. For many of us who live in urban South Africa, the harshness of grinding poverty is not our daily reality as it is for many millions of South Africans trapped in the peri-urban and rural areas. The closest many of us get to poverty is when we come face-to-face with crime and possibly unemployment. But we are in this mess together and together we need to find a solution to our problems.

Eating the elephant

I readily admit that there is no overnight solution to poverty, crime and unemployment. But, as we say in the jungle, it is possible to eat an elephant, if you do it piece-by-piece, and step-by-step. We know that the way towards prosperity in South Africa is not through BEE deals or the hope of a benevolent trickle-down from the wealthy (including a monopolistically minded developmental state) to the poor. Neither is the solution a welfare state where the majority of the nation live on hand-outs rather than the sweat of their brows.

It is therefore imperative that we refocus our economy and find creative ways to employ all levels of skill and ability. The way to achieve this is through a radical mindshift, from racial entitlement to industrial consciousness. I believe we can only do this if we, as a nation – black and white alike – are all of one mind, one soul and one spirit.

This book has served as a primer. Its intention was simply to signal the domain where the solutions lie and, like all geological reports for prospecting miners, it will only be useful and potentially profitable after the exploration has started and the valuable minerals have been unearthed. We all have different roles to play as we rebuild our country. However, the key issue is to ensure that we are all fighting the same enemy – and not each other.

Is patriotic solidarity possible?

This book has traversed many disciplines, resulting in many and varied proposals for consideration. The depth of the crisis we are facing with regard to crime and unemployment is such that it will require every bit of imagination possible to get to a solution which excites our patriotic juices and which will mobilise us into constructive action. Whatever I have proposed cannot be more inflammatory and inciting than the unacceptably high levels of crime and unemployment that we have become used to as citizens of our wonderful country. In fact, we often trade stories of victimhood – trying to tell an even worse story of crime and misfortune than the one we have just heard. Tragic!

Nothing is more inflammatory than tolerating the incompetence of public servants who are tasked with serving us, the citizens, and yet they think they are doing us a favour just by turning up for work. I would like to think that I am like millions of ordinary South Africans who are very sober about the gravity of the problems we are facing as a nation and the growing culture of entitlement and laziness that is engulfing us.

The situation we face in South Africa is much too serious to be flippant and nonchalant about. I believe we are beyond the need to be politically correct for fear of offending someone. Of course, we must not use our perceptions about the levels of the problems we face as an excuse to be racist or rude. I am the first to acknowledge that such caution is necessary. But let's not be so cautious that we fail to realise that we are facing a crisis. This is not the time to score cheap political points.

I also don't think that it is too far-fetched to nurture the view that if we don't find a solution to crime and unemployment very soon – a solution that is embraced by all the citizens of South Africa – we are likely to find ourselves with a war on our hands. If we don't mobilise ourselves into positive action, it is likely that some opportunistic economic terrorist grouping or religious fundamentalist group will grab the attention of our jobless and starving masses for their own ideological cause and purposes.

An almost last word ...

My vision for South Africa is a healthier and wealthier nation for all. I believe it is possible to achieve this, but a necessary first step is that we must all be united by the same belief and understanding – and that understanding and belief is what makes me a South African – not the colour of my skin, but the fact that I am a member and supporter of a curiosity-driven industrial army – a South African team that is going to win the war on poverty, crime and unemployment.

The tradesman, pastor, teacher, professor and wannabe capitalist CEO in me says:

> ***Sit up and pay attention to what I have to say! Change your mindset. Let us reclaim our country from the jaws of poverty and hopelessness. Let us collectively create a country where there is health and wealth for all.***

Postscript: For our children's sake

What we believe about reality motivates us either to change it or protect it.

What we believe

With this final postscript I wish to signal the need to extend the discussion concerning industrial consciousness into the realm of the spiritual – a matter currently under discussion within my limited group. Such a discussion will necessitate a different book expressing thoughts and contributions no less significant than the above, since it is ultimately what we believe about reality that motivates us either to change or to protect our current reality. Our ability to move the economy towards prosperity and away from poverty, among other things, will require a radically new industrial and industrious work ethic. A key element in such a discussion is the issue of African, and other forms of spirituality and attitudes to work (i.e. work ethic), and how these either impede or support industriousness or entitlement. A key concept to be further explored must be the notion of ubuntu and its impact on or conflict with the call for industrial consciousness as a new basis for South Africa's national identity. Controversially, one should ask whether ubuntu, the much acclaimed and celebrated African concept of humanism is not in fact heresy. Perhaps the African spirit of accommodation and tolerance is the major problem and impediment to economic growth. This is a thorny question likely to evoke a very strong reaction.

The purpose of this book, among other things, is to call to every South African citizen to make an informed and conscious decision to create an industriousness or industrial consciousness that permeates every aspect of the South African being.

South Africa needs a nation of patriots determined to rid our society of the scourge of poverty. To be a true South African patriot must mean that our entire existence and being is focused on the economic liberation of our country, so that all who live in our land can partake in its wealth to the extent that they put in the effort rather than to the extent that they have a particular racial identity, preference or entitlement. This is what industrial consciousness and a new standard for nationhood is all about – a quest to be judged by what we want to be rather than what we were.

But can we make this shift or are our spiritual minds trapped in a value system that more readily accommodates and absorbs slavery and racial capitalism than the wild, thrilling and adventurous spirit of entrepreneurial exploration – the very cornerstone of a successful economy.

Creating a legacy in the midst of complexity

When one is desperate to motivate people into action, the last court of appeal is often the plea: "Let's do it for our children". To some extent I am guilty of this by adding this postscript. However, motivating us to do it for our children is more sobering when one considers that over 60% of South Africa's population is considered to be youth (i.e. between ages of 14 and 35 years). So, doing it for our youth is in fact doing it for our nation. The alternative is becoming a nation governed by an ill-advised youth – which is a very real possibility given the age profile of our country.

What kind of future do we want to create for our children? Just as importantly, what will South Africa look like in 15, 30 and 60 years' time? What will the profile of our population look like given the ravages of HIV and AIDS, and the fast-dwindling industrial skills base so sorely required to grow the economy? What will our children say when they discover that we knew the solution – we knew the success formula for a better South Africa – but because of our sensitivities, we simply were not motivated enough to "make it happen" for our country? What will future generations say about us, the first generation of post-apartheid nation builders?

What I have attempted to show in this book is that there is a known and sustainable solution to South Africa's most significant challenges – crime and unemployment. Neither apartheid nor the first 16 years of democracy applied such a solution.

Instead, former and current solutions are characterised by more fire-power for the police, more aid, more welfare, more social grants, more BEE, more pro-poor rhetoric, more housing, more money for education, more anti-retrovirals, etc. But not much measurable success. The only success we have achieved is to create an even bigger gap between the rich and the poor.

Deep down we know that more money and more policy is not the solution. Yes, a higher degree of implementation will certainly help. But I believe we need a brand new approach. It is an approach that says the key solution to our problems is, in the first instance, a change of our mindset as individuals and then as a nation. I am not fussy about which comes first. All I am interested in is that a shift takes place – from our current politically charged race-conscious paradigm to an industrial consciousness and paradigm.

Our country has the money – not a bottomless pit – but more than enough (even though our officials will tell us differently); we have the policy documents; we have the systems in place; we have good international friends; we still have enormous goodwill among the citizens of South Africa (even though we are frustrated at times); and we have the skills. As South Africans we are essentially good and loyal people. So where's the problem? Why are we not succeeding in dealing with our problems when we have almost everything imaginable to make this country the most successful and prosperous country in the world? Part of the explanation is that we are not united in our efforts to rid our society of the scourge of poverty and its twin manifestations of crime and unemployment.

There may be commentators who firmly believe that government is not interested in addressing structural poverty at all. I don't share this sentiment. I also do not wish to echo the predictable chorus line which says we need to fix corruption in government first. Of course, I agree that corruption in government must be rooted out. But even if we did fix corruption in government and even if the ruling party did change hands through the ballot, as it did from the National Party to the ANC, the problem of unemployment and crime will continue to plague us because we are using the wrong formula to address our problems. Barry Smith's dated comment captures well the ongoing contradictions and complexity which persist in a free South Africa:

> In the midst of political stability and strong economic growth, post-apartheid South Africa is faced with the stubborn reality of widespread poverty and growing inequality. As economic empowerment benefits an expanding, mainly urban black middle class, the majority of people continue to live in poverty and mass unemployment. As the country's remarkable and peaceful transition to democracy unfolds, millions – both urban and rural – are trapped on the margins of society, contending with the multiple crises of unemployment, landlessness, homelessness, lack of basic services, HIV/AIDS, food insecurity and unacceptable levels of crime and violence.
>
> All these contradictions persist under the leadership of a government that has unprecedented legitimacy, democratic credentials and popular support. If nothing else, this vexing

situation confirms that we continue to underestimate the depth and complexity of the problems we face.[1]

We have asked in previous chapters what the basis was for the unprecedented support enjoyed by the ANC-led government. Is it a historical sympathy vote or an aspirational vote that keeps the ANC in power? It will always be difficult to definitively state the basis for the support enjoyed by the ruling party. The fact of the matter is that the masses have made their vote clear and have given the ruling party a mandate to govern. The ruling party enjoys legitimacy regardless of what we may personally feel or think. The question is whether or not the overwhelming vote in favour of the ANC translates into a policy framework that benefits the supporters of the ruling party only, or whether the ruling party re-engineers government systems to benefit all citizens of the country, of whom the ANC support base, based on the voting patterns, is by far the majority.

This may be a pedantic and semantic point, but it is nevertheless important as we contemplate a democratic order and existence in South Africa. So a pertinent question in this regard would be: Is the civil service the delivery arm of government or the ANC?

To conflate these two entities would be fallacious in theory although in practice it probably does not matter. Interestingly, there is a shift in the thinking expressed by some that the civil service should be managed by professionals and not by cronies of the ruling party.

The reason I rehearse these matters here is to acknowledge that there is already a shift taking place from a race bias towards a competency bias. Whether this is out of sheer desperation or a long-term policy shift remains to be seen. My proposal for industrial consciousness is a long-term, sustainable and deliberate solution as opposed to a short-term politically expedient proposal.

I believe that a positive future is possible for our country. It's going to take hard work combined with honest and robust engagement. Let's do it – even if only for the sake of our children.

Notes
1   Smith B (2007) Finding solutions to complex social problems in South Africa http://www.synergos.org/knowledge/07/findingsolutionsinsouthafrica.htm

Determine your own list of priorities

Name of exercise: In, alongside and out-of-the-box solutions
The following exercise is designed to enable you to navigate your away through what can sometimes be a very explosive discussion and which can easily degenerate into a deeply emotional and politically charged exchange. And yet, we all have our own views on what we consider to be the most important priorities to be tackled by the country at large.

The exercise below is designed to help you to develop your own list of priorities and view of what is most important and urgent.

Aim:
To identify what you think is most important for the country and what the priorities of the new South Africa should be in terms of an emergency rescue plan to fix crime, unemployment and ultimately poverty.

What will you discover through this exercise?
You will discover that you, and not just management professionals and consultants, have the ability to think about solutions that are IN, ALONGSIDE and OUT of the box.

Who should do this exercise?
You can do this alone or in a group. It's more fun in a group.

Tools and equipment needed for exercise:
- At least 20 small pieces of paper on which you can at least write one sentence.
- A pencil or pen.

The challenge
Sometimes we are so overwhelmed by the magnitude of the problems facing our country that we don't think that what we have to say will matter or ever be able to change the direction of the country. With this little exercise I want to show you that you not only *have* a solution, but that you *are* the solution to many of the problems facing South Africa.

To help you realise your analytical potential I have developed an exercise for you to do in your own time. The only cost attached to this exercise is courage, honesty and integrity, which, if you are reading this book, you already have lots of.

Instructions

I propose that you first do this exercise on your own. You can then get five to ten close family members or friends together, and ask them to help you identify 20 things which must be done in South Africa in order for us to fix our crime and unemployment problem, and ultimately our poverty problem. You will find that in no time you may well have a list of 100 things or more. But set yourself a target of 20 as a start.

Write down one suggestion (or action step) per piece of paper. Remember, just let your mind run wild and make a list of everything you can think of that can be done to fix crime and unemployment. It does not matter how insignificant you may think your idea is. Just write it down. You will find there are others who share your views. In fact, others may say: We thought about that but did not have the courage to write it down because it sounded so silly. Remember, it is sometimes the "silly" things that provide the real answers and solutions.

Once you have written down all your suggestions and actions (remember: one suggestion per piece of paper) and have used up your 20, 30 or 100 pieces of paper, I want you to categorise the papers into three groups:

- **In**-the-box category
- **Out**-the-box category
- **Alongside**-the-box category.

IN-THE-BOX solutions – write an "I" next to each proposed solution which you have identified that fits into this category. This category is for all those suggestions which need to and can be remedied within the existing system. So, for example, you may say that we need to improve the quality of the nursing in our public hospitals. This would be an "I" category issue since we have public hospitals and nurses already. All we need is a different work ethic, perhaps, or a different pay scale. But if you say that we must fire all nurses, this will be a different solution – probably an "O" category solution which is an out-of-the-box solution.

OUT-OF-THE-BOX solutions – write an "O" next to each of the proposed solutions that fall into this category. These solutions generally refer to those creative, innovative, unique or never-before-thought-of or implemented solutions. You will know when it is out of the box when someone responds by saying "I never thought of that – that's fantastic".

Sometimes these are suicidal proposals, but let your mind run wild. Only your friends or family will think you are mad. An example of an "O" category item would be, for example, the amnesty tax for all BEE beneficiaries, or a ban on the export of non-beneficiated raw materials.

ALONGSIDE-THE-BOX solutions – These are solutions which are difficult to implement in the current system and for which you would almost need to run parallel systems for them to work. A good example would be the following: *Government needs to adopt a performance-monitoring system that is not linked to a political party.* This is something that is linked to, but must be run alongside the normal systems of government to work. I am, of course, referring to the newly introduced Performance Monitoring and Evaluation Ministry created by the Zuma administration.

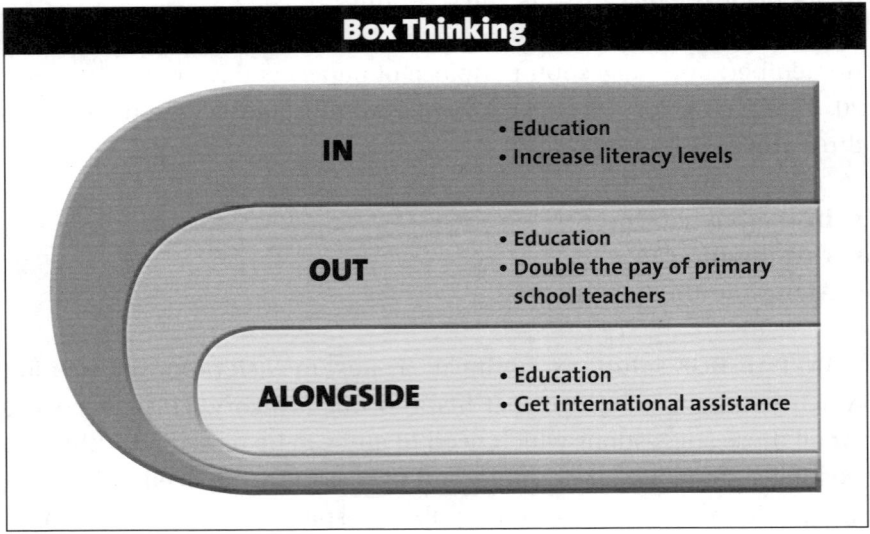

Figure 7: Box thinking

Final comment

Don't be scared or shy. Give it a go and see what you come up with. See if you and your closest friends share the same view of the nature of the problems faced by our country. You may be surprised to know that you share common views and solutions.

Remind yourself that you are part of the solution to our country's problems. Your view does count. It may be more rewarding to do this exercise with young adults or first-year university students who think that they can still change the world. It's even more fun doing it with young children who are at their creative best before they become teenagers and who have no political or cultural baggage.

Have fun and feel the energy. Solutions are what the country desperately needs. Perhaps you have to start your own political party or organisation of like-minded people that you can gather around yourself. Who knows, you may be the next President of South Africa!

Outcome
Count up how many I's, O's, and A's you have identified. You may surprise yourself!

Select bibliography

Akoojee S & Brown H (2009) Accelerated Artisan Training at the Manufacturing Coalface: responding to the Skills Challenge in South Africa (unpublished paper) Presented to the AATP Steering Committee of the Merseta, Johannesburg, August 2009.

Altbeker A (2007) *A Country At War With Itself: South Africa's Crisis of Crime*. Johannesburg & Cape Town: Jonathan Ball Publishers

Altman M (2008): Time to mobilise frustrated jobless youth. *HSRC Review*; Vol 6. (3). September; pp. 19 -20

Araie F (2009) Fight this assault on our freedom – Article in *Sunday Independent* November 1, page 9

Asmal K, Asmal L & Roberts RS (1996) *Reconciliation Through Truth: A Reckoning Of Apartheid's Criminal Governance*. Cape Town & Johannesburg: David Philip Publishers & Mayibuye Books

Auerswald EH (1985) Thinking about thinking in family therapy. *Family Process*, 24, 1, 1-12.

Barron C (2010) Gordhan takes advice from victim of red tape. *Sunday Times Business Times* February 21, page 10

Barron C (2010) Link between crime and unemployment is exaggerated. *Sunday Times*, February 14, page 9

Bernstein A (2008) (Ed.).South Africa's Door Knockers: Young people and unemployment in metropolitan South Africa. Centre for Development Enterprise. *CDE in Depth* No 8.

Bhushan K (1999) The industrialisation of Africa.(landmark conference on industrial partnerships and investment in Africa)(Cover Story) *African Business* (November 1)

Bochner A (1997) It's about time: narrative and the divided self. *Qualitative Inquiry*, 3, 4, 418-438.

Boesak A (2009) *Running with Horses: Reflections of an Accidental Politician*. Cape Town: Joho Books

Bond P (2000) *Elite Transition: From Apartheid to Neoliberalism in South Africa*. Pietermaritzburg, South Africa: University of Natal Press

Booysen V (2008) BEE a failure (18 September) http://www.fin24.com

Boraine A (2000) *A Country Unmasked: Inside South Africa's Truth and Reconciliation Commission*. Oxford, England: Oxford University Press.

Botman HR and Petersen R (1996) (Eds) *To Remember and to Heal: Theological and Psychological Reflections on Truth and Reconciliation*. Cape Town: Human & Rousseau

Boyle B (2010) Will Mr Delivery deliver? *Sunday Times* February 14, page 4

Boyle B (2010) Zuma offers first look at industrial policy plan. *Sunday Times Business Time* February 21, page 3

Boyle B (2010) A growth path that has a longer-term vision for SA. An interview with the new Minister of Economic Development, Ebrahim Patel, and his search for a sustainable formula that will create jobs for the poor. *Sunday Times Business Times*, March 26, 2010, page 4.

Braverman H (1974) *Labor and Monopoly Capital: The Degradation of Work in the Twentieth Century*. New York: Monthly Review Press

Bunting I & Cloete N (2008): Governing Access to Higher Education - Country Report: South Africa. (unpublished paper)

Burns J (2008) *Getting incentives right: the role of wage and employment subsidies and job search assistance programmes in reducing youth unemployment*. Cape Town: HSRC

Cawthra G (1993) *Policing South Africa: The South African Police & the Transition from Apartheid*. London & Cape Town: Zed Books & David Philip

Cawthra G (2003) Security Transformation in Post-apartheid South Africa in Cawthra G and Luckman R (Eds). (2003) *Governing Insecurity: Democratic Control of Military and Security Establishments in Transitional Democracies*. London & New York: Zed Books

Cawthra G (2009) (Ed) *African Security Governance: Emerging Issues*. Johannesburg: Wits University Press

Cawthra G and Luckman R (2003) (Eds.) *Governing Insecurity: Democratic Control of Military and Security Establishments in Transitional Democracies*. London & New York: Zed Books

Chabane C (2010) Focus now on delivering the right stuff. *Sunday Times* February 14, page 8

Chang H J (1996) *The Political Economy Of Industrial Policy*. London: Macmillan

Chang H J (2002) *Accelerating Growth And Development: The Contribution Of The Integrated Manufacturing Strategy*. Pretoria: Department of Trade and Industry.

Chipkin I (2007) *Do South Africans Exist? Nationalism, Democracy and the Identity of 'the people'*. Johannesburg: Wits University Press

Chonco N (2010) The long wait for transformation. *Mail & Guardian* December 23 to January 7, page 4

Cloete N (2009) (Eds) *Responding to the educational needs of post-school youth: determining the scope of the problem and developing a capacity-building model*. Council for Higher Education and Training

Coleman M (1998) *A Crime Against Humanity: Analysing the Repression of the Apartheid State* (Maudsley Monographs). Human Rights Committee

Concept Note: Expert Group Meeting on the Industrial Investment Policies in Africa. Addis Ababa, Ethiopia 8-9 July 2009. Organised by the African Union (AU) in collaboration with the United Nations Industrial Development Organization (UNIDO)

Cramer T (2010) Big business wants doubling of SA economy by 2040 to be new national goal. *Engineering News* February 23 http://www.engineeringnews.co.za

Davenport J (2010) Cabinet to consider new growth plan by midyear. *Engineering News* March 2 http://www.engineeringnews.co.za

Davies R (1978) The class character of South Africa's industrial conciliation legislation in E Webster (Ed) *Essays in Southern African Labour History*. Johannesburg: Ravan Press

Davies R (2009) Statement by Dr Rob Davies, Minister of Trade and Industry during the 13th General Conference of the United Nations Industrial Development Organisation (UNIDO) 7 December 2009. Department of Trade and Industry htpp://www.thedti.gov.za

Davis G (2009) Economy to bleed more jobs before year closes. *Sunday Independent* November 1, page 7

De Gruchy JW & Villa-Vicencio C (1983) (Eds.) *Apartheid is a heresy*. Grand Rapids: Eerdmans

Dixon B and van der Spuy (2004) (Eds) *Justice Gained? Crime and Crime Control in South Africa's Transition*. Cape Town: University of Cape Town Press.

DTI *National Industrial Policy Framework*. (with the Executive Foreword by Minister of Trade and Industry Mandisi Mpahlwa. Department of Trade and Industry

DTI *South Africa's Economic Transformation: A strategy for broad based black economic empowerment* http://www.thedti.gov.za

DTI (2001) *Driving Competitiveness: An Integrated Industrial Strategy For Sustainable Employment And Growth* http://www.polity.org.za http://www.thedti.gov.za

DTI (2002) *Accelerating Growth and Development: the contribution of the integrated manufacturing strategy*. Pretoria: Department of Trade and Industry.

DTI (2003) Broad-Based Black Economic Empowerment Act, No. 53 of 2003 http://www.thedti.gov.za

DTI (2007) Implementation of Government's National Industrial Policy Framework: Industrial Policy Action Plan August 2007.

DTI (2007) Update on the process towards the launch of the National Industrial Policy Framework (NIPF) 19 April 2007 – The Developmental State http://www.info.gov.za

DTI (2010) *National Assembly statement on Industrial Policy Action Plan (IPAP2)* by Dr Rob Davies, Minister of Trade and Industry 18 February 2010

DTI (2010) 2010/11 – 2012/13 Industrial Policy Action Plan , February 2010 http://www.thedti.gov.za

du Toit R & Roodt J (2008) *Engineering professionals: Crucial key to development and growth in South Africa* - Scarce and critical skills research project commissioned by Department of Labour South Africa

Economic Justice Network of FOCCISA Newsletter - *Policy Series* 3/2009, page1.

Ellis C & Bochner AP (2000) Autoethnography, personal narrative, reflexivity; researcher as subject. In Denzin NK & Lincoln YS *Handbook of qualitative research* (2nd ed.) Thousand Oaks, California: Sage Publications

Ellis S (1998) The historical significance of South Africa's third force. *Journal of Southern African Studies* 24/2, pages 261 - 299

Enslin-Payne S (2009) No quick fix to recover a million jobs – Employment growth to lag economic revival. *Business Report*, November 2, page 1

Erasmus Z (2001) (Ed.) *Coloured By History – Shaped By Place: New Perspectives On Coloured Identities In Cape Town*. Cape Town: Kwela Books & South African History Online

Eskom contractor accused of importing Chinese workers. March 19, 2010 http://www.busrep.co.za

Fitzgerald P, McLennan A and Munslow B (Eds.) (1995) *Managing Sustainable Development in South Africa*. Cape Town: Oxford University Press

Flatters F (2005) The Economics of the MIDP and the South African Motor Industry. Paper prepared for TIPS/NEDLAC South African Trade and Poverty Programme (SATPP) Policy Dialogue Workshop, Johannesburg, November 1-18.

GCIS (2006) *Accelerated and Shared Growth Initiative South Africa (ASGISA) - Background Document: A summary*. Pretoria: Government Communication and Information Services

Glenister H (2008) Urgent interdict launched to prevent disbanding of Scorpions. *Legalbrief Today* March 18 http://www.legalbrief.co.za

Gobodo-Madikizela P (2010) A wounded nation. *Mail & Guardian* 23 December to January 7, page 17

Gordhan P (2010) *Budget Speech 2010* - Minister of Finance. Pravin Gordhan, 17 February 2010 http://www.treasury.gov.za

Graybill LS (2002) *Truth and Reconciliation in South Africa: Miracle or Model?* London: Lynne Rienner Publishers

Hall S (2010) Definition of Performance Measurement. http://www.ehow.com

Harris M (2010) A degree is an advantage but not essential for a job. *Sunday Times / Careers* February 14, page 7

Haussman R, Hwang J and Rodrik D (2006) What you export matters. NBER Working Paper 11905, Cambridge, Mass: National Bureau of Economic Research.

Hawkey I (2010) Africa lack confidence in local coaches. *Sunday Time Sport* March 14, page 3

Hazelhurst E (2010) Gordhan reveals new growth path. *Business Report* February 18, page 1

Hemson D, Carter J & Karuri-Sebina G (2009) Service delivery as a measure of change: State capacity and development. In Kagwanja P & Kondlo K (Eds) *State of the Nation: South Africa 2008*. Cape Town: HSRC Press

Hills A (2000) *Policing Africa: Internal Security and the Limits of Liberalization*. London: Lynne Reinner Publishers

Hubbard RG & Duggan W (2009) *The Aid Trap: Hard Truths About Ending Poverty*. New York: Columbia University Press

Kagwanja P (2008) South Africa: Gap Between the Rich And Poor Too Wide http://www.southafrica.info/business

Kaplan D (2004) Manufacturing in South Africa over the last decade: a review of industrial performance and policy. *Development South Africa* 21(4)

Kaplan D (2007) The constraints and institutional challenges facing industrial policy in South Africa: a way forward (Accelerated an Shared Growth Initiative for South Africa). *Transformation*. HighBeam Research. 8 Dec. 2009 http://www.highbeam.com

Keeney BP (1983) *Aesthetics of Change*. New York: Gilford Press

Kgosana C (2010) State offers 30% extra to skilled foreigners. *Cape Times* January 6, page 1

Khuzwayo W (2010) Too few black and women directors. March 3 http://www.busrep.co.za

Ki-moon B (2009a) *Still not lived up to potential*, UN Secretary-General Ban Ki-moon's remarks at the 20th Africa Industrialisation Day panel on "Industrialisation Strategies and Policies: A Key to Economic Transformation of Africa", in New York, today, 20 November 2009 http://www.un.org

Ki-Moon (2009b) *Ban says Africa will benefit from economic recovery if it industrializes* (UN Secretary-General Ban Ki-moon's remarks at the 20th Africa Industrialization Day panel on "Industrialisation Strategies and Policies: A Key to Economic Transformation of Africa", in New York, 20 November 2009) http://www.afriquejet.com

Kirsten M (2006) South Africa's Second Economy – DBSA http://www.idc.co.za

Kondlo K & Maserumule M (Eds) (2010) *The Zuma Administration: Critical Challenges*. Cape Town: HSRC Press

Kondlo K (2010) Introduction: political and governance challenges. In Kondlo K & Maserumule M (Eds) *The Zuma Administration: Critical Challenges*. Cape Town: HSRC Press, pp.1-14

Krog A (1998) *Country of my skull*. London: Jonathan Cape

Le Roux M (2008) SA battles national identity crisis. Internet article *Mail and Guardian* February 17 http://www.mg.co.za

Lolwana P (2010) *Post-school Education and Research in Labour market Skills (PEARLS) - Concept Document* – (Wits University, Department of Education, unpublished paper)

Lunsche S (2010) AsgiSA's quiet death. *The Wits Business School Journal* 1/2 pp.43-44

Malefane M (2010) No more excuses on service delivery. *Sunday Times* March 14, page 4

Manila Bulletin(2005) Editorial – Industrialisation, too late? Manila Bulletin Publishing Corp (March 18). *HighBeam Research*. 8 Dec. 2009 http://www.highbeam.com

Mantashe G (2006) *Jipsa an intervention in the skills revolution* – Conference Presentation - Sandton- 21 November www.idc.co.za

Manual T (2007) *Economic Policy And South Africa's Growth Strategy - New Growth Paths*. A speech by Trevor Manual, Minister of Finance, delivered at the Gordon's Institute of Business Leadership, Johannesburg, 19 March 2007.

Marais JS (1968) *The Cape Coloured People (1652 - 1937)*. Johannesburg: Witwatersrand University Press (first published in 1939)

Mashigo P (2010) Socio-economic development and poverty reduction in South Africa. In Kondlo K & Maserumule M (Eds) *The Zuma Administration: Critical Challenges*. Cape Town: HSRC Press, pp.107-144

Masuku T (2006) Targeting Foreigners - Xenophobia among Johannesburg's police - Centre for the Study of Violence and Reconciliation - *Crime Quarterly No.15*. http://www.iss.co.za

Mbalula F (2009) Asmal's attack on ANC smacks of double standards, chauvinism. *Sunday Independent*, November 1, page 4

Mbeki M (2009) *Architects of Poverty: Why African Capitalism Needs Changing*. Johannesburg: Picador Africa

Mbola B (2008) Chinese South Africans qualify for BEE (18 June) http://www.southafrica.info

Meiring P (1999) *Chronicle of the Truth Commission: A journey through the past and present – into the future of South Africa*. Johannesburg: Carpe Diem Books

Merseta (2009) *External Review of the Accelerated Artisan Development Project (AATP) – Draft Report* (unpublished) – tabled at the January 2010 sitting of the Steering Committee of the Manufacturing, Engineering and Related Services Skills and Training Authority of South Africa chaired by Dr Raymond Patel.

Mills G (2002) *Poverty to Prosperity: Globalisation, Good Governance and African Recovery*. Cape Town: Tafelberg Publishers

Motlhabi M (1988) *Challenge to Apartheid: Toward a morally defensible strategy*. Grand Rapids: Eerdmans

Mukora J (2008) *Artisans/Trades*. Scarce and critical skills research project commissioned by Department of Labour, South Africa

Naidu E (2009) Universities face a crisis at every turn – and those who don't drop out can't get work. *Sunday Independent* November 1, page 5

Naidu E (2009) White men still cling to control of tertiary institutions – report. *Sunday Independent* November 1, page 1.

Ncana N (2010) No more excuses on service delivery. *Sunday Times* March 14, page 4.

Nel F & Bezuidenhout J (1997) (Eds) *Policing and Human Rights*. Cape Town: Juta & Co, Ltd

Nevin T (1999) SA's second industrial revolution in *African Business* 1 November

Nzimande B (2010) Nzimande on South Africa's seven day war http://www.politicsweb.co.za

Onyeani C (2006) *Capitalist Nigger: the Road to Success – A Spider Web Doctrine*. Johannesburg & Cape Town: Jonathan Ball Publishers

Ormond R (1985) *The Apartheid Handbook: A Guide to South Africa's Everyday Racial Policies*, England: Penguin Books

Pauw J (1997) *Into the heart of darkness: Confessions of Apartheid's Assassins*. Johannesburg: Jonathan Ball Publishers

Pelser E (2000) *Operation Crackdown: The new policing strategy*. Nedbank ISS Crime Index 4,2 March - April

Posel D (2002) The TRC Report: What kind of History? What kind of Truth. In Posel D and Simpson G (Eds) (2002) *Commissioning the Past: Understanding South Africa's Truth and Reconciliation Commission*. Johannesburg: Wits University Press, pp.147-172

Presidency (2003) *Towards A Ten Year Review – Synthesis Report On Implementation Of Government Programme – Discussion Document* (Policy Coordination and Advisory Services). http://www.10years.gov.za

Presidency (2006) *Brief Synopsis - Clarifying The Second Economy Concept*. http://www.thepresidency.gov.za

Presidency (2006) Khampepe Commission of Enquiry into the mandate and location of the Directorate of Special Operations ("The DSO"). http://www.thepresidency.gov.za

Presidency (2007) A Nation in the Making. A study commissioned by the Presidency of South Africa – coordinated by J Netshitenzhe and F Chikane.

Presidency (2007) *Jipsa Annual Report for 2007 - Background and highlights* (A Presentation). The Presidency. April 2008

Presidency (2008) *Jipsa - Report on activities in 2007*. Issued by the office of the Deputy President of South Africa

Presidency (2008) *Resignation speech 21 September 2008 - Address to the Nation by the South African President - Thabo Mbeki*. http://www.politicsweb.co.za

Presidency (2008) *Towards An Anti-Poverty Strategy For South Africa - A Discussion Document*.

Presidency (2009) - Revised Green Paper: National Planning Commission http://www.info.gov.za

Presidency (2009) *Address by His Excellency Mr Jacob Zuma on the occasion of his Inauguration as fourth President of the Republic of South Africa*, 09 May 2009 http://www.politicsweb.co.za

Presidency (2010) *Opening remarks to the inaugural to the meeting of the President's broad based economic empowerment council*. Speech delivered by Deputy President Mothlante at the Presidential Guest House 4 February

Presidency (2010) *State of the Nation Address by His Excellency JG Zuma, President of the Republic of South Africa; Joint Sitting of Parliament, Cape Town* 11 February 2010 http://www.thepresidency.gov.za

Rakgoadi PK (1995) *The Role of the Self-defence Units (SDUs) in a Changing Political Context*, Research report written for the Centre for the Study of Violence and Reconciliation, January 1995. http://www.csvr.org.za

Rawoot I (2010) Shoot to kill: when it is reasonable? *Mail & Guardian* March 5 to 11, page 16

Reinert ES (2007) *How Rich Countries Got Rich ... And Why Poor Countries Stay Poor*. London: Constable

Repath J (2004) *The Scorpions: Analysing the Directorate of Special Operations*. ISS Monograph Series No.96

Richards RR (1998) Heilende Wahrheit: Das Selbsverständnis der südafrikanischen "Wahrheits und versöhnnungskomiission. In Wustenberg RK (Ed) *WAHRHEIT, RECHT und VERSOHNUNG: Auseinandersetzung mit dem Vergangenheit nach den politischen Umbruchen in Südafrika und Deutschland*. Frankfurt am Main: Peter Lang Publishers, pp.33-47

Richards RR (1994) National Reconstruction And Literary Creativity In Ezra-Nehemiah: A black South African perspective in *Old Testament Essays* (Journal of the Old Testament Society of South Africa) 7,2, pp277-301

Richards RR (2007) *The Challenge Of Critical And Scarce Skills Training In The Marine And Ship Repair Industry: A Perspective Of A Once Upon A Time Artisan Turned CEO*. Keynote presentation to the first national critical and scarce skills summit, Cape Town, 2007 hosted by Knowledge Faqtory, The Pavilion Conference Centre, BMW Pavilion V&A Waterfront Cape Town, 19 April 2007

Rodrik D (2004) Industrial policy for the twenty-first century. Discussion Paper No. 4767. London: Center for Economic Policy Research.

Rodick D (2006) Understanding South Africa's economic puzzles, Working Paper No. 130. Cambridge: Harvard University, Center for International Development.

Russel A (2009) *After Mandela: The Battle for the Soul of South Africa*. London: Hutchinson

Sakoana T (2007) SA identifies key growth sectors http://www.southafrica.info/business

SAPS (2009) *The Crime Situation in South Africa (2008/09)* - Annual report. http://www.saps.gov.za

Shaw M (2002) *Crime and Policing in Post-Apartheid South Africa: Transforming under Fire.* Bloomington: Indiana University Press

Smith B (2007) Finding solutions to complex social problems in South Africa http://www.synergos.org

South Africa: Strategies for stopping country's runaway crime (opinion) (October 25) http://africanpress.wordpress.com

Sparks A (2003) *Beyond The Miracle: Inside the New South Africa.* Johannesburg & Cape Town: Jonathan Ball Publishers.

Stats SA (2006) - Income and Expenditure of Households 2005/2006 – Stats SA report http://www.statssa.gov.za

Stats Singapore (2008) "Key Household income trends for 2008 - Department of Statistics, Singapore http://www.straitstimes.com

Tabane R (2010) Goodbye, faded rainbow. *Mail and Guardian* December 23 to January 7, page 25

Totten S, Parson WS & Charny IW (Eds) (1997) *Century of Genocide: Eyewitness Accounts and Critical Views.* New York & London: Garland Publishing, Inc

Tregenna F (2006) *The Contribution of Manufacturing and Service Sectors to Growth and Employment in South Africa.* Cape Town: Human Sciences Research Council

Trümpelmann M H (1991). *The Joint Matriculation Board – seventy five years - achievement in perspective.* Cape Town, National Book Printers

Truth and Reconciliation Commission (1997): T*ruth and Reconciliation Commission of South Africa Report.*, Cape Town

Tutu D (1999) *No Future Without Forgiveness.* South Africa: Random House.

Urbach J (2007) South Africa's poverty and unemployment battle. http://www.moneyweb.co.za

Van Beek UJ (2005) *Democracy under construction: Patterns from four continents.* Pretoria: Van Schaik

Van der Spuy E (2009) Transforming Safety and Security in Southern Africa: Some Trends and More Challenges in Cawthra G (Ed) (2009) *African Security Governance: Emerging Issues.* Johannesburg: Wits University Press, pp.37-56

Villa Vicencio C & Ngesi (2003) A South Africa: Beyond the Miracle. In Doxtander E & Villa Vicencio C (Eds) (2003) *Through Fire with Water: The roots of division and the potential for reconciliation in Africa.* Cape Town: Institute for Justice and Reconciliation

Villa Vicencio C and Verwoed, W (2003) (Eds) Looking back, Reaching Forward: *Reflections on the Truth and Reconciliation Commission of South Africa.* Cape Town: University of Cape Town Press

Williams R, Cawthra G and Abrahams D (2003) (Eds) *Ourselves to Know: Civil-Military Relations and Defense Transformation in Southern Africa.* Pretoria: Institute for Security Studies

Yumkella KK (2009) Industrialization key to Africa's full integration into global economy, says UNIDO Director-General Tuesday, 17 November 2009. http://www.unido.org

Zuma freezes Simelani's NPA strategy (May 14, 2010) http://www.newstime.co.za

Index

AATP 263-265
Accelerated Artisan Training Programme (AATP) see AATP
Accelerated Shared Growth Initiative of South Africa (ASGISA) see ASGISA
Acquired Immunodeficiency Syndrome (AIDS) see AIDS
Acts
    Competition Act 18
    Employment Equity Act 18-19
    Extension of Security of Tenure Act 18
    Minerals and Petroleum Development Act 18
    National Empowerment Fund Act 18
    National Empowerment Fund Act, 105 of 1998 19
    Preferential Procurement Policy Framework Act 18
    Restitution of Land Rights Act 18
    Telecommunications Act 18
    The National Small Business Act 18
    The Promotion of Equality and Prevention of Unfair Discrimination Act 18
affirmative action 19, 145
Africa Industrialisation Day 45
African National Congress (ANC) see ANC
African Renaissance 40, 185
African Union (AU) see AU
Afrikaner Weerstandsbeweging (AWB) see AWB
AIDS 195, 279-280
ANC 17, 60, 65, 100, 137-138, 163-165, 167-168, 184, 201, 206, 218, 220-221, 228, 254-255, 262, 280-281
ANC Youth League 79, 184
apartheid 17-18, 20-21, 28, 38-39, 48, 54, 58, 60-61, 65, 67, 72, 75, 78-79, 100, 113-114, 116, 126, 134, 136-139, 146-148, 150-153, 158-159, 162-166, 168-169, 181-182, 185, 194-196, 201-203, 206-207, 211-212, 218-224, 226, 228-229, 235-237, 240, 244, 252, 254-255, 262, 266, 271, 279- 280
AsgiSA 77, 86-87, 89, 108, 114, 253-254, 256-257, 259
Asset Forfeiture Unit 79
AU 26, 34, 291
AWB 225
Ban Ki-moon 33, 45
B-BBEE 22, 58-69, 146-148, 152, 168-170
BEE 18-21, 32-33, 58-61, 63-64, 66, 74, 76, 78-79, 90, 100-101, 106-109, 145, 148, 152-153, 160, 168, 175, 200, 256, 263, 273, 279, 286
    abandon 107-108
    critique of, a 61-62
    definition 59
    psyche 58-59
Black Economic Empowerment (BEE) see BEE
Broad-Based Black Economic Empowerment (B-BBEE) see B-BBEE
Chief of Police 41
Competition Act 18
comrades 17, 169, 210, 223
Constitution, the 20, 35, 73, 79, 127, 135, 163, 165-167, 174, 186, 218, 227, 235, 238, 245
crime 16-17, 21-22, 24-25, 28-29, 31, 33, 41-43, 46, 48-54, 72-73, 77, 79-81, 84, 86-88, 91, 93-94, 100, 115-116, 122-123, 135-136, 139, 144-145, 153, 161-165, 174, 181, 183, 196-197, 200, 203-204, 208, 218, 234-237, 252, 261-262, 270-275, 279-280, 284-285
DDG 209
definition
    BEE 59
    industrial consciousness 23
    prosperity 22

Deoxyriboneuclic Acid (DNA) see DNA
Deputy Director General (DDG) see DDG
Deputy National Director of Public Prosecutions (D-NDPP) see D-NDPP
Directorate of Special Operations (DSO) see DSO
disadvantaged 18-19, 43, 160, 168-170
    historically 18-19
    previously 168, 170
DNA 48, 229
D-NDPP 234, 240
DSO 234, 240, 248-249, 294
education 17, 23, 39, 41, 53, 61, 64-65, 77, 84, 87, 92, 106, 113-114, 125, 136, 149, 165, 170, 177, 183, 197, 199, 203-206, 211, 246, 254-255, 257-259, 262-263, 271, 279, 286
EMF-SA 107-110
Employment Equity Act 18-19
Entrepreneurial Millionaire's Fund – South Africa (EMF-SA) see EMF-SA
Extension of Security of Tenure Act 18
FBI 209, 234, 242, 244
Federal Bureau of Investigation (FBI) see FBI
Fédération Internationale de Football Association (FIFA) see FIFA
FET 260
FIFA 46, 79, 94
freedom fighters 17-18
Further Education and Training (FET) see FET
FW de Klerk 17, 225
GDP 87, 94, 96, 253
green industrialisation 29-30
Gross Domestic Product (GDP) see GDP
Hawks, the 79, 183, 243, 247
health 17, 41, 73, 93, 127, 176, 275
HIV 195, 279-280
HRD 183, 257, 266
HRD-SA 183
Human Immunodeficiency Virus (HIV) see HIV
Human Resource Development (HRD) see HRD
Human Resource Development South Africa see HRD-SA
IDC 175
IDOC 243
IDSEO 243
industrial consciousness 22-24, 42, 44-45, 47-49, 52, 72-73,75-76,80,85,101-104, 107, 123-127, 139, 144, 154, 167, 169, 174, 180, 183, 187, 229, 252, 254, 261, 263, 270-273, 278-279, 281
industrial development 25-26, 29, 31, 43-45, 48, 72, 103, 109, 113, 175-176, 183, 270-271
Industrial Development Corporation (IDC) see IDC
industrial investment policies 26-27
Industrial Policy Action Plan (IPAP) see IPAP
industrial zones 110
industrialisation 26-27, 29-32, 44-45, 48, 51, 80, 84-85, 93, 112, 164, 256
    Africa Industrialisation Day 45
    green 29-30
Investigating Directorate – Organised Crime (IDOC) see IDOC
Investigating Directorate – Serious Economic Offences (IDSEO) see IDSEO
IPAP 87, 257
Jacob Zuma, president 17, 18, 38, 39, 40, 163, 181, 184
JIPSA 76, 108, 180, 181-183, 252-254, 256-259, 261, 263-266, 270
Jipsa moment, the 252-266

Joint Initiative for Priority Skills Acquisition (JIPSA) seeJIPSA
Julius Malema 79, 184
Kempton Park negotiations 17, 78, 225
key priorities 43
Manufacturing, Engineering and Related Services Education and Training Authority of South Africa (MERSETA) see MERSETA
Mbeki, president 18, 39-40, 79, 137, 160, 163, 165, 207-208, 234, 253-254, 262
MERSETA 263-264
Minerals and Petroleum Development Act 18
Minister of Safety and Security 42
Minister of Trade and Industry 25, 30, 41, 87
MK 220-221
Motlanthe, Kgalema, president 18, 40, 59-60, 62
national crisis 41, 91
National Director of Public Prosecutions (NDPP) see NDPP
National Empowerment Fund (NEF) see NEF
National Empowerment Fund Act 18
National Empowerment Fund Act, 105 of 1998 19
national identity 20-21
National Opinion Research Center 39, 55
National Party 17, 138, 163, 166, 225, 280
national unity 16, 24, 38, 42, 63, 215, 219, 221
nation-building 16-17, 38, 41-42, 44, 46, 54-53, 58, 81, 84, 92-93, 116. 138-139, 159, 162, 165, 180, 192, 197,209-210, 228-229, 270-271, 273
    cornerstone issues 46-47
nationhood 16-19, 38, 42, 52, 63-65, 72, 74, 80, 83-95, 159, 167, 170, 180, 252, 278
    performance standard, new 84-95
NDPP 234, 240
NEF 19
Nelson Mandela, president 17, 202, 219
NGO 203, 222, 223
Non-Governmental Organisation (NGO) see NGO
Patriotism 16, 23-24, 33, 38, 52, 63, 72, 112, 115, 180, 261, 273
POCA 242
poverty 16, 21-23, 25-26, 28-29, 31, 38, 43, 45-46, 49-51, 58-59, 72-75, 80-81, 85, 87, 93, 103, 110, 112, 122-124, 127, 139-140, 145, 164, 166, 168, 170, 174-175, 183, 213, 230, 252-253, 256, 261-262, 266, 270-273, 275, 278, 280, 284-285
Preferential Procurement Policy Framework Act 18
President
    FW de Klerk 17, 225
    Nelson Mandela 17, 202, 219
    Jacob Zuma 17, 18, 38, 39, 40, 163, 181, 184
    Thabo Mbeki 18, 39-40, 79, 137, 160, 163, 165, 207-208, 234, 253-254, 262
    Kgalema Motlanthe 18, 40, 59-60, 62
Prevention of Organised Crime Act (POCA) see POCA
prosperity 22-23, 25, 28, 32, 43, 45, 49, 58-59, 72-75, 81, 134, 162, 196, 252, 261, 266, 270, 273, 278
race consciousness 20, 23, 25, 124, 144
raw materials 27, 85-86, 106, 111-113, 177, 286
renewal 39-42, 54
    the president's call for 39-41
Restitution of Land Rights Act 18
rural development 17-18, 41, 93, 165
Scorpions, the 79, 180, 183, 194, 200, 207-209, 234-237, 239-244, 246, 270
    Scorpions, creating 207-209

SDU 206
Sectoral Education and Training Authority (SETA) see SETA
Self-Defence Units (SDU) see SDU
Self-Protection Units (SPU) see SPU
SETA 264
Small, Medium & Micro Enterprises (SMMEs) see SMMEs
SMMEs 18, 26
Solidarity 122, 127, 168, 212, 274
SPU 206
state, the
    state, the role of 30-31
Telecommunications Act 18
ten commandments, the new 176
The National Small Business Act 18
The Promotion of Equality and Prevention of Unfair Discrimination Act 18
transformation score card 16-19
TRC 24, 78-79, 88, 103, 133, 151, 180-183, 187, 193-194, 196, 200-204, 207-208, 218-230, 234-235, 252, 258, 270
    TRC overview of 219-221
Truth and Reconciliation Commission (TRC) see TRC
UDF 150
Umkhonto we Sizwe (MK) see MK
unemployment 16-17, 21-22, 24-25, 30, 41, 43, 46, 48, 50-54, 72, 80, 86-88, 91, 93-94, 100, 103, 123, 135-136, 139-140, 144, 153, 161-165, 174, 177, 181, 183, 196-197, 218, 234, 252-253, 255-256, 261, 270-271, 273-275, 279-280, 284-285
    rate 48, 86
UNIDO 25-26
United Democratic Front (UDF) see UDF
United Nations Industrial Development Organisation (UNIDO) see UNIDO
United States Dollar (USD) see USD
United States of America (USA) see USA
USA 39, 45, 113, 140, 160, 193, 196, 199, 211-213
USD 50
voter apathy 162
xenophobia 88, 145, 182, 185-188

MUTLOATSE arts heritage trust

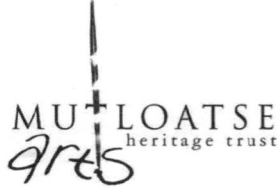

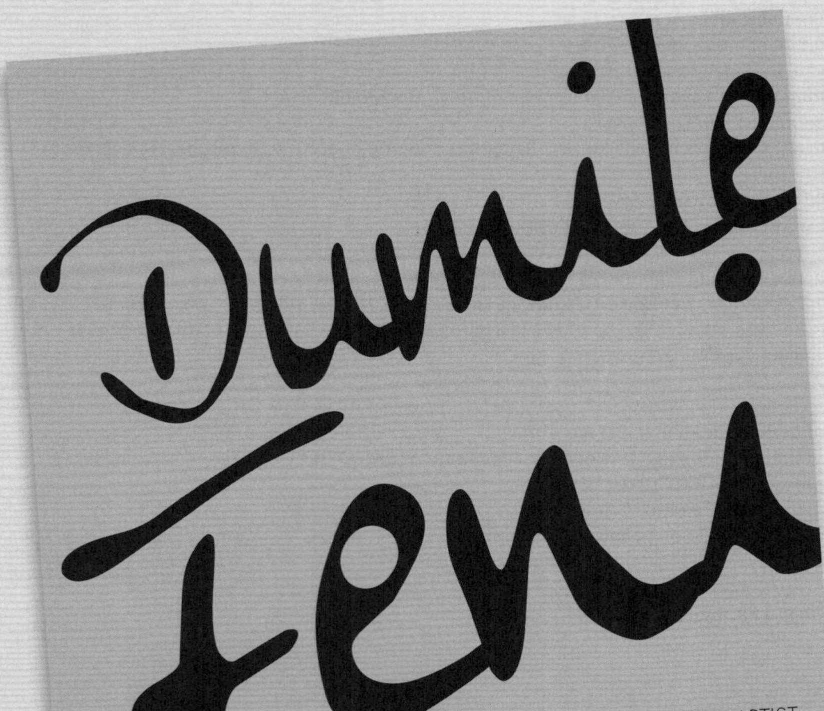

Dumile Feni
THE STORY OF A GREAT ARTIST
Prince Mbusi Dube | VOLUME 1

FOSATU
A TRADE UNION - THAT'S ALL?